MANAGING FOR THE LONG RUN

Danny Miller
Isabel Le Breton-Miller

MANAGING FOR THE LONG RUN

Lessons in Competitive Advantage
from Great Family Businesses

Harvard Business School Press
Boston, Massachusetts

Library of Congress Cataloging-in-Publication Data

Miller, Danny.
  Managing for the long run : lessons in competitive advantage from
great family businesses / Danny Miller and Isabelle Le Breton-Miller.
     p. cm.
  Includes bibliographical references.
  ISBN 1-59139-415-5
  1. Family-owned business enterprises—Management. 2. Success in
business. I. Le Breton-Miller, Isabelle. II. Title.
  HD62.25.M54 2004
  658'.04—dc22
                                                              2004019789

Contents

List of Figures and Tables

Acknowledgments

This book is a product of so many people. It was John O.Whitney, Professor Emeritus, Columbia University, and former CEO of Pathmark, who convinced us that our ideas warranted a book and kept encouraging us to write it. John went through several drafts of the manuscript, giving detailed and unfailingly helpful suggestions. The fact that he is clinically blind and had to use his Kurzweil reader to go through the text is a testament not only to his belief in our project but to the character of the man.

Nathaniel Foote, Managing Director of the Center for Organizational Fitness, and former principal and head of the organization design practice at McKinsey & Company is a busy man. But he kept making time throughout this project to provide us with his deep insights, and pushed us to highlight the configurational aspects of our findings. Chapters 2, 8, and 9 strongly reflect his involvement.

Lloyd Steier, Director of the Center for Entrepreneurship and Family Enterprise at the University of Alberta, got us interested in family business, served as a personal tutor about the challenges and merits of the breed, and gave us useful advice on virtually every chapter of this book. We are in his debt.

Luc Farinas was our senior research assistant for the pilot study and the early phases of the book, and his insights are reflected on many of these pages. He was a joy to work with and a real and valuable contributor.

Mike Beer of the Harvard Business School, Bill Starbuck of New York University, and Russ Eisenstat of the Center for Organizational Fitness all provided guidance; and Mike shared his contacts. John Ward of Northwestern University and Kelin Gersick and Ivan Lansberg of Yale are among the most informed family business thinkers and consultants in the world. They kindly provided their reactions to our ideas and to earlier versions of parts of this manuscript. Marjorie Williams, Virginia A. Smith, and Jean-Marie Toulouse were also most generous with their moral support and sound writing and positioning advice. Ming-Jer Chen of the University of Virginia and Kenneth Craddock of Columbia University shared their refreshing ideas about family businesses, as did good friends Bob Feinstein, Peter H. Friesen, Anil Miglani, Robert C. Payette, Joseph Rose, and Chen Wei-Cheng. We are indebted, too, to executive editor Kirsten D. Sandberg of Harvard Business School Publishing and our agent Jim Levine for their creative advice and unflagging support.

We would also like to thank our anonymous respondents and clients, whose experiences and wisdom we hope are reflected in these pages. We are especially thankful to Bill Bone and James Houghton for sharing their ideas and contacts.

Research support from HEC Montreal, the University of Alberta Center for Entrepreneurship and Family Enterprise, and the Social Sciences and Humanities Research Council of Canada (Grant 410-2002-0007) is most gratefully acknowledged.

Finally, Danny would like to acknowledge his profound debt to his former teachers, the late Tom Kubicek and Henry S. Tutsch, who stimulated his critical interest in business, and to the late Jon Hartwick, who was a close friend to both authors and a helpful critic during the initial stages of work. Like the courageous leaders we write about, these men taught even more by example than by word.

—Danny Miller and Isabelle Le Breton-Miller
Montreal
January 2004

This book is dedicated to the memory of Johanna and Jean Weymiers and to Bernard and Evelyne Le Breton.

In Search of Long-Term Winners

W E'RE STILL LICKING our wounds from the crash of 2001 to 2003. The stock market collapsed, once-touted companies like Enron, WorldCom, and Global Crossing failed, and even old standards like GE and Time Warner fell on hard times. Jobs were lost by millions of people, and the economy, not to mention our pension plans, reeled. Of course there are explanations: crooked greedy executives, the bust in telecoms, and global competition. But for many companies, the problems went deeper.

It is paradoxical that some of the most celebrated enterprises were hurt the most. These had been taken to be paragons of best practices: ABB, Nortel, Vivendi, and, again, Enron among them. Experts had pointed to the entrepreneurial energy and bottom-line discipline of their CEOs, whose stock-price-based compensation "heightened accountability." Strategy scholars praised the rapid growth being garnered by complementary acquisitions and the efficiencies being wrought by lean, "reengineered" operations. Then there were in-depth studies describing can-do, action cultures, in which every manager was an entrepreneur with his or her own unit and profit-based incentives. In short, these companies seemed to be doing everything right. But subtly, they began to move toward excess: too much risk taking, too much focus on the short term, too little time to digest opportunities, too many balls to juggle. Their accountabilities, strategies, and incentives, it seems, had not prevented these enterprises from getting into trouble. They may even have contributed to the problems as managers gamed the system, focusing too narrowly on massaging the numbers to earn their bonuses instead of building up core competencies and delivering value.

Such occurrences highlight a very old problem: Companies have a devil of a time staying successful. No sooner do books like *In Search of Excellence, Built to Last*, and *The Discipline of Market Leaders* appear

1

than their stellar examples begin to fade. In *The Icarus Paradox,* one of us argued that the very elements that foster success, as well as the attitudes bred by success itself, can precipitate failure.[1] The systems that built great companies often worked to destroy them. So we set out to answer one compound question: Who, if anyone, manages to *sustain* success, and how?

Seeking Out a Different Breed

To that end, we decided to look where others had not—where there was no spotlight, little glamor, and more grizzled survivors than shooting stars. After some searching, we found such a place: the domain of major family-controlled businesses (FCBs)—businesses, whether public or private, in which a family controls the largest block of shares or votes and has one or more of its members in key management positions. These businesses fulfilled two key criteria:

1. As a group, they *outperformed* nonfamily peers on many performance dimensions of interest, and vastly outsurvived them as well.
2. As a class they have been *dismissed* as role models, written off as obstacle-ridden, old-fashioned, and rife with conflict. FCBs that defied this description might have lots to tell us.

Take the point about obstacles. The great business historian Alfred D. Chandler has blamed the economic decline of Great Britain partly on family businesses—on their lack of scale, backwardness, and inability to preserve capital.[2] His unflattering view still dominates. Experts on FCBs today write mostly about these businesses' problems and special challenges. At a recent academic conference, we listened to ten presentations on FCBs.[3] Each paper highlighted the challenges and disadvantages of that organizational form: from corruption to misplaced altruism to governance conundrums to shortsighted coddling of the kids. A few weeks later, in discussing family businesses with us, the editor of a national business publication suggested that FCBs are not his readers and do well only when they behave like regular public companies. His publication could be missing out on a large audience. FCBs make up 35 to 40 percent of the *Fortune* 500 and S&P 500.[4] They account for over half the employment in the United States and 78 percent of the new jobs created.[5] Comparable figures for Asia, Europe, and South America are significantly higher (see table I-1).

Table I-1

Percentage of Companies Controlled by Families

Notes to this table are found in "Table I-1" in Notes.

FCB Prevalence	Sample	FCB Definition
35%	S&P 500 (2003)	Founding family on board as executives or as significant owners [a]
32%	S&P 500 (1992–1999)	Members of founding family on board and hold shares in absence of outside blocks of >5% [b]
37%	*Fortune* 500 (1992)	Top executive is family member or descendant of founder [c]
35%	*Fortune* 500 (1987)	Founding family in top management position or on board [d]
47%	*Fortune* 500 (1965)	5% family ownership, representation on board, and multiple generations of involvement [e]
21%	*BusinessWeek* CEO 1000 (1993)	Top executive is family member or descendant of founder [f]
60%	54,000 public companies in the United States (1996)	Under close family control [g]
20% United States 25% Canada 55% Italy 70% Hong Kong	20 largest publicly traded companies (1990s)	Families control >20% of the shares and are the largest stockholders by more than a factor of 2 [h]
44% Western Europe 65% Germany 65% France 56% Spain	5,232 publicly traded firms in Western Europe (1996)	Families control >20% of the votes [i]
57%	Top 250 firms on Paris Stock Exchange (1993–1998)	Families control >10% of equity [j]

Time and time again, FCBs have been shown in systematic studies to outperform public nonfamily-controlled businesses (non-FCBs). This is true in revenue growth, market valuations, return on assets, return on equity, and total shareholder returns (chapter 1 presents the details). Do they accomplish that performance by running down their resources or taking excessive risks? The research evidence suggests not. FCBs seem to invest more than NFBs in human resources and training, in social benefits for their people, and in modernizing plant and equipment. They also enjoy better cash positions, more stable earnings, and lower debt to equity. It is no surprise then that FCBs outsurvive others by a factor of two. The overall consensus and weight of this growing body of evidence is too impressive to ignore. Many of these companies, far from being underdogs, are real "contenders."

So our research team set out on a multiyear journey to study this underrated animal. We identified more than forty large, family-controlled businesses, half public, half private, that had done well for long periods of time; that is, they had come to lead their industries in market share as number one or two for at least twenty years. Furthermore, more than half these companies had survived for over a century (median age 104 years). Firms included Cargill, Bechtel, Michelin, Hallmark, the New York Times Company, Timken, Fidelity Investments, W.L. Gore, Estée Lauder, S.C. Johnson, L.L. Bean, Wal-Mart, Tyson Foods, and IKEA—exceptional companies by any definition. We also examined the practices of these and other FCBs during intervals of poor performance to better understand what it took for them to succeed. These firms—again, substantial companies that had been stars—had fallen, at least for a while, on hard times; among them Motorola, Corning, Nordstrom, and Levi Strauss.[6]

Deviants All

It didn't take us long to figure out why this breed had been ignored in the best-practice literature. As we began to accumulate hundreds of pages of historical files on each of these enterprises, the reasons for their neglect became apparent, while the sources of their successes became more baffling. Perhaps, we thought, we should have listened more attentively at that conference or to our editor friend? The firms, seemingly, had skirted most aspects of modern management practice. Far from acting accountable, the CEOs were often secretive. They disliked explaining themselves to shareholders or even giving financial data to their bankers. They resented being questioned and sought enormous discretion to do what they believed was right for the company—which was, they insisted, "their business." Many took only a passing interest in quarterly financial statements, and just as many mistrusted the numbers. Leaders then used their freedom to stubbornly ignore market trends or to make moves that were radically out of step with what the rest of industry was doing. When it came to strategy, firms lived as much in the past as the future: Some traditions were sacrosanct, and fulfilling a family mission was almost always more important than any bottom line—in fact it *was* the bottom line. Then there were the primitive organizational arrangements—scary informality, rudimentary controls, overworked managers, blurred roles and reporting relationships, smarmy clubbiness, and a profound intolerance of doubters of family ideals. Relationships with outsiders seemed "cronylike," with contracts based on personal attachments rather than competitive bargaining. What century were these companies living in, we wondered? Who *are* these guys?

We were sorely tempted by this time to look elsewhere and dismiss these firms as anomalies living on borrowed time. But there was too much evidence to the contrary. Again, their streaks of "good luck" had lasted an incredibly long time and taken them to the pinnacle of a multitude of industries, high-tech and low, where some seemed almost to take up permanent residence. Moreover, it was clear that these firms had mastered very different types of competitive advantage—not just stable ones like efficiency and quality, but innovation, brand building, and entrepreneurship. They sustained their advantages as markets and technologies altered and the rosters of rivals churned. All the while, the materials we gathered on these firms over their long histories showed an amazing consistency in their practices. They had embraced a peculiar pattern, stuck with it, and got away with it—time and again. And of course there were those pesky non-FCB performance comparisons. Maybe *we* were the problem? Maybe we were using the wrong lenses to study the companies—standards that do not apply to FCBs. If those standards could be so profitably ignored by our winners, might those firms not possess an alternative worth examining?

Searching for a Different Model

It was time to get beneath the surface and examine the world not through our non-FCB filters but by viewing what the great FCBs and their leaders thought was critical and, more important, by studying the concrete actions that reflected these choices. Instead of looking at criteria based on the prevailing model, why not look at accomplishments, track records, policies, stories, histories, and managers' explanations? Why not just listen to the data instead of asking leading questions?

Before long, that data started to reveal a softer set of very different dimensions. Things like inspiring ideals, a passion for the substantive over the pecuniary, a culture of mutual loyalty, interminable executive apprenticeships, a concern for the collective over the individual, patience and perfectionism, religious unorthodoxy, Spartan parsimony, and permanent tenures. We also found systemic role ambiguity, top to bottom: channelled intolerance, transaction phobia, and a host of other qualities and behaviors rarely discussed in management textbooks. Moreover, these peculiarities were blended to back a specific strategy and carefully counterbalanced to prevent excesses. They were, in effect, orchestrated to form harmonious and robust configurations.

In essence, our winners, to varying degrees, demonstrated four driving priorities or passions, each giving rise to a thematic set of remarkable policies and practices. We call these priorities command, continuity, community, and connection—or "the four Cs." Take *command*. Our FCB leaders and their top teams insist on the freedom to be decisive, speedy, and innovative in running and renewing the firm. They serve their shareholders not by being slaves but independent "people of action." They also cherish the *continuity* of the business and its contribution to the world. First is the desire to keep pursuing the dream—a heartfelt substantive mission and the core competencies needed to achieve it. The dream, of course, can only be realized through the firm, and so it too is safeguarded via farsighted investment and solicitous stewardship. *Community*, another driving priority, is the desire to unite the tribe—to get everyone inside the company psyched to achieve the mission. This attitude spawns not financial incentives or bureaucracy but cohesive clan cultures, shaped by authentic values, incessant indoctrination, and a deep concern for employees at all levels. Finally, a desire for *connection* plays out in the firm's relationship with outsiders. Rather than opting for one-shot, opportunistic transactions, many of these firms strive to be good neighbors—to contribute generously to secure win-win, enduring relationships with clients, suppliers, partners, and the broader community.

Far from being shortcomings, these four Cs and their elements— if blended or "configured" correctly—translated over the long run into profound sources of vitality, supporting strategies that wrought competitive advantage not just for years but in many cases for more than a century. The FCBs that really did well incorporated all of these Cs, but they prioritized them differently depending on the strategy they embraced. Then they combined practices to offset the gaps or potential excesses of one with the complementary strengths or counterbalancing effects of another.

The Book

This book documents our findings. It isn't a litany of a bunch of qualities or strategies, but a set of models, or configurations, revealing some paths less traveled that managers can take to achieve enduring competitive advantage. The major managerial lessons of the book include:

- How to configure and shape the C priorities and their elements to support a specific chosen strategy, be it brand building, product and operations excellence, innovation, or entrepreneurial deal making
- How to spot when things go wrong and evaluate your own company to troubleshoot problems
- How every manager can build on our findings to manage for the long run, starting Monday morning

Scope and Limitations

This book is *not* about the average family-controlled business, but about the great ones—large, old companies that have achieved market share leadership. We look only at businesses in which, for most of our period of analysis, the family controlled the largest block of shares or votes *and* was involved in top management. We do not argue that all FCBs are superior. As everyone knows, family businesses have their problems. The well-publicized frauds at FCBs like Adelphia Communications and Parmalat show that family businesses can be as imperfect as any other enterprise. Even some of our great FCBs occasionally have exhibited excesses of conservatism, rashness, antiunionism, sexism, and racism. But as we will see, the long-term FCB winners *do* have something to teach us all, and that is what we will be concentrating on: how to manage not for short-term profits but for very *long-term* market success and for the benefit of *all* organizational stakeholders.

To that end, we have focused our investigation on the organizational and strategic advantages of some *thriving* FCBs. We do not grapple with important FCB challenges such as family governance, succession, family boards and councils, family conflict resolution, and so on. A vast and useful literature on family enterprise has taken on these topics and made real progress. In particular, the integrative works by Gersick and colleagues, Lansberg, and Ward have done an especially fine job of laying out and addressing these issues, which must be confronted before even thinking about strategy and organization.[7]

To oversimplify, we can categorize family business concerns as either *hygiene issues*, those that lie below an imaginary line, or *strategic issues*, those that rest above it. Hygiene factors, such as family governance, succession, and conflict resolution, must be got right to assure survival. Unless these challenges are addressed, few advantages are apt to be realized. How, for example, can the benefits of independent command be attained when relatives are fighting for leadership? How can the dream of a substantive mission be realized while impatient family owners haggle about their share of the profits? And how can a corporate culture be harmonious when different factions support different family members? Although this book addresses the strategic issues above the line, these rely on foundations of good governance below it.

A Note About Our Study

Our approach was to find out as much as we could about the histories of the sample companies by systematically analyzing book accounts, streams of articles, and financial reports. When possible, we also spoke to managers, ex-managers, customers, and suppliers. For a number of our FCBs we either served directly as consultants or worked with others involved at top levels of the organization. Although those experiences helped shape our frameworks and understandings, the details garnered there must remain private. That constraint, and the secrecy of many of the FCBs we write about here, necessitated that we take many examples from secondary sources. But we have gathered overlapping sources for each company and focused on fine-grained facts rather than opinions. Indeed, it is these telling details that provide the most actionable lessons for managers.

Contents

Chapter 1 compares an increasingly common non-FCB paradigm with that of our great FCBs, contrasting the opportunistic owners, tactical strategies, and individualistic cultures of the former with the stewards, substantive missions, and collective cultures representative of many great family firms. Chapter 2 focuses on the four thematic priorities—the afore-mentioned four Cs—that drove our FCBs, the remarkable policies and practices to which they gave rise, and their roots. Chapters 3 to 7 deal with specific strategies: brand building, craftsmanship, operations excellence, innovation, and deal making, respectively, and how our firms were able to sustain competitive advantage in these realms by tailoring and blending the four Cs. Each of these chapters presents our analyses of four to six different firms and is full of details about what these companies did to become and stay great. At first, some of the policies and ventures recounted may appear to be odd and extreme, but the details throughout each chapter will show the context or *configuration*—the *blend* of ele-ments—needed to make a strategy work. Chapter 8 describes what happened to some of these companies when they mismanaged the priori-ties, taking some to excess while ignoring others. Chapter 9 tells all managers what they can start to do right now to begin their journey in governance, managerial incentives, strategy, organization, and the func-tional areas. Appendix A describes our research methods: our sample, sources of data from secondary sources and interviews, and our way of extracting the patterns and findings. Appendix B presents assessment grids that managers may use to evaluate their own company and to deter-mine how it stacks up against some thriving and faltering examples from our sample. Finally, extensive, annotated footnotes—especially for chap-ters 1, 2, and 9—connect our work to some of the exciting academic literature in economics, sociology, strategy, and organizational theory.

Chapters 3 to 7 can be read in any order. As our five strategies all rest on the C priorities, the themes of continuity, community, connection, and command keep recurring—albeit often in different guises and with assorted functions. Therefore, busy managers might want to determine from appen-dix B which of the strategy chapters most pertain to their own organization, and begin there.

We'd love to hear from our readers about what they like and dislike about this book. Learning is an ongoing process, and we're sure to benefit from your feedback. E-mail us at:

Danny.Miller@hec.ca and lebreton@generation.net

Chapter 1

What Distinguishes
Great Family Businesses?

A T FIRST GLANCE, the Michelin tire plant and its surroundings in the sleepy French town of Clermont-Ferrand take one back to another age. There are ancient red-roofed buildings, winding roads, and people dressed in the garb of another century. Here also is a company that ostensibly and in fact lives on its traditions. Its focal tire business is what it was a century ago, and the company is run by the same family with the same values. Many Michelin employees reside in a nineteenth-century company town in which the family has built houses, schools, and hospitals, and imposed a cradle-to-grave welfare system.

Archaisms are apparent, too, within the enterprise. Departments are denoted by letters, not names, which would imply "too much of a division." So, apparently, would position titles. Ex-CEO François Michelin had the same title as all his other managers: "manager." He refers to his company as a "house," in the style of the guilds, and his business as a "craft." Many of the workers are third-generation Michelin employees, some of them forty-year veterans. Relationships with numerous suppliers and clients are even more enduring. And when it comes to making tough decisions, these are decided not by considerations of the market, the investment community, or world economic conditions, but according to the enduring beliefs of the family. Oddly, all this happens under a veil of secrecy that should be the envy of the CIA. Sounds quaintly anachronistic, doesn't it?

Yet Michelin has thrived for over a century as a quintessential family business. It has gone from underdog to the dominant international player in the hypercompetitive tire business by consistently out-innovating its competitors in both products and processes. It is Michelin that developed the demountable bicycle tire, the rubber carriage tire, the radial tire, and the space-age indestructible tires for the NASA shuttle and the Concorde (after its crash in July 2000). It also completely reinvented the process of tire manufacturing several times over—ultimately making it completely portable in one self-contained machine, and reducing the number of distinct manufacturing steps from seven to one. All of these marvels occurred in the context of stable strategies, clan cultures, and unencumbered family ownership.

It is this kind of story, repeated in dozens of family-controlled businesses we studied, that got us thinking: How is it that these supposed family drudges so often beat their nonfamily counterparts?[1] In this first chapter, we begin to unfold clues to that mystery, contrasting the fundamental operating philosophies of many of today's non-FCBs with those of our long-term winners. The later chapters will "put meat on those bones." But first, let's outline the mystery—acknowledge the negative opinions of FCBs and reveal some very contrary evidence.

Family Plots

Until now, the writing and thinking about family-controlled business has fixated on its problems and pitfalls. Daily newspapers have been rife with stories of feuding family owners and managers, prodigal children, and tales of excess and woe. In fact, the majority of articles over the last ten years in the highly regarded *Family Business Review* and *Family Business Magazine* have concentrated on the challenges peculiar to FCBs. Small wonder family businesses as a class get little respect.

FCBs are said to have a unique potential for conflict. Contrary interests are inevitably brought to the table by the likes of a family owner with managerial responsibility, versus the one who merely lives on dividends and possesses less patient capital. Also, there is the temptation and capacity among some family executives to do what is profitable for the family but damaging to the minority shareholder.[2] Aggravating the situation are emotion-driven battles between parents and next-generation managers, as the grudges of childhood are dragged into the present. Sibling rivalries can fester within a context of high financial stakes or arise as a fight for turf in the business. If cousins get involved, the scenario becomes even messier as ownership diffuses and aunts and uncles advocate for their offspring.[3]

Lurking always are succession problems that manifest when an appropriate heir is not available or can't get backing from the family.[4] Nepotism too is a threat, and family leaders may get away with behavior that is whimsically excessive because of their kinship status.[5] Even amassing capital may be a problem when a family's financial needs grow geometrically while the business grows arithmetically.[6] The list goes on.[7]

Things Are Brighter Than They Seem

How strange it is, therefore, that so many FCBs go on to thrive for decades, besting their competitors and changing not only the competitive landscape but fundamental business practices. The *New York Times* and *Washington Post* are widely considered to be the best newspapers in North America. Cargill reigns as the world's biggest commodity intermediary, while J.R. Simplot in potatoes and Tyson in chickens dominate their industries with original business models. At the customer end, Wal-Mart and IKEA are burgeoning retailers, each having pioneered bold service concepts.

It's no surprise then that best-sellers such as *In Search of Excellence* and *Built to Last* take numerous examples from FCBs.[8] Yet they rarely mention their family-controlled status. When, via a mutual friend, we passed on this observation to one of the authors of these books, his response was, "The companies were successful *despite* being FCBs." Like many business scholars, he seemed to be missing the point.

As noted in the introduction, systematic evidence is emerging about the FCB edge. Hermann Simon discovered that of the 500-odd midsized European firms that dominated their markets, more than 75 percent were controlled or run by families. Daniel McConaughy and his colleagues found that FCBs had higher margins, more stable earnings, and better cash flow and sales per employee than the rest of the *BusinessWeek* 1000. Jose Allouche and Bruno Amann confirmed this with French data and found that FCBs also grow faster than other firms and have higher returns on assets and on equity. Superior returns and market valuations were also discovered by Ronald Anderson and David Reeb, Belén Villalonga and Raphael Amit, David Kang, and Dirk Junge. Paul Bornstein found FCBs to outperform in share appreciation and Robin Mackie found they survived twice as long as non-FCBs. Dirk Junge decided to take advantage of these facts by establishing a fund that invests only in family businesses.[9] Table 1-1 lists telling summary statistics comparing FCB and non-FCB performance.

Table 1-1

Financial Performance of FCBs Versus Non-FCBs

Notes to this table are found in "Table 1-1" in Notes.

FCBs Versus Non-FCBs	Sample	FCB Definition
FCB annual returns to shareholders 16.6% versus S&P 14% (understated as FCB one-third of S&P)	Family Business Stock Index of 200 largest U.S. FCBs, 1975–1995	Founding family involvement in top management[a]
76% TSR for FCBs, 9% for non-FCBs	Paris Bourse largest 250 firms, 1989–1996	Family control[b]
31/50 wins for FCBs in TSR	50 major U.S. FCBs versus peers in industry, 1972–1983	Family owned 30% or more[c]
Higher profit margins, higher ROE, faster growth in sales and assets	325 large industrial firms in the United Kingdom, 1980s	Ownership control[d]
FCBs 33% more profitable and 15% faster growing than industry average	Biggest 800 publicly traded firms in U.S., early 1990s	Member of founding family is the CEO[e]
Higher ROA and higher ratio of market value of firm to replacement cost of assets	*Fortune* 500 firms, 1982–1994	If one of five largest shareholders is family; also helps if owner is non-CEO chairman[f]
FCBs have greater TSR, ROA, sales growth	205 traded FCBs from Value Line versus S&P 500, 1989–1994	Family has >10% of shares and ≥ two officers[g]
Superior ROS relative to industry if family ownership and family CEO	U.S. publicly held textile firms 1983–1992 (N=595 company years)	If one of five largest shareholders is family, also helps if owner is CEO[h]
Higher market-to-book value ratio for FCBs	109 matched pairs from *BusinessWeek* CEO 1000, 1987	CEO is founder or member of founder family[i]
Higher ROS—8.8% versus 3.3%; higher ROE—27% versus 6%	104 family businesses in Spain versus 4,702 others reported by Bank of Spain, 1991	More than 50% of stock owned by the family; one family member on top management team, sales > 40 million pesetas[j]
Superior ROA, higher Tobin Q—market value to replacement value of assets	S&P 500 1992–1999	Helps if CEO is both founder and descendant[k]
FCB mean revenues up 50% in last five years, in an often down economy	1,000 U.S. FCBs 1997–2002	Firm controlled by family members; 94% also run by them[l]

Table 1-1

Financial Performance of FCBs Versus Non-FCBs *(continued)*

FCBs Versus Non-FCBs	Sample	FCB Definition
ROE 25.2% versus 15.8% ROA 7.6% versus 6.1% ROC 18.5 versus 12.6 ROS 5.4% versus 3.6%, faster revenue growth	47 pairs matched by size and industry of largest 1,000 industrial French companies, 1982–1992	Firms under family control[m]
ROA 5.4% versus 4.1% TSR 15.6% versus 11.2% Revenue growth 23.4% versus 10.8% Income growth 21.1% versus 12.6%	S&P 500, 1992–2002	Firms with founding families on board in executive role or as significant shareholders[n]

TSR = total shareholder returns; ROS = return on sales; ROA = return on assets; ROE = return on equity; ROC = return on total capital

From the facts so far, it seems there may be two kinds of FCBs: those that have overcome the special survival challenges we mentioned, and those that haven't. Some of the latter experience abysmal performance, as they lack the governance mechanisms even to survive, let alone thrive. The first group, however, is much tougher to understand, as mastering survival hurdles does not explain success; solving problems one's rivals don't confront can hardly confer advantage! And stories like Michelin's, in which stellar success is to be found in a paternalistic, stubborn, strangely organized company, only add to the mystery.

Why Do So Many FCBs Become and Stay Winners?

This is the puzzle that drove us to look further into FCBs to understand why, despite the enormous challenges facing them and despite their aberrant behavior, so many do so well for so long. In looking at long-thriving FCB winners, we found a number of fundamental qualities, each suggesting distinct advantages over many of today's common organizational practices.

In the broadest terms, there are two remarkable aspects to our findings:

- First, because of their family control, successful FCBs have embraced *very different* ownership, business, and social philosophies—distinctive approaches to leadership, strategy, organization, and relations with the environment that contrast sharply with the conventional wisdom and practices of many public, nonfamily-controlled businesses (non-FCBs).
- Second, exactly those distinctive aspects are often viewed as the primary *weaknesses* of the FCB form. One of the best-kept secrets, we discovered, is that they in fact serve as pillars of competitive advantage for the most successful firms.

Let's take a closer look.

The Grasshoppers Versus the Ants

To better reveal the distinctiveness of our winners, it is useful to compare how they operate with some increasingly common practices. First we compare the governance arrangements of many non-FCBs with those common within our sample of *outstanding* FCBs. Then we show how these arrangements may give rise to steep contrasts in the business philosophies and social philosophies of the two groups of enterprises. Table 1-2 summarizes these contrasts between some of the non-FCB "grasshoppers," which, like the live-for-today, self-absorbed fiddlers of Lafontaine's fable, failed to prepare for a brutal winter; and the successful FCB "ants"—those purposeful, industrious social creatures whose preparation and sacrifice kept their pantries well stocked.

Bear in mind that the basis for the following comparisons are the successful FCBs we studied, not *all* FCBs, some of which may be very shortsighted indeed. Nor do we in any way deny that some NFBs are truly enlightened and managed for the long run. Nonetheless, our comparisons do seem to reflect more general tendencies—modal differences between FCBs and other organizations.

Ownership Philosophy

The underlying contrast between enduring FCBs and most other companies is in governance—in the owners who control the company, in their objectives, and in the mechanisms they use to get managers—their "agents"—to pursue those objectives.

Non-FCB Traders. In a memorable scene from the movie *Wall Street,* buyout specialist Gordon Gecko shouts, "Greed is good." Today, mutual funds, hedge funds, and wealthy traders own large chunks of major NFBs. For the most part, these investors are, if not greedy, impatient. Often, they have little loyalty to a company; their primary purpose is to make their money and get out. Even the smaller shareholders are there mostly for regular, quick capital appreciation and dividends. These "financially driven" investors have a trading mentality: They are happy with their holdings as long as share prices keep mounting, but they have no enduring interest in the organization.

Table 1-2

The Approaches Compared

This table contrasts the practices common among many public, nonfamily businesses with those demonstrated by our thriving FCBs. Some of the difficulties with the former and advantages of the latter follow the arrows after the first phrase for each cell of the last two rows.

	Popular Practices: The Grasshoppers	Winning Ways: The FCB Ants
Ownership Philosophy: Shareholders	Owners as traders: want quick profits; little loyalty to the enterprise or its people	Owners as stewards: more committed to and involved with the enterprise; there for the long haul
Business Philosophy: Top Managers	Tactical: financially driven; quick-results-oriented ↓ Managing the quarterly numbers via expedients like downsizing and acquisitions; tougher to sustain core competencies and preserve competitive focus and advantage	Strategic: driven by a substantive mission; long-term results-oriented ↓ Managing for the future; profound investments in the business and its people, push to develop, sustain, renew unique core competencies
Social Philosophy: Staff and Relationships	Individualism: bureaucratic or market control, extrinsic incentives; one-shot transactions with external partners or clients ↓ Employees act in their own narrow interests; potential mistrust, poor collaboration, high turnover, and leakage of knowledge; competitive relationships with outsiders	Collective: shared values, clan control, intrinsic incentives; lasting relationships with outsiders ↓ Employees act in the interests of the organization; higher levels of motivation and collaboration, lower turnover, tacit knowledge kept within firm; win-win connections with outsiders

Over the years, the more influential among these investors have shaped how top managers are rewarded in many public corporations. They have made sure that it is in the CEO's interests to keep earnings rising steadily and briskly, quarter by quarter. That is what stock analysts and potential investors like to see; that is what drives the price of the stock. Thus, at many firms, executives are compensated and punished on the basis of short-term earnings. Common incentives to do that include stock options and bonuses linked to earnings. Today, American CEOs are paid on average almost 500 times that of the first-line workers, up from 40 times in 1970; and 80 percent is now incentive pay.[10] Executive compensation is also linked closely to the size of the company, and so there is a pull to grow quickly.

But there are penalties as well as incentives: CEOs who do not deliver immediately and consistently on the bottom line may be sidelined. In fact, the average tenure of CEOs in public companies has shrunk down to three to four years, about a third of what it was ten years ago.[11] And when earnings grow too slowly, multiples fall and the firm may become susceptible to a hostile takeover. The pulls and pressures to produce lock-step bottom-line growth, it seems, are becoming more and more intense.

Unfortunately, this is a dangerous system. The newspapers are filled with articles about CEOs who have retired with multimillion-dollar packages because they've done well for their shareholders. Many of these executives, however, have been induced to choreograph, or "manage," company earnings. The firm hits its numbers while the CEO is in office—but only at the expense of its long-run competitiveness—and its other stakeholders. In the extreme cases of Enron, WorldCom, Vivendi, Global Crossing, Nortel, and so many of the dot-coms, CEOs departed with lucrative packages just when their companies were collapsing. These are not isolated examples. At the end of the day, researchers have found no correlation between executive compensation and shareholder returns.[12]

Although the temptations are great, there is nothing essential about this opportunistic ownership philosophy. Warren Buffet is one of the richest men in the world. In his annual report commentaries for his publicly traded Berkshire Hathaway, he has for years criticized the short-term orientation of many companies, and made managing for the long term a key part of his strategy. But such stewardship has become increasingly rare, as impatient investors have become more powerful and CEOs are corralled mostly by short-term incentives and the threat of termination. Changing the system would require a change in thinking by major shareholders and directors alike (see chapter 9).

FCB Stewards. Like traders, the major owners of our great FCBs want to see the value of their company increase. But unlike traders, they are deeply and personally attached to the business and its mission. The business represents a treasured institution that is intended to sustain the family, employees, and other key stakeholders into the future. It is something to nurture, not a holding to be sold for a fast capital gain or exploited in order to draw a fat paycheck. Thus, financial policy is conservative, with low debt, high liquidity ratios, and, ultimately, higher survival rates. Table 1-3 presents the details.

Table 1-3

Financial Policy and Stewardship

Notes to this table are listed in "Table 1-3" in Notes.

	FCBs Versus Others	Sample	FCB Definition
Risk	Lower debt to equity: 0.56 versus 1.53	104 family businesses in Spain versus 4,702 others reported by Bank of Spain, 1991	More than 50% of stock owned by the family; one family member on top management team; sales > 40 million pesetas[a]
	Lower debt to assets; lower short-term debt to assets; lower dividend payout	109 matched pairs from *BusinessWeek* CEO 1000, 1987	CEO is founder or member of founder family[b]
	Lower debt to equity; lower dividend payouts	205 traded FCBs from Value Line versus S&P 500, 1989–1994	Family has >10% of shares and ≥ two officers[c]
	55% of FCBs have debt of less than 25% of equity	1,000 U.S. FCBs, 2002	Controlled by family members—94% also run by family[d]
	Less debt to total assets	S&P 500 1992–1999	CEO is founder or descendant[e]
	Liquidity ratio: 1.3 versus 1.1; leverage 0.9 versus 1.5	47 pairs matched by size and industry of largest 1,000 French industrials, 1982–1992	Firms under family control[f]

continues

Table 1-3

Financial Policy and Stewardship *(continued)*

	FCBs Versus Others	Sample	FCB Definition
Efficiency	Higher sales per employee, asset turnover, working capital to sales, gross margin	109 matched pairs from *BusinessWeek* CEO 1,000, 1987	CEO is founder or member of founder family [9]
Survival	Twice as high a percentage of FCBs survived to 30 and 60 years	All firms in Kirkaldy County, Scotland manufacturing or mining, 1870–1970	Family-owned firms [h]
	Life expectancy of all firms is 12 years; FCBs, 24 years. (Our 41 winners: 104 years and counting. Firms in book, including losers: 94 years.)	All European and Japanese companies in Stratix study versus all FCBs assessed by the Family Firm Institute (FFI)	Various [i]
	Of the firms over 300 years old, most are still family businesses	U.K. Tercentenarians Club, 1997	Firm controlled by family members [j]
	Over 60% of FCBs very optimistic about future in a down economy	1,000 U.S. FCBs 1997–2002	Firm controlled by family members [k]
	Average age of FCBs growing	Firms on Paris Stock Exchange, 1993–1998	Families control >10% of equity [l]

Of course, family owners are interested in having the business succeed. But typically they are broader in their definitions of success and more patient in their desire for returns. "Returns" to them are counted in the form of substantive social or technological accomplishments and the long-term health of the enterprise. They are tallied in the conduct of the business in a way that reflects well upon it, and the development of the company to provide opportunities for treasured family members and employees. Profits and revenues are neither ends in themselves nor a means of goosing the stock price, but outcomes from achieving these other priorities.

So the incentives here are quite unlike those at many other companies. CEOs are appointed as stewards of the most important economic and reputational asset of the family. Given this key role, and their emotional bond and their financial stake in the business, leaders generally have every desire to act in the long-run interests of the enterprise. And as their jobs typically are secure and their tenures very long (often more than twenty years), they guard against doing anything in the short run that might compromise the future of the business.[13]

Business Philosophy

These contrasts between our FCB winners and other public firms in owner priorities and incentives often give rise to profound differences in business philosophies—philosophies that define the primary objectives and strategies of the business.

Financial Tactics at Non-FCBs. Given their compensation incentives and the short-term financial targets their boards and shareholders impose, it is little wonder that many CEOs focus on the short run—on quick, easy ways of getting top- and bottom-line growth during their brief tenures. Some executives emphasize tactics over strategy: cost cutting, reengineering, and downsizing to quickly enhance profits, and making acquisitions to grow revenues. In the near term, earnings may grow, but in the long run downsizing depletes and demoralizes human resources, and merger integration problems fester. The vast majority of *Fortune* 500 companies have downsized their workforces over the last twenty years, many losing valuable talent, incurring steep rehiring costs, and, in the end, reaping no benefit.[14] Even General Electric has run into trouble recently, in part because former CEO Jack Welch put a higher priority on cutting costs and people than developing new patents and products.

A related difficulty with this time-restricted, dollar-driven approach is that many firms do not invest deeply enough in their future. There is a failure to develop unique competitive capabilities or to be courageous and original—necessary ingredients of competitive advantage. Because CEOs are penalized for missing their numbers, some are loath to try anything that requires time to come to fruition—in other words, anything that makes for a distinctive, competitive company. So many firms become victims to the first seriously committed rivals to come along.

An especially dangerous shortcut is acquisition. Certainly, industry consolidation and globalization have made takeovers increasingly popular, as have modern financial techniques such as leveraged buyouts. Also increased has been the desire of CEOs to have higher-profile jobs and better compensation. But unless an acquisition is purchased at a reasonable price and truly complements the business, and unless it is managed to build overall competencies, it ends up hobbling the acquirer, particularly where growth is the primary motive. Study after study has shown that most acquisitions fail, especially those only remotely related to the core business. Research also shows that the more the firm is controlled by managers, as opposed to owners, the more common are these problematic "unrelated" acquisitions.[15] This became apparent first during the acquisitions wave of the 1970s and 1980s at conglomerates like Litton Industries, LTV, Gulf & Western, and even the once-vaunted ITT. More recently, the same problems cropped up as bricks-and-mortar companies bought shaky dot-coms, or big firms tried to buy innovators rather than be innovative themselves. Lucent, Nortel, Vivendi, and BCE all undertook "sexy" acquisitions that made their CEOs look good for a few quarters. But before long, problems came home to roost in the form of poor fit, hidden defects, and billions in write-offs. By then, many of the executives of acquirer and acquired alike had gone on to the next company or a country club retirement.[16]

Substantive Missions at FCBs. As we have seen, most leaders of our outstanding FCBs, by dint of their stewardship duties and status, respectively, have both a heavy responsibility and a good deal of security and discretion. They are less likely therefore to be distracted from their purpose by impatient, numbers-obsessed investors.[17]

Many FCB leaders are at the helm for decades, during which they are expected to improve the strength and reputation of their organizations. They are charged to do this by furthering a substantive mission—some real contribution the company makes to its customers, employees, or society at large. That mission, be it technological advancement, quality, or service, is the soul of the enterprise. It is at once something the firm stands for and the backbone of company strategy and competitive advantage. To realize this mission, these leaders are not afraid to invest deeply and for the long run, sacrificing and focusing to build capabilities, and doing whatever it takes to excel. In fact, studies have found that, on average, FCBs invest more than non-FCBs in long-term improvements to their plant and equipment, research and development, and their people. They do this with 60 percent less debt than other firms and 20 percent more liquidity.[18] Unlike many of their rivals, their concern is not just with today's profits, but tomorrow's; not just with growth, but excellence and renewal.

The Timken Company and its five generations of Timkens have, for over a century, manufactured the finest tapered roller bearings in the world. Its rather grand mission, conceived by the founder and propounded by his son H. H. Timken was: "To contribute materially to industrial progress . . . by making things run smoothly for others." Translation: to reduce mechanical friction and improve America's productivity. Timken's unique, indestructible bearings for trains, cars, machinery, and even satellites and disk drives, did exactly that. Said H. H.: "If there [was] any one thing that fixed in my mind [it was] that we must continue to make our product better and better; it was the thought that it carried the family name." Those were not just words. That pride in the mission and products of the company and the impetus it gave to constant improvement and capability renewal epitomized corporate purpose. For the Timkens, profits were significant, but largely as a means to the mission. At the end of the day, the Timken Company's sense of identity centers on its social purpose, the technological legacy of its pioneers, and the continuity of Timken family leadership.[19]

The business philosophy at firms like Timken is born not of a tactical game of tweaking the numbers but a passion for making a substantive contribution. Timken, the New York Times Company, Michelin, Cargill, and many other FCBs we studied sacrificed for decades to become great. They spent years of their best profits and even endured losses not only to improve their products, but to hone processes and skills. Time and again Michelin reinvented the tire—and its mode of manufacture. Cargill, over a century, built up much of America's grain-handling infrastructure. Ultimately, such sacrifice and investment led to reputation and capabilities no one could match. And the families kept building on those to sustain advantage for generations to come.

Social Philosophy

These contrasts in ownership and business philosophies tend to give rise to major differences in social philosophies, especially in the way managers think about and treat their employees.

The Individual at Non-FCBs. So far we have been concerned mostly with the relationships among owners and managers. Now employees enter the equation—the people needed to actually do the work. Owners, top managers, and employees frequently diverge in their interests. The former are concerned with managing profitability, increasing productivity, and holding down costs; the latter want to earn good wages under comfortable conditions and have job security. Although all are members of the same company, most are, in significant measure, working for themselves. To ensure that they are *also* working for the organization, bureaucratic controls and incentives are put into place. Under bureaucracy, breaking the rules carries punishment. Under incentives, superior output yields superior rewards. Within both these systems the inducement is often extrinsic: People behave *in order to* get rewarded or avoid punishment, too rarely because the behavior itself is gratifying.

Unfortunately, bureaucracy is costly and cumbersome to administer. It can make jobs boring and reduce the scope for employee initiative. It also can be slow if many decisions are routed through the vertical chain of command. Incentives pose problems as well, with people so focused on short-term targets and self-interest that staff may act for themselves, not the organization. This makes collaboration difficult and has employees behaving in opportunistic ways that hurt a company. The classic example is that of the piecework employee who holds back good ideas to keep the piece rate up. Perhaps more significantly, some managers and profit centers too work to maximize their own rewards at the expense of the firm.

Models of decentralization such as ABB and Citicorp were hobbled by such factionalism in the 1990s, as selfish regional managers and subunits were unwilling to sacrifice or even cooperate to serve multinational clients. They fought over transfer prices and revenue splitting, and ignored any requests that wouldn't enhance the local bottom line. In both companies the "solution" was to reshape the incentive system to reward and make managers accountable for serving, say, a key customer or geographic unit. But these solutions tended to be incomplete as managers still favored those tasks for which they were most highly rewarded. Emerging functions such as new competency development fell into the cracks. In serving Peter, the units now ignored Paul. Simple accountability, it seems, works only in a simple world.

Another problem is that individualism breeds conflict. Managers with truncated, financially driven perspectives are poor stewards of corporate resources, including human resources. Too often, they see employees as tools for achieving quick results rather than human beings who need to be nurtured and developed for the long-run good of the company. Consequently, many firms unleash downsizing and reengineering projects and design stressful or monotonous jobs, creating real ill will among the staff. Labor's work-to-rule practices at General Motors during the 1980s and 1990s, for example, were a product of such treatment. Even in its more benign forms, individualism reduces loyalty to the enterprise and results in higher turnover rates and a consequent loss of good people and their knowledge.[20]

The FCB Collective. Our FCB winners adopt a more collective orientation. The leadership knows that the only way it can realize its cherished mission over generations is with a stable cadre of motivated, loyal employees. Excellence is impossible without enthusiastic, committed people willing to use their initiative in the best interests of the company. Thus, employees are induced not just to serve the boss or serve themselves but to do both by serving the mission. A sufficient number are recruited to a common crusade whose pursuit satisfies *intrinsically*.

In many of our winners, employees are seen as cocombatants in a holy war, so they are more cherished and better cared for than elsewhere (see table 1-4). They are also developed to their full potential and thoroughly indoctrinated in company values. In fact, studies have shown that major FCBs pay their employees more, give them better benefits, train them more intensively, and retain them longer (they also pay their top executives 20 percent *less* than non-FCBs, and other staff about 10 percent more).[21] Employees soon sense that they are in a reciprocal, encompassing relationship with a family that is there for them even during the hard times. This personification of the business nurtures loyalty and commitment—a win-win attitude, whereby people feel that by contributing to the business, everyone benefits.

It would be misleading to say that these firms do not use bureaucracy or incentives to organize. They do. But for most of them a third alternative is more useful: "clan control." People do what's right for the business and its mission because they are true believers. While individual rewards remain important, rewards from furthering the mission are even more enriching. People know that (1) the pursuit of the mission has intrinsic value; (2) it benefits the company that cares for and is loyal to them; and (3) if they are not completely onboard, they do not fit and should leave. These beliefs induce staff to use their initiative productively. There is less need for restrictive controls or incentives that would extinguish or localize motivation. Staff are also more loyal, and so it's easier to keep great people.[22]

Table 1-4

Human and Capital Investments—for the Long Run

Notes to this table are listed in "Table 1-4" in Notes.

Statistics and FCB Versus Other Comparisons	Sample	FCB Definition
Family long-run involvement: 94% of FCBs run by family members; 85% say successor will be a family member; 90% plan to keep the business in the family	1,000 U.S. FCBs, 1997–2002	Firm controlled by family members [a]
More investment in plant machinery and electronic data interface for FCBs	U.S. publicly held textile firms, 1983–1992 (N=595 company years)	If one of five largest shareholders is family; also helps if owner is CEO [b]
FCBs R&D US$618 million versus US$539 million for others	S&P 500, 2002	Firms with founding families on the board, in executive role or as significant shareholders [c]
Training 4% of staff costs versus 3% for NFBs; training hours/year 56 versus 43; training expenses per employee 7.4 versus 4.7 thousand francs	24 pairs matched by size and industry of largest 1,000 industrial French companies, 1982–1992	Firms under family control [d]
Commitment to employees: no reduction in staff levels in an often poor economy	1,000 U.S. FCBs, 1997–2002	Firm controlled by family members; 94% also run by them [e]
Benefits: 15 versus 9.4 thousand francs; but 34% less short-term benefits (entertainment), 60% more long-term (health care, disability)	24 pairs matched by size and industry of largest 1,000 industrial French companies, 1982–1992	Firms under family control [f]
CEO tenure six times that of non-FCBs	1,000 U.S. FCBs, 1997–2002	Firm controlled by family members, 94% also run by them [g]
Lower CEO equity-based pay for FCBs	S&P 500, 1992–1999	CEO is founder or descendant of founder [h]
Pay 10 top execs: 70 versus 87 thousand francs; middle managers: 12.4 versus 11.4 thousand francs	24 pairs matched by size and industry of largest 1,000 industrial French companies, 1982–1992	Firms under family control [i]

Today, Levi Strauss (Levi's) faces major problems (see chapter 8). But until recently it has thrived. Although Levi's, like every firm, made use of rules and dollar incentives, its employees were especially motivated by firm values and ethics. Ex-CEO Robert Haas chafed at the idea of being just a jeans company, intent instead on showing that a firm driven by social values could outperform companies bent on profit alone. Said Haas: "Everyone looks at the wrong end of the telescope, as if profits drive the business. Financial reporting doesn't get to the real stuff—employee morale, turnover, consumer satisfaction, on-time delivery, consumer attitudes, perceptions of the brand . . . I believe that if you create an environment that your people identify with, that is responsive to their sense of values, justice, fairness, ethics, compassion, and appreciation, they will help you be successful . . . I will stake all my chips on this vision." He has done exactly that. When Levi's found out that two of its subcontractors in Bangladesh were employing child labor, it decided to take the children out of the factories, continue to pay their wages, and set up schools for them. The company also guaranteed their jobs. Decades of no-layoff policies, open avenues for equal opportunity career advancement, and racially integrated factories since the 1940s also put employees on the side of the firm. People did not, however, identify with a department but an organization— one that didn't just make jeans but worked all over the world for social justice and economic development. There was also a profound understanding that the family would look after its employees. If not in name, then in spirit, they were a part of the Haas family. This personification of the business nurtured pride and commitment. Levi's for many years thrived with the lowest turnover and highest job satisfaction in the business, having been ranked as one of the top twenty places to work in America.[23]

The inclusiveness of these businesses also has an impact on their relationships with outsiders. Firms' substantive missions require help not only from devoted employees but also from value chain partners or joint venture partners. So, unlike organizations that emphasize the one-shot transaction—the best deal today—FCBs invest generously in open, enduring relationships, relationships that ultimately bring access to valuable resources. Furthermore, when a family that cares about its public image is in charge, the company reaches out to be helpful to the broader community. This jibes with firm values and reflects well on the business.

Our discussion is summarized in table 1-5 and encapsulated in an article critical of Timken. The piece contrasts Timken's policies with the preferences of a hard-nosed investment community. "The rap on The Timken Company from Wall Street analysts is that it could be even more profitable if it would only be more aggressive in downsizing its workforce . . . if it were not so preoccupied with striving to produce the top bearings and steel products in the world and if it was less worried about the people of Canton [Ohio]."[24] It certainly would make higher profits if it resisted these tendencies—for a few quarters. But eventually it would also alienate its excellent staff, many of whom have twenty-five years or more with the company; it would degrade quality, its premier asset; and it would relinquish preferred access to community resources. Timken, in short, would become like other companies and lose its edge.

Qualifications

We should reiterate that our comparisons are overly stark. Certainly, many public, nonfamily firms have avoided or overcome the governance limitations we describe, and embraced substantive missions and collective cultures. Many family-controlled businesses, moreover, are hardly ideal places to work, especially where there are conflicts among family owners and managers or an inability to find a talented leader. But among the enduring FCBs we studied, cherished missions and inclusive, energizing collectives were very common—and very rewarding. It is exactly those advantages that are lacking in so many of today's troubled companies.

Mistaking Strengths for Weaknesses

The paradigm of great FCBs runs counter to what many today consider best management practice. In an era of hardball capitalism, analysts and some stockholders find it disconcerting for top executives not to make every quarterly target. Too often, it is considered "naïve" to lock onto a proud social mission and "limiting" to embrace a craft. It is also, perhaps, deemed expensively sentimental in a culture of downsizing to be too loyal and generous to ones' employees, and counterproductive to give too much away to outside partners (see table 1-5).

It is remarkable, then, that exactly these *maligned qualities of the winners' paradigm* seemed central to the success of these businesses. Independent direction, focused, substantive missions, and caring clan cultures not only consistently distinguished most of our thriving FCBs from many non-FCBs, but also from many of the troubled FCB performance intervals we describe in chapter 8. It is these qualities that created an edge and contributed vitally to competitive advantage.

Table 1-5

Weaknesses into Strengths: Two Views of the FCB Paradigm

	Critique of FCBs	Advantages of Great FCBs
Ownership philosophy	Owners don't care enough about the bottom line	Owners cherish the business, invest in it, and manage for the long run
Business philosophy	Naïve mission, no economic or growth focus, failure to meet near-term financial targets	Persistent capability building, distinctive strategies and competencies
Social philosophy	Excessive coddling of staff; high costs; clannishness, insularity	High motivation, loyalty, initiative; privileged partnerships inside and out

Indeed, we have already flagged some of these advantages in describing the winners' paradigm. Independent direction revealed itself not in aberrant leaders prone to excess or stagnation but in care for the mission and craft of the enterprise, and persistent capability building and renewal. Clannish organization translated into a deep concern for the people in the company. It did not lapse into cultism but provoked value-driven performance, initiative, and rich collaboration.

Another Way to Manage

As we will see, by avidly pursuing such priorities, even passions, in an orchestrated way, our winners have done incredibly well. They have succeeded by using a different paradigm of management, in some ways more in tune with administrative thought at the first half of the twentieth century than the second. They have embraced another mode of developing strategy, organizing, coping with the external environment, and directing an enterprise: one that is more antlike—more inclusive, more collective, and more focused on the long term. These enterprises are not victims of a myopic economic calculus but businesses with a heart and soul; feeling institutions that stand for something, have moral fiber, look after all their stakeholders, and are there for the long run. Happily, this makes them especially effective at such quintessentially modern pursuits as developing distinctive core competencies, partnering along the value chain, organizing around powerful customers, and promoting a culture of learning, creativity, and speedy initiative.

Perhaps by devoting so much attention to the special challenges of FCBs, we have all been missing out on what they have to teach us about different ways of managing and competing:

- Leadership that is independent and courageous rather than imprisoned by quarterly financial targets
- Strategies that are focused on and orchestrated for long-run capabilities, rather than distracted by tangential opportunities
- Cultures that are cohesive, caring, and single-minded, rather than individualistic or bureaucratic
- Enduring, win-win relationships with the external environment, rather than fleeting transactions with it

This book is all about the revealed priorities and remarkable practices of great FCBs and how today's managers can develop and configure them to build powerful strategies that produce competitive advantage. In other words, we believe that the thriving family-controlled enterprise offers a strong alternative model for *many* kinds of companies. It is indeed a road less traveled, but with a worthy destination—and an increasingly attractive and scenic one, now that the NFB highway is in growing need of repair. The mission of this book is to guide managers along this exciting road: one that stresses long-run contribution and performance over short, and addresses the interests of *all* stakeholders. The next chapter begins to describe the legs of the journey.

Chapter 2

Potent Priorities at the Great Family-Controlled Businesses

The Four Cs

T O MANY OUTSIDERS, family businesses seem to behave in incomprehensible ways. The *New York Times* knowingly put its very existence into jeopardy publishing Pentagon documents the government and its own lawyers deemed treasonous. It was their public duty, the owners said—a part of their mission. Hallmark and Levi Strauss sometimes seemed more like clans than companies: Values and loyalty were deemed as important as competency; employees were kept on the payroll for life; and the family looked after their people from cradle to grave. Where would the money come from? IKEA and Wal-Mart didn't just buy from their suppliers, they went in and redesigned their plants and bought them new equipment. Then we have firms like Fidelity Investments, Cargill, and W.L. Gore and Associates that embraced business models so bold and unorthodox as to invite both ridicule and sympathy.

Yet it was just these distinctive approaches that we kept finding in successful family companies—approaches that emerged from the contrasts we drew in chapter 1. These, we discovered, reflect the four driving priorities or even passions of our great FCBs and their leaders that we called "the four Cs." Each C priority engendered remarkable policies and practices that we encountered with extraordinary frequency in our research.

- *Continuity: Pursuing the dream.* Our long-lived FCBs commit enduringly and passionately to a substantive mission—to do something important exceptionally well. They invest deeply and for the long run in the competencies needed to attain that mission. And because the company is the vehicle for achieving their dream, families strive to ensure corporate health and continuity, exercising careful stewardship over resources and encouraging long executive apprenticeships and tenures. Short-term tactics and quarterly earnings are furthest from their minds.

- *Community: Uniting the tribe.* To realize their missions, thriving FCBs often insist on building a cohesive, clanlike team. They embrace strong values that rally people around what is important, socialize staff to assure that these values will prevail, and often pamper employees to elicit loyalty, initiative, and collaboration. Bureaucratic rules and financial incentives are secondary.

- *Connection: Being good neighbors.* Many great FCBs cherish enduring, open-ended, mutually beneficial relationships with business partners, customers, and the larger society. These relationships vastly exceed the time span, scope, and potential of episodic market or contractual transactions.

- *Command: Acting and adapting with freedom.* FCB leaders desire the discretion to act independently—quickly and in original ways—often to renew or adapt the firm. They typically work with an empowered top team whose members are similarly free to communicate openly and make decisions. Unlike at many non-FCBs, these leaders do not face hobbling constraints from shareholders.

These driving priorities, and the practices they engender, collectively blend into a kind of symphony that supports powerful strategies common among FCBs. Just as notes can be combined to form a variety of melodies, so can the four Cs and their elements be orchestrated to gird different strategies such as innovation or quality leadership. Now this is a critical point. Volumes have been written about recipes for corporate success that signal the benefits of a whole list of individual practices, including some of the ones we will discuss here. Unfortunately, there are many firms out there that employ these practices and perform miserably. The reason is twofold: First, depending on the strategy and the capabilities the company demands, some priorities and practices are far more important than others; and second, a *wide variety* of complementary and counterbalancing elements acting in concert are required to make any organization work. Firms that ignore these two lessons, including some of our once-great FCBs, soon become victims of gaps and excesses.

We raise these points here because they signal a major difference between our approach and the typical "best practices" literature. Our stance, quite simply, is that although the individual practices of long-lived FCBs have something to teach us, they are utterly incomplete without specifying the *configuration* in which they must play a role—specifically, the strategy they are intended to realize and the many complementary elements needed for its pursuit. So this chapter is only about the notes, not the melody. Chapters 3 to 7 then will play some very popular melodies—songs of brand leadership, craftsmanship, superior operations, innovation, and stellar deal making.[1]

For now, we will discuss the Cs, as well as their roots in the preoccupations and values of successful family owners and executives. They are summarized in table 2-1, and our method of discovering them is related in appendix A. Although more "natural" for FCBs, the Cs certainly are not universal there, nor are they beyond the reach or experience of non-FCBs wishing to embrace them.[2] Our winning FCBs *do,* however, pursue them with rare passion and integrity.

Continuity: Pursuing the Dream

Great FCBs are unusually devoted to their dream—their mission. They are willing to sacrifice profoundly to attain it, and to safeguard the organization that is its instrument. Take the *New York Times.* Despite its recent snafu with reporter-cum-plagiarist, Jayson Blair, the *Times* rests on a long-standing tradition of journalistic excellence, one based on thoroughness, truth, and good judgment. The paper's century-old mission is, at first glance, a simple one: "To give the news impartially, without fear or favor, regardless of any party, sect, or interest involved."[3] But that's a tall order. To fill it, the *Times,* at great expense and risk, keeps taking on powerful interests, from the U.S. attorney general in the Pentagon Papers case to, on countless occasions, New York's civic administration and police department. The credo at the paper is that the public has the right to be informed. Leads are to be followed whatever the consequences. Period. The owning Sulzberger family's original mission of truth comes above personal politics, connections, friendships, and profits—and every editor knows that.

Table 2-1

Overview of the Four C Priorities

	Priority	Practices
Continuity: **Pursuing the dream**	Pursue an enduring, substantive mission and ensure a healthy, long-lived company to realize it.	Embrace a meaningful mission and build the core capabilities it depends on by sacrificing and investing patiently; exercise careful stewardship; foster lengthy executive apprenticeships and tenures.
Community: **Uniting the tribe**	Nurture a cohesive, caring culture with committed and motivated people.	Stress clarion values; socialize persistently; create an enlightened "welfare state"; foster informality that frees initiative and teamwork; enforce intolerance of mediocrity.
Connection: **Being good neighbors** **and partners**	Develop enduring, win-win relationships with outside parties to sustain the firm in the long haul.	Partner intimately with major clients and suppliers; network broadly; stay in touch with customers; be generous to society.
Command: **Acting and adapting freely**	Preserve the freedom to make courageous, adaptive decisions and keep the firm spry.	Act with speed, boldness and originality; exploit a diverse and empowered top management team to do so.

The Sulzbergers not only took courageous stands, they invested hundreds of millions of dollars and gave up about a billion dollars in personal capital gains (see chapter 4) to make the *Times* the most reputable and thorough paper in America. To fulfill their "public trust," they found and retained for career lifetimes independent and brilliant editors like Arthur Gelb and Abe Rosenthal, whose honesty made the *Times* an integral part of the conscience of the nation. They recruited the best journalists, set up the largest number of international news bureaus of any news organization in the world, and kept expanding coverage to neglected domains such as health and science, even as their rivals opted for "news lite." And because the *Times* is the family jewel, the Sulzberger children spent decades learning how to continue this tradition of excellence.

Elements of Continuity

The example of the *Times* evokes a number of continuity elements common to many thriving FCBs. First, firms are so passionate about their mission that they are doggedly persistent and highly vigilant in its pursuit. That's what continuity is all about—chasing a cherished dream. This inspiring mission motivates a relentless development of the capabilities needed to realize it. It also draws forth intensive, patient investment in these capabilities, as well as total-immersion leader apprenticeship programs to impart the spirit to the next generation. Because owners so treasure the company that *realizes* the dream, they impose exacting policies of stewardship: Risks are controlled and products and practices are constantly improved to maintain a healthy enterprise into the future.[4] In the following subsections, we express each of these elements as an imperative, as that is very much how our managers perceived them.

Embrace a Mission That Matters. Substantive missions are not concocted by some strategic planner, nor are they financially driven. They flow from values residing in the bellies of family proprietors. And like all bulwarks, they are immovable. Although missions are manifested in objectives such as making a superb product, pioneering technologies, or establishing an effective brand, they are more fundamental than that. Their ultimate purpose is to make a difference in how people live, in social or scientific progress, even in the joyfulness of life. The Michelins had as a mission to transform travel into a safer, happier experience. The Timkens wanted to make bearings to reduce the friction that impedes global industrial progress. The *Times* wanted to create nothing less than an enlightened electorate. For these firms, it is not a matter simply of having a clear or ambitious mission, but one of real and enduring substance.

Relentlessly Pursue Core Capabilities. Because they are of pivotal significance to the owners, these missions motivate constant capability development. All firms pursue skills, but few do so with the dedication of our winners. Here the lion's share of funding goes to core capabilities—even in dire economic conditions, even when the company is strapped. Nothing can stop the train. During the Great Depression, while its rivals and customers cut back and adopted a fetal pose, Timken kept enhancing its superior competencies in bearings design, metallurgy, and manufacturing. Having hoarded cash and eschewed debt, it saw the crisis as a great chance to extend its leads. So instead of laying people off, Timken put many of them to work at research, developing alloys that years later became the mainstay of jet engine manufacture, and inventing the dominant technology for seamless tubing. At the same time, the research and development (R&D) staff busied themselves writing internationally heralded bibles on high-temperature metallurgy and corrosion, which, incredibly, remain classics after fifty years. Fast-forward four decades and we find Timken outspending rivals in R&D by a factor of 5 or 6, and building, during the economic crisis of the 1980s, a steel plant three times more efficient than the Japanese mills.[5] Given such dedication, it is no wonder the firm has been a market leader for over 100 years.

Invest and Sacrifice Patiently. Profound core competencies may take ages to develop and longer to pay off. So it wasn't unusual for our FCBs to invest all their profits in capability or product development, or to endure losses until the projects bore fruit. In 1978, *Times* editor Abe Rosenthal had the "crazy idea" of introducing a science section to keep readers informed of an increasingly vital part of society. This initiative would demand costly plant facilities at a time when the paper was hurting. The business end of the *Times*, moreover, had made it clear that it would be virtually impossible to sell advertising for the section, which then had no link to commerce of any kind. Although Punch Sulzberger acknowledged that fact, he said, in effect, "not to worry": the family had the money and the faith. So the *Times* went ahead with its new addition, which so clearly fit its information mission. With increasing use of the personal computer, the section became more and more popular. By the mid-1980s, the investment had paid off handsomely in increased circulation and advertising.[6]

Exercise Stewardship. Clearly, the dream is fulfilled via the organization. So organizational health and continuity are primary imperatives. To promote long-term survival, firms are assiduous resource stewards and risk managers. They minimize debt and build up mountains of cash to last out the dry spells. When they do take risks, they mitigate them by partnering, subsidies, sticking to areas of expertise, and buying countercyclically. Firms also keep their physical assets shipshape. Michelin maintained state-of-the-art facilities by using the steepest depreciation schedule in the business.

Foster Lengthy Executive Apprenticeships and Tenures. Two other striking aspects of stewardship over the firm and its mission are uniquely lengthy top executive apprenticeships and tenures. Typically, one generation runs the company until the next is ready to take over. This luxury of time allows the old generation to embed its principles in the organization and to train the newcomers. Punch Sulzberger served for twenty-nine years as the *Times* publisher, twenty of them ensuring that son Pinch learned the business. The Nordstrom, Michelin, Lauder, and Cargill kids spent decades at the feet of their parents—in the office and the living room—all the while absorbing a passion for the mission and the company, under emotionally riveting conditions. The result: Family members, like Pinch Sulzberger, feel not that the business belongs to them, but that they belong to the business, and that they must prove themselves worthy of the association.[7]

All these elements of continuity supported key advantages among our star FCBs: a striving to do something important exceptionally well; the persistence to create superior competencies; and the capacity to sustain these competencies across the generations. In an economy that has suffered from myopic opportunism, the notion of continuity and its elements warrant revisiting.[8]

The Family Roots of Continuity

The mission elicits remarkable sacrifice in part *because* it is so closely linked with the family: its dream, principles, well-being, and reputation—sometimes even its religion. There are few things as compelling as the legacies of our forebears and the future of our children. Given their upbringing, family executives see themselves both as caretakers and crusaders. The onus on them is palpable. In speaking about the *New York Times* and all it stands for, Publisher Arthur Sulzberger Jr.'s wife said of him, "He knows how fragile it is; he knows how remarkable it is. It's daunting." Said a *Times* editor: "Deep in Arthur's soul, he firmly believes that if he blows this, he will burn in hell."[9]

Continuity in FCBs has distinct past and future components. The past takes the form of a proven legacy handed over from the previous generation—an heirloom to be respected and treasured—as is the *Times'* mission of being a public trust. Matriarch Iphigene Sulzberger, who died in 1990 at the age of ninety-eight, spanned all the generations of the paper back to Adolph Ochs, who first purchased the *Times*. She saw her purpose as transmitting to the "kids" Adolph's core values of "duty, unity, and the central importance of nurturing the *New York Times*." Iphigene had conveyed to the family "the conviction that they and the newspaper were one seamless identity." Grandson Arthur Jr. joked that the family had "grown up with tape recorders under their pillows chanting, 'You are one with the paper, you are one with the *Times*.'"[10]

The future component of continuity is a family's commitment to nurture the business to support subsequent generations. Such commitment pushes family members to conserve resources and build for the years to come. To that end, these families made sacrifices and substantial investments, often living with penurious dividends and plowing back virtually all profits. Because the family is in control, opportunistic shareholders cannot undermine these commitments.

Community: Uniting and Tending to the Tribe

Another core priority for winning FCBs, that again results in effective practices, is to build a cohesive, gung-ho community of employees. Community is a manifestation of the collectivist social philosophy we discussed in chapter 1. It is epitomized by the Hallmark Cards Company, which seems, at times, more like an energized volunteer association than a thriving enterprise. Hallmark is staffed by a corps of motivated believers who, with rare delicacy, fashion greeting cards for those who "Care enough to send the very best." That did not happen by accident. The Hall family tutors and nurtures their devoted clan using powerful levers. First they articulate in their credo very clear values and intentions, *ordered* for all to see. "Enriching people's lives and enhancing their relationships" (at the very top of the list), "creativity and quality in products," "people are our most valuable resource," and "distinguished financial performance is a must, *not* as an end in itself, but as a means to accomplish our broader mission."[11]

The Halls champion these values in their everyday contacts. They comment personally on the taste and style of *every one* of the thousands of cards and products designed each year by a creative staff of 800 strong, endlessly fretting over how the product enhances human relationships and fits the Hallmark image. Tolerance is zero for the tawdry or sensational.

The Halls also have drafted meticulous guidelines for card design: how to use sentimental language, match cards to situations, and compose messages and verse. Then there is the company university, Creative U, where employees go for weeks at a time to be steeped in the Hallmark way and the subtleties of writing, drawing, poetry, and even artistic collaboration.[12]

Such indoctrination means little unless people are willing to work all-out for the company. So Hallmark pulls its staff on board by caring for them not only with excellent compensation and working conditions, but unusual loyalty and professional opportunities. Since its founding in 1910, and until very recently, Hallmark never laid anyone off. And because the Halls want to foster an environment for long and successful careers, all promotion is from within. Every effort is made, moreover, to place people wherever their passions lie. Thus, as people's interests develop, so too do their jobs. Hallmark has been named as one of the twenty best places to work in America, and it comes as no surprise that the turnover rate is minuscule.[13]

One of the biggest attractions of Hallmark's culture is that staff are committed to building social harmony with their products and services. They thrive on using their initiative in the fine products they design, the painstaking way they produce them, and the honest and tasteful means by which they sell them. Because everyone resonates with the same values, there is no need for stifling, formal controls or tall hierarchies. The organization is flat and lean, informal and energized.

Elements of Community

The Hallmark example illustrates the key elements of a tribal community in an outstanding family business: strong values, not just stated, but pervasively enacted; incessant socialization in those values; a welfare state to enlist employees in the good fight; and an informal way of operating that engages initiative and collaboration.[14]

Manifest Strong Values. In an FCB, it is often hard to separate mission from values. Typically, the mission reflects the family's values, which are central to what the company does. Hallmark embraces the values of family harmony in the messages of affection on its cards, its employee benefits for young mothers, its family counseling programs, and its charitable work to aid families. Similarly, outfitter L.L. Bean's values—preservation and enjoyment of nature, honesty, and quality—show up everywhere: in how Bean locates its facilities in sylvan settings, recycles, manufactures ecologically, trains its employees to be outdoorspeople, and even fills its catalogue with stunning natural panoramas.

Socialize, Indoctrinate, and Select. To have impact, values need to be diffused. Not only do the Halls critique every card, their corporate university pulls staff in constantly, imparting norms and beliefs as well as skills. To celebrate the family spirit, the daily *Noon News* keeps everyone current about the people, products, and deeds that register high on Hallmark's value meter. Also, there are those fifty years' worth of classy commercials and Hall of Fame television broadcasts that radiate the company's morality, not just to customers but every employee.

This, of course, is no place for the blasé, and the Halls plan to keep it that way. They themselves control the personnel function by setting precise "people criteria" and interviewing candidates for jobs. Thus staff members buy into the values and work well together. Those who don't soon begin to feel uncomfortable, and leave. So for almost a century now, this has been a haven for Pollyannas to fashion products evoking the "warmer" side of life.

Establish a Welfare State. "God is our personnel manager," said Punch Sulzberger of the *Times*. "People only leave when they die."[15] Many families are unusually generous to their staff—the people charged with accomplishing the cherished mission and assuring the firm's survival. To get the staff on their side, they foster a spirit of unity. They pay well, share the wealth, design interesting jobs, and open paths to advancement. They also "absorb misery." When the business gets into trouble, the family often takes a big hit to keep people onboard. In 1956, Hallmark initiated what *Fortune* magazine deemed America's most liberal employee benefits and profit sharing plan. In 2002 the stock valuations in the plan declined. The Halls offered to fund retirements by purchasing shares from the plan at a huge premium, thereby forfeiting a significant percentage of their personal wealth. S.C. Johnson, Levi Strauss, Hallmark, and so many great FCBs have kept people on during recessions, depression, and war, when revenues were abysmal. Such loyalty retained talent and motivated people to give their best when things picked up.

Encourage Informality, Initiative, and Teamwork. When people are motivated and share common values, they can be trusted to use their initiative and collaborate in the best interests of the company. There is less need for the long chains of command or bureaucratic controls that are such anathema to FCBs. Indeed, job descriptions are often open-ended: People contribute when and wherever needed and are encouraged to follow their interests and talents. The Coors family, for example, were control freaks when it came to quality. But they did not micromanage people or set up layers of bureaucracy. When Adolph Coors issued a handwritten memo assigning titles to his managers, he concluded the note by stipulating that titles "mean nothing and should not be displayed. We all have equal responsibility as individuals and as a group."[16] That was how all people were expected to behave. Even by the 1970s, the Coors Brewing Company, a $350 million business, eschewed administrative paperwork and bureaucracy. A mammoth industrial plant with thousands of workers was in many respects run like a mom-and-pop corner store. People were just expected to pitch in and do what was right. And, bolstered by values and training, they did.

All of these elements of community confer advantage. People's hearts and minds are engaged to work for the organization, thereby enhancing learning, initiative, and quality. There is also minimal turnover, and thus an ability to keep proprietary skills and knowledge within the company. The results are best described in Tifft and Jones's portrayal of the *New York Times*:[17]

> *For many, working for the* New York Times *was both a mission and a substitute family. Those who retired or left for other jobs made regular pilgrimages to West Forty-third Street to visit old friends, to catch up on the gossip, and reconnect, if only for a moment, with something larger than themselves. In this respect, those who worked for the Sulzbergers worshipped in the same pew as the family . . . When Punch's secretary [suggested building] a nursing home for former* Times *employees, she was only half joking. "The* Times *is a haven for them; they just never want to leave."*

The Family Roots of Community

Many family owners in our study strive to create a cohesive community because they care so deeply about the company and those who sustain it. Take the company first: It is what the family has built over decades. It is something that reflects on them, and its values and mission are their own.

It is also an institution that supports them and their valued stakeholders. Small wonder the family are so solicitous to select, socialize, train, and care for their employees; it is the latter, after all, who must nurture the precious enterprise and strive to achieve its hallowed mission.

François Michelin put it best when he said that a business concerned with short-term profits will try to exploit its employees. But for a company in it for the *long run,* the more it invests in its people, the more it will reap from them.[18] Our families invested in their employees because of the importance to them of the jobs these people did, and because they wanted the right ones to stay with the company and contribute over an entire career.

Then there is the personalization of the business that is often wrought by family ownership. Employees work for those who care for them, people to whom they can turn when things go wrong. So generous acts are attributed to personal intentions, not bureaucratic requirements, and thereby evoke loyalty. An understanding takes shape to the effect that the family will look after employees and employees will do their best for the institution. This is not, however, a transactional understanding of the form, "If you do A, we'll give you B." Rather it is a moral commitment to enter into an enduring relationship of broad reciprocity—like friendship or even kinship. There is a felt bond between employer and employee, not between a faceless legal entity and a depersonalized staff.

But if many of our FCBs coddle their people to sustain the business, some also do so out of *altruism.* Family members may believe they should share their bounty with those who made them successful because it is the right thing to do. The Haas family at Levi Strauss always said it *owed* its workers loyalty and superior working conditions. It would be not only unwise but "unfair," they felt, not to share generously.[19]

Connection: Being Good Neighbors and Partners

Just as many outstanding FCBs strive to foster enduring, mutually beneficial relationships with employees, they also seek to develop them with business partners, customers, and broader society. This brings them reputation and resources that help ensure a long and healthy future. Therefore firms aim to be "good neighbors" and indispensible partners. And they achieve that with an ancient toolkit: being honest, farsighted, and generous. Bechtel Group, one of the largest engineering and construction companies in the world, thrives by cultivating friends in high places. Rather than going after one-shot deals, Bechtel invests in enduring, open-ended associations with clients and co-contractors. It makes itself invaluable to its initial contacts by providing advice and intelligence, often at no charge. And it is meticulously honest in its dealings, many times delivering more than it promises. It also invests its people and money into relationships very early on to earn the gratitude of its partners. As a result, its contacts grow into contracts, and its contracts into age-old partnerships.

From its earliest years under Warren Bechtel, the firm went after megaprojects such as the Boulder and Grand Coulee dams. Because these were complex jobs that demanded considerable capital, Warren partnered to finance and execute them with industrialists such as Henry J. Kaiser and Felix Kahn. He committed vast resources on the basis of a handshake. Said Kaiser of Bechtel, "He hated to sign papers, on the theory that if you couldn't trust a man's word, you couldn't trust his signature."[20] Such partnerships placed within reach massive contracts ranging from the Trans Arabian pipeline to the $30 billion Jubail Industrial City in Saudi Arabia. Other Bechtel relationships are with clients. More than 75 percent of the firm's projects today represent repeat business with "old friends," in large part because of Bechtel's ongoing efforts to be helpful, even between contracts. Its connections with government agencies are legendary: from long associations and financial partnerships with the Saudi royal family to hires of high-level U.S. officials such as George Schultz and Caspar Weinberger.[21] It is no surprise that, in 2003, Bechtel landed major contracts for the rebuilding of Iraq.

Elements of Connection

The larger point here is that many great FCBs favor long-term, win-win relationships over transactions—links with clients, value-chain partners, providers of capital, and the outside community. They want the business to last and they are willing to put time and money into potentially sustaining associations that take a long time to pay off. They also act with honesty, generosity, and sometimes fraternity, to build a reputation that attracts and prolongs partnerships. The elements of connection follow, in descending order of required commitment.

Be a Benevolent Partner. The most intensive relationships are enduring, open-ended partnerships that demand significant investments of capital and time. Such partnering sometimes happens with suppliers. Ingvar Kamprad at IKEA obsessed about keeping costs down and controlling the designs and quality of his furniture. But he did not want IKEA to be a low-margin furniture maker. So, wisely, he became not just a buyer but a teacher and generous benefactor to his Polish suppliers, who lacked equipment and expertise. Kamprad certainly was liberal in funding these vendors; but he also provided comprehensive technical support and staff to modernize their plants and train their workforce. In building up his suppliers, he was really investing for the long term—convinced that enduring relationships would ensue and pay off. They have, for decades, with a devoted cadre of supply chain soulmates.

Be Responsive and Solicitous. Sometimes connection takes the form of trying to do more for smaller clients by attending more closely to their needs. Here, there are no major investments or dedicated resource commitments to a single party, just a willingness to be more responsive and connected. Even companies like Nordstrom, L.L. Bean, and Estée Lauder, which deal with thousands of clients, personalize their services. Their sales staffs maintain detailed books on individual customer preferences so that they can target offerings and make available more efficient and appropriate service and advice. Follow-ups are often personal, with the same representatives building relationships by calling regularly on a specific set of clients. The object is repeat business from forming a closer bond with the customer.

Network and Stay in Touch. Some relationships, although long term, are intermittent. They simply involve an exchange of information and small favors with old or prospective clients and partners. These contacts are revived whenever needed. Bechtel, for example, maintains contacts with former clients and bankers just to stay knowledgeable and in touch, and to keep the network alive. It occasionally provides useful information or a government contact in the hope that the favor might be returned down the road in the form of additional business. Here, there is no such thing as an ex-customer.

Be a Good Citizen. Firms also connect with the broader community, making contributions to the causes they believe in. Hallmark and L.L. Bean are especially generous in the areas of family support and conservation, respectively. They are, in essence, giving back to the community that has treated them so well—and they view this not as a favor but an obligation.

Inevitably, the company image is enhanced as a result, bringing clients and eager job applicants.

Advantages of connection—of relationships over transactions—include more loyal partners, an ear to the ground, and reputation born of mutual familiarity. The trust built up makes it possible to dispense with cumbersome legal agreements. It also affords a useful interchange of privileged information that can be of great benefit to both parties and a basis for further business. And relationships provide access to resources and business based on loyalty accumulated across the years.[22]

The Family Roots of Connection

Family-controlled businesses invest in relationships to reap all these advantages. They also use them to survive the hard times. Certainly, FCBs have an edge in building these connections. First, partners are drawn to their stability. As noted, family enterprises survive twice as long as other firms.[23] And because their CEOs have such long tenures, there is a "permanent," fully accountable face behind each commitment. Notable, too, is the investment families are willing to make during the formative phases of relationships.

In contrast to non-FCBs where connections may last only as long as an executive is in office, FCBs may transfer contacts across the generations. Status and reputation thus flow to younger family members, and extend the web of contacts. Warren Bechtel passed on his contacts to son Steve, who passed them on to Steve Jr., who in turn passed them on to his son, Riley. Sometimes this happened through personal introductions and membership in exclusive associations such as the Bohemian Grove in California's Sonoma County, a secluded retreat where the country's corporate and government elite gather.

Command: Acting Independently and Adapting Freely

Leaders at the great FCBs insist on the freedom to act decisively and courageously. They view this prerogative as a vital source of competitive originality and business renewal. Take Corning. Although it is still suffering from over-expansion by some nonfamily leaders, Corning has led its industry in innovation for over a century. According to CEO James Houghton, his family and their scientists and engineers have spent the last hundred years altering the technological landscape of the United States. And they accomplished this with a material that is over a thousand years old: glass. Corning has innovated boldly around that substance, moving from the very first light bulbs and radio and picture tubes to heat-resistant Pyrex to the revolutionary fiber optics and now to photonics for the laser manipulation of DNA. Always fast off the mark and tolerant of risk taking, the company is now working on photonics projects with twenty- to thirty-year time horizons—projects that sound as utopian today as fiber optics did back in the 1960s.

The command discretion accorded executives at many FCBs allows them to act quickly, unconventionally, and courageously.[24] This discretion often accrues, as well, to a diverse and frank top management team (TMT), so that decisions are not just bold, but also responsive and intelligent. Our command elements all reflect a theme of independent initiative and renewal.

Elements of Command

Act Speedily. The independence of family executives allows them to make decisions very quickly—providing important first-mover advantages in getting new business and fostering innovation. The Bechtels could raise and commit capital to a megaproject at the drop of a hat—there were no approval hoops or board meetings to go through. Fidelity Investments could launch a major new mutual fund in the time it took to pronounce its name. It knew that timing and being first could be critical in attracting funds to new offerings—from specialized funds like Japan Small Companies to a variety of mid- and small-cap innovations.

Be Original. Many great FCBs march to a different drum and embrace unorthodox ways of doing things. Estée Lauder believed that department stores would be opportune places to sell cosmetics. Ridiculous, many said, in a world that shopped for lipstick in drugstores. S.C. Johnson (Johnson's Wax) and Hallmark sponsored the first radio and television broadcasts to promote their products. Crazy, their competitors thought: What's wrong with print advertising, and how could anyone possibly brand a greeting card anyway? Wal-Mart's business model relied on establishing big department stores in small towns and selling cheaply. Where would the volume come from? In each case, leaders persisted in doing something very distinctive—breaking the rules.

Act Courageously. Independent command has firms acting while others are taking cover. The recent stock market collapse has seen major cutbacks in staff and capital spending at banks, mutual fund companies, and brokerages. But that was not happening at Fidelity. The Johnson family viewed the slowdown as an opportunity to extend Fidelity's lead in Internet client interfaces. While its rivals were pulling back, Fidelity kept pouring millions of dollars into its massive information technology department, thereby extending its service leadership. That same courage also is shown when change is required and strategies need to be questioned.

Keep Renewing. Although our successful FCBs pursued their core competencies for decades, they also innovated a great deal. Estée Lauder introduced edgy new brands for different market segments and bought promising brands from others. Those brands today account for more than half of Estées revenues. Corning and Motorola, too, kept coming up with new products as they deliberately made obsolete the old.

Establish a Diverse but Cohesive Top Team. The speed and soundness of decision making is aided by a diverse but cohesive top management team. In many FCBs, executives have grown up together, so they can understand and trust each other, debate openly, and operate as an effective team. During their heyday, the Coors brothers partitioned the job of running the brewery such that Bill could exploit his brewing brilliance, while the more affable Ad could take care of the distributors. The brothers would pull each other into line whenever either went overboard. A major advantage was that executives could communicate frankly and work quickly together. And no one worried about getting fired. Team members, moreover, believed in each other: They knew all were acting for company, not career.

In the end, independence of command gives rise to profound advantages: an ability to adapt and stay current, be original, and beat competitors to the punch in seizing opportunities.[25]

The Family Roots of Command

The family roots of command issue from owner independence. Unlike executives elsewhere, and much like entrepreneurs, the leaders of many FCBs are at liberty to take risks and make changes. They can adopt ingenious, unorthodox strategies and accomplish big things fast. During deliberations about one of his initiatives, a *Times* executive was overheard to ask Punch Sulzberger: "How will the [public] shareholders react?" His response: "They can always sell their shares."[26]

Unlike many entrepreneurs, however, our FCB leaders feel more responsible for the long-run viability of the business and the reputation of the family. François Michelin said: "The fact that I am responsible for the well-being of 120,000 souls who work for us is a horrific onus."[27] He feels very keenly, too, responsibility for the millions of people whose lives depend every day on the soundness of Michelin tires. He also knows that the extended family will lose all their material assets—down to their homes and furniture—should anything happen to the business.[28] So several family members serve on the top team to condition and inform action and prevent independence from becoming an ego trip. Thus, boldness takes form not in gambles, but in programs of courageous, targeted adaptation.

What We Did *Not* Find Among the Great FCBs

In examining our long-term winners, many things we might have expected to find were, in fact, quite uncommon.

- We did not find much talk about competitors, competitive analysis, or market "positioning." Firms were far more driven by their mission and how to make it relevant to their customers than by the initiatives or "best practices" of the competition. Strategy was "from the inside out."
- There were few charismatic leaders—at least in the traditional sense. Certainly, many family leaders were very visible in their companies, and their deeds were the subject of lore. But, always, the mission was what was important; and the leaders were there to serve it, rather than vice versa. Also, in many cases, firms were run by a cohesive top team rather than a single strong individual; sometimes there were even co-CEOs.
- Sophisticated organizational designs were rare. Firms relied on the initiative of value-driven people to get the job done, not on complex control systems and incentives, detailed job definitions, or bureaucratic rules.
- We found little "grand strategizing." The emphasis was on execution—getting things done, fulfilling the mission. Everyone knew what the mission was and which core competencies had to be

developed to achieve it. Deliberation and action took place within that context.

- Competition often took a back seat to collaboration. Certainly that was true among units and people inside the companies, but it was also true of dealings with outside partners and customers. Firms did not so much try to get the last penny of margin as to form enduring, win-win associations.
- Diversification was sparse and selective. These were meat-and-potatoes companies that knew exactly how they wanted to distinguish themselves, worked assiduously to do it, and were not tempted by distractions. We found little evidence of fads of any sort. And diversification away from areas of core competency was especially rare.
- Reorienting changes, too, were rare. Firms got better at their core capabilities and renewed their product lines and market foci. But they competed on the same basis—brand, innovation, quality, or operations, decade after decade. The president of the Hundred Year Association of New York said most non-FCBs on the list were products of multiple restructurings and survived in name only. "But those that are family-controlled seem different," he said. "They tended to continue in the basic business line, while adapting successfully to change."[29]
- We did not find excessive "bottom-line" discipline. Most managers rarely mentioned profit, which was an expected outcome and a means to keep the business going, not an end in itself. They were mission- and "feel"-driven, not numbers-driven.

As we said, these are strange animals. Firms emphasize the long-term benefits over the short. They address the interests of *all* of the stakeholders needed to keep a company healthy and relevant—not just top executives but all employees, customers, partners, society, and owners. This *long-term, encompassing philosophy* is what our winners are all about.

A Delicate Balance

The four C driving priorities, and the practices they engender, support powerful competitive advantages. Excellent books such as *Built to Last* and *The Living Company* have endorsed some of the elements highlighted here.[30] But were the story so simple, many more businesses, family-controlled or otherwise, would be successful. Each of the priorities, when taken alone or to excess, has a sinister side: Continuity can bring tunnel vision; cohesive community may beget insularity; tight connection some-times invites dependence; and independent command can induce care-lessness (we discuss these pitfalls in chapter 8). Such excesses are the result of an *absence of checks and balances*.

As noted at the beginning of the chapter, and as we will see in the rest of the book, the four C priorities and their elements work only as a config-uration—a melody: when there is a complementary interplay within and across them. First look within categories. Continuity must preserve both past and future orientations: a respect for the core mission and traditions as well as for the long-term future of the business. Community must indoctri-nate with strong values, but it also must liberate with informality and initiative. Connection must not only be to business partners and clients but to the broader community that affords the firm its resources. Command must encompass independent initiative as well as an empowered top team to keep that initiative on target (see table 2-2). These notions, now some-what abstract, will become clearer over the next few chapters.

Looking across the Cs, the natural tensions among them become appar-ent. Continuity is mostly about a stable dream and mission and the *momentum* to carry it out; but command, its natural counterpoint, is about the freedom to *act* and *redirect*. Community concerns the *internal* cohesive-ness of an organization's tribe—the forces that pull its membership together to accomplish the mission. Connection, by contrast, is about relationships to *external* "neighbors," to what is often called the "environment." It is the interplay among these categories—continuity and independent command, internal culture and external connection—that sustains viability (see fig-ure 2-1).

Table 2-2

Opposing Pulls Within the C Priorities

Continuity	*Past:* Mission and traditions	*Future:* Long-term capability development
Community	*Pull:* Core values and indoctrination	*Push:* Informality and initiative
Connection	*Narrow:* Close relationships with business partners and clients	*Broad:* Links with markets, community and public
Command	*Bold:* Independence, courage, originality	*Careful:* Input from a diverse and frank top management team

Figure 2-1

Contrasting Themes Across the Cs

C	Dominant Theme
Continuity	Mission momentum
versus	versus
Command	Action and redirection
Community	Internal cohesiveness
versus	versus
Connection	External relationships

Enduring missions, for example, must be renewed and energized by free command. The threat of community insularity must be offset by close connection to the market.[31] It is this dynamic tension that lies at the heart of our winners' durability.

Strategy and the Four Cs

This is a book about how managers can orchestrate the four core priorities, and the remarkable practices and policies to which they give rise, to support potent competitive advantages. Our main interest in the Cs, then, is in their ability to serve as the pillars of an effective strategy. As we said, although the thriving companies did not rely on a single "note," neither did they play a random assortment of notes. The best family businesses, we found, orchestrated, or "configured," their four Cs around a specific strategic melody. Each strategy was *driven and supported* primarily by two "major" or focal Cs, *backed up by* two "complementary" or balancing ones to complete the organizational arsenal, instill resilience, and prevent excesses in the majors. In chapter 8 you'll find a summary table mapping the Cs onto the five dominant strategies embraced by our FCBs.

Defining Strategy

Before proceeding, we need to say a few words about what we mean by strategy, and its relationship to the Cs. Strategy is (1) the basis upon which the firm chooses to distinguish itself or its offerings to gain advantage in the market, and (2) the set of distinctive capabilities that enable it to do so. Superior returns to the firm may come from higher prices and/or lower costs that are the result of offerings being distinguished, say, by unsurpassed quality, product performance, brand seductiveness, or economy. The bundle of capabilities going into a brand-building strategy, for example, includes the ability to differentiate, build, preserve, and leverage the brand. The strategy literature argues that such capabilities will lead to sustainable profitability only if they are rare, valuable to the market, inimitable by rivals, and nonsubstitutable.[32] They are rendered that way by the practices spawned by the Cs and by their subtle configuration.[33]

Chapters 3 to 7 deal with strategies of brand building, craftsmanship, superior operations, innovation, and deal making, respectively. The chapters begin with a description of the strategies—the bundles of product-market choices and complex capabilities. They then proceed to the four C priorities and practices that are the driving, actionable fundamentals supporting the strategies. Among the winning FCBs, you'll find companies that were later to run into trouble. We include the latter to compare their healthy states to their travails—the topic of chapter 8.

Chapter 3

Brand Builders

O N AN ESPECIALLY COLD, damp day in December, we ducked
into Bloomingdale's in midtown Manhattan. At once, we
encountered a vast array of cosmetics counters, each with its own
character—urban hip, clinical, back-to-nature, French chic, Generation X.
The layouts, posters, "beauty consultants," sales styles, and even fragrances
of each brand seemed so complementary, and yet so very distinctive.

In their white lab coats, Clinique representatives counseled customers
on skin care products, extolling their "hypoallergenic" high-tech ingredients. Slim, stylishly dressed, and quite persistent men and women offered
spritzes of Aramis's exotic, masculine scent. At the same time, dignified,
almost matronly, Estée Lauder advisers gently patted patrons' faces,
preparing them to look more beautiful. We passed the Prescriptives,
Origins, and Bobbi Brown counters, each with unique and beautifully
packaged wares. At every location, the salespeople played their roles con-
vincingly and enthusiastically, their niche appeal apparent. On leaving,
one of us remarked: "Impressive, but I'd hate to compete in a business
with so many options and intangibles." Said the other: "No problem. Every
one of those brands is owned by Estée Lauder."

Estée Lauder, clearly, is a master of branding. In less than thirty years,
the company has come to dominate the U.S. cosmetics market with a share
of 40 to 45 percent. It did this not with one striking success, but time and
again with twelve major brands. Similarly, Levi Strauss made its jeans the
most successful branded product in history, and the company's Dockers
are not far behind.[1] Hallmark, with 55 percent of the U.S. greeting card
market, is the only brand of card 80 percent of the population can name.
In fact, Hallmark is so good at creating emotional brand attraction that its
fastest-growing arm is a consulting division that teaches other firms how
to do just that.[2]

What do these "brand builders" have in common? They are image masters. They create perceptions of themselves and their products that prompt customers to buy. This image, as much as a product's objective features, adds value. The indefinable quality of a brand, so devilishly difficult to create, can prove highly sustainable as a competitive resource. But how do these FCBs do it? How do they become brand leaders?

Family-Controlled Brand Builders

The Estée Lauder Companies Inc.

- Founders/Family: Joseph and Estée Lauder/Lauder
- Founding Year: 1946
- Revenues (2002): $4.74 billion
- Market Share: World's number-two/America's number-one prestige cosmetics firm

With the steely determination of a Jewish mother, Estée Lauder, née Josephine Esther Mentzer, founded her cosmetics empire in Queens, New York. The first to score with brash perfumes and push into luxury department stores, she built the foundation for one of the world's leading manufacturers and marketers of skin care, makeup, fragrance, and hair care products. Estée's son, and now a third generation of Lauders, police the brand's presentation down to the last scintilla. Their products sell in over 120 countries under such names as Estée Lauder, Clinique, Prescriptives, Origins, M.A.C., Bobbi Brown, Jane, and Aveda.

Hallmark Cards, Inc.

- Founder/Family: Joyce Hall/Hall
- Founding Year: 1910
- Revenues (2002): $4.20 billion
- Market Share: Number-one greeting card business worldwide

Joyce Hall's probity, reserve, and uncompromising precision were the foundations of his company's reputation for good taste and its ability to deliver value. Hallmark Cards, Inc. is a privately held company; its 20,000-odd employees own 25 percent of the stock. Through its network of subsidiaries and licensees, it operates in more than 100 countries and publishes in more than 30 languages. The third generation is currently managing the firm.

S.C. Johnson & Son, Inc.

- Founder/Families: Samuel Curtis Johnson/Johnson and Lewis
- Founding Year: 1886
- Revenues (2002): $5 billion
- Market Share: World's number-one or number-two consumer household brands in fifteen product categories

From their landmark Frank Lloyd Wright–designed building in Racine, Wisconsin, five generations of Johnsons have popularized such household brands as Johnson's Wax, Windex, Ziploc, Pledge, Glade, OFF!, and Edge. For over a century, S.C. Johnson & Son has been successfully introducing bold new categories of consumer goods ranging from floor wax to insect repellent, and has pioneered their marketing through retail channels and relentless advertising.

L.L. Bean, Inc.

- Founder/Families: Leon L. Bean/Bean and Gorman
- Founding Year: 1912
- Revenues (2002): $1.07 billion
- Market Share: World's number-one outdoor speciality products and sport catalogue retailer

With its personalized homespun catalogues, well-made sporting clothes, and yuppie favorites like the Maine Hunting Shoe, L.L. Bean has earned a reputation as a concerned status merchandiser—an amalgam of outdoorsmanship, the leisure class, the state of Maine, and stellar corporate ethics. The family, now into its third generation, has enforced the principles of honesty and service, attracting clients with a no-questions-asked return policy, free lifetime repairs for select items, and profound ecological consciousness.

Levi Strauss & Co.

- Founder/Families: Levi Strauss/Strauss, Stern, and Haas
- Founding Year: 1853
- Revenues (2002): $4.14 billion
- Market Share: World's number-one brand-name apparel manufacturer

Founded by a Bavarian immigrant, Levi Strauss & Co. has turned Levi's jeans into a cultural icon and Dockers into indispensable wear for casual Fridays. A workforce of 16,000 extends across 100 countries. In 1873, the company put rivets into pants for strength, thereby creating the first "Levi's," now the world's most widely recognized label in apparel. It continues to offer products ranging from the legendary 501 Blues to the more upscale Dockers Recode. Among the most socially conscious employers in the industry, the controlling Haas family, descendants of Levi Strauss, has invested as deeply in Levi's people as in its brands. Although struggling today to renew itself (see chapter 8), Levi's shares rose from $2.53 to $265—almost as much as Microsoft—in fifth-generation Robert D. Haas's first thirteen years as CEO (1984–1997).[a]

a. Stratford Sherman, "Levi's: As Ye Sew, So Shall Ye Reap," *Fortune*, May 12, 1997: 104–116; Ed Cray, *Levi's* (Boston: Houghton-Mifflin, 1978).

A Strategy of Brand Building

The first step in brand building is strategy—the competitive positioning choices and distinctive core capabilities a firm embraces in order to:

- Create a brand that stands out as different and attractive
- Keep building market share to add to the brand's critical mass and economies of scale
- Protect brand integrity
- Leverage the brand to exploit its power

We will detail how our companies excelled at these choices and capabilities before going on to describe the four C priorities that enabled them to do so.

Brand Creation and Differentiation

Companies choose a variety of ways to differentiate their brands—to make them stand out. S.C. Johnson sells a demonstrably superior product and a positive consumer experience. Hallmark stresses unfailing tastefulness. And Levi's "authentic" jeans celebrate a youthful lifestyle. L.L. Bean combines all of these attributes: quality, taste, lifestyle. Each of these businesses uses a broad set of levers to distinguish their brands: the product itself, the features surrounding it, and creative marketing in all its guises.

A Distinctive Product. There is a popular view that brands are fluff—all smoke, magic, and advertising. Sometimes that's the case. But not among these thriving FCBs. To create a distinctive image, the firms first sell a distinctive product, unique in both its features and performance. And quality is a key component of that uniqueness.

Joyce Hall designed the first greeting cards to convey subtle sentiment. There had been joke cards and picture cards, but none that expressed intimate personal feelings for significant human occasions. Hallmark's products spoke for the senders in words they were too tongue-tied or shy to speak themselves. The cards were imbued with quality, not just in the paper and ink, but the sensitivity and tone of their messages: never gushy, never presumptuous, never off-color. But neither did they shy away from expressing emotions appropriate for life's milestone occasions: births, birthdays, anniversaries, holidays, and deaths. The messages were composed by literary writers, not gagmen, and the images were drawn by skilled artists. And the cards were laboriously pondered over by Hall and his staff to ensure their tastefulness—a tradition Hall family members continue to this day.[3]

On a less exalted plane is Samuel Curtis Johnson, who sold the first floor waxes and insect repellents. Johnson dreamed up and formulated some of these now-universal consumer goods over 100 years ago, but his firm still insists on uniqueness in any new offering. S.C. Johnson will not sell a product unless it has demonstrated real superiority vis-à-vis its rivals—the Product-Plus policy. Today's Sam Johnson relates how, while new product director, he tried to get his dad to introduce an aerosol insecticide that "was a damned good product." The son made a powerful case, explaining that, with Johnson's national distribution and reputation, it could blow away its smaller rivals. The father replied: "But is the product clearly superior?" When told no, he said: "Then take it back to the lab, and when you have got something better, come back and we'll talk about insecticide." Today, Product-Plus is the primary competitive advantage behind all Johnson products and the basis of their promotional appeals.[4]

The chatty L.L. Bean catalogue stems from founder Leon Leonwood Bean's twin passions of hunting and fishing. In 1911, fed up with the soggy shoes he got on his outings, Bean developed a rubber-bottomed shoe, got a roster of nonresident hunters from the state of Maine, and compiled his first mailing list. The Maine Hunting Shoe's rubber soles and leather uppers make their wearers look a little like ducks, but they last forever and keep wading hunters warm and dry in the muck. Then there is icon-maker Levi Strauss, who invented those thick, riveted, denim jeans with incomparable durability. These were not fashion goods when they came on the scene over a century ago, but work clothes that outlasted all competing products.[5]

None of our winning brand builders, in short, succeed with copycat products. None of them get by with goods that lack consistent quality. They shun mediocrity and are embarrassed to "sell smoke"; after all, they reason, reputation and longevity are at stake.

An Emotional Link with the Client. Unlike the craftsmen of chapter 4, brand builders must rely on more than product functionality and quality to attract the customer. The psychological relationship with the client is every bit as central, and honesty and assurance are key components of that relationship. Nowhere is this more apparent than at L.L. Bean. Of the first 100 pairs of the Maine Hunting Shoe sold, 90 were returned because the rubber was weak. Leon Bean gave everyone a full refund. He then borrowed $400 from his brother and made a better boot. This, in 1912, was the birth of the 100 percent lifetime money-back guarantee—potentially a catastrophically generous policy that came to define Bean to generations of clients. According to Bean's 1916 motto: "I do not consider a sale complete *until the goods are worn out and the customer is still satisfied* [italics ours]. We will thank anyone to return goods that are not perfectly satisfactory . . . Above all things we wish to avoid is a dissatisfied customer."[6] To this day, under the lifetime guarantee, Bean reconditions and mends its Maine Hunting Shoes at company expense, repairing more than 10,000 in the year 2000 alone. So, of course, the incentive to build in quality is very strong.

Some brand builders attract clients by fostering more personal relationships with them. At Estée Lauder, intimacy with prospective clients takes form in the thoroughly trained beauty counselors who help clients to choose the right products for their needs and intentions. The counselors compile detailed cards on the preferences of their best 100 customers and call them whenever there are sales or new products that might be of interest, or after they have tried a free sample or have likely used up their supplies.[7]

Sometimes the relationship with clients is further personalized by an explicit connection with the family. Thus S.C. Johnson in its advertisements keeps emphasizing that it is a family company. Levi Strauss and Estée Lauder also play up the family connection. They create among customers the sense that the company is not an impersonal entity but a group of caring human beings who stand behind their product.

We must be careful not to oversimplify, because a great brand normally is a product of many things. An editor at a family publisher we worked with expressed it well. He said that they are very cognizant of both the style and content of the articles they want to publish. He clarified that the publisher's trademark style is not just subject matter but point of view, writing style, educational takeaways, lifestyle examples, presentation, the whole impact and ambience of each issue—including the letters to the editor. Similarly, for L.L. Bean, the affection and loyalty of its customers seems to come from a uniquely effective brew of factors: merchandise, price, style, the return policy, the funkiness of the catalogue, and the state of Maine itself. But the mystique cannot be expressed in any or all of those things, but in the way they blend to create the image of an enterprise that actually likes its customers.[8] Levi's, in the same way, makes a simple pair of denims into a statement about authenticity, quality, fashion, and even political awareness and social conscience.[9] That is the magic of a brand. And promotion, as we are about to see, can figure prominently in the equation.

Brand Building: Unorthodox Promotion to Develop Critical Mass

Having established a basis for brand identity, brand builders go about capturing "share of mind" in the target market. Where this cannot be done via individual relationships, mass promotion and broad distribution play dominant roles. But for these efforts to be effective, they demand expenditures that vastly exceed industry standards. The moral here is not that it pays to advertise, but that these businesses proceeded fearlessly to promote in ways that no one else had thought of or had the courage to pursue. They invested much more intensively than their rivals, boosting cost structures but winning in the long run.

In essence, the companies initiate "virtuous circles": They know brand awareness drives market share, which makes promotion and distribution more economical, which in turn further boosts market share. So they fund lavish advertising and distribution programs that launch these circles— and withstand the glacial payoffs that are such anathema to their rivals.

Unconventional Promotion. Our winners were stunningly original and unorthodox in their advertising, which often marked the first use of a particular medium by a product category. Joyce Hall wrote the first Hallmark advertisements himself, for the *Ladies' Home Journal* in 1928. By the mid-1930s, he began talking to ad agencies about sponsoring a radio broadcast. Most said they were not interested. One agency head told Hall, "You'll never be able to advertise greeting cards if you expect people to turn them over and read the [company] name." Another said, "Greeting cards can't be sold for a brand name like other products." Still another objected: "You can't afford to justify the expense of advertising."[10] And these skeptics were in the advertising business! Needless to say, Hall's competitors had the same reservations. But finally, a brave agency went along with the plan. In October 1938, radio station WMAQ began to broadcast *Tony Won's Scrapbook* three times a week. Won talked informally, recited poetry, and read from Hallmark's cards. At the end, he would say: "Look on the back for the identifying mark—a Hallmark card." The approach was subtle and very new. But before long, people began to take notice.

Later, Hallmark would go on to sponsor one of the first television broadcasts, the *Hall of Fame* series—with seventy-eight Emmies under its belt, the most honored program in the history of the medium. Unlike firms that sponsor lowbrow entertainment, Hallmark makes its audience stretch. Featuring everything from Shakespeare's plays to classical dramas and quality miniseries, each presentation attracts between 10 and 20 million households, solidly reinforcing the brand's image of good taste and sincerity. The broadcast of "Hamlet" in April 1953 drew more viewers in one evening than had seen the play in all of its preceding 300-plus years.[11]

L.L. Bean's marketing has been just as original. From the beginning, the company boosted revenues by pioneering direct mail catalogue sales for sporting goods and embracing the new notion that huge retail businesses do not need an army of stores. The catalogues incorporated Leon Bean's own homespun tips on hunting, fishing, and camping—all the while describing the products and personalizing the relationship between Bean and its customers. "This is the shirt I personally use on all my hunting and fishing trips," he would write. Or, "A white handkerchief is dangerous for a hunter to use. They have been the cause of many shooting accidents." And although the catalogue seemed disorganized—following Leon's narrative accounts and advice more than the logic of a product category, that just made it more fun for readers to go through, and compelled them to take their delightful quests from one end of the publication to the other.[12]

Intensive Promotion. If promotion is original, it is also intensive. Leon Bean was one of the first large-scale advertisers in sports and adventure magazines. His grandson, Leon Gorman, has continued the founder's tradition to include sophisticated but costly prestige publications such as *Barron's*, the *Wall Street Journal*, and even the *New York Review of Books*. L.L. Bean also publishes more than fifty catalogues per year worldwide, sending out hundreds of thousands of copies, all precisely targeted to their audience based on the data meticulously gathered from each and every client. The sales trajectory at Bean was almost a perfect reflection of the company's promotional expenditures.[13]

Although Estée Lauder's (EL's) gross margins still approach 75 percent, its net can be less than 7 percent—the difference being the enormous amount spent on advertising, sales training, and free samples and gifts (EL was the first in the business to offer these). These expenditures enabled EL to mushroom, ultimately to rule the U.S. prestige cosmetics market with 40 to 45 percent shares—more than twice that of its closest rival, L'Oréal.[14] Yet because of their unusual scale, and the potentially slow and uncertain payoffs, these are the sorts of promotional investments that EL's public competitors simply refused to make.

It is worth noting that some of these firms also distributed in novel ways. Estée Lauder took the radical step of trying to break into department stores when cosmetics queens like Helena Rubinstein sold their products through drugstores. S.C. Johnson was the first to sell its wax and insect repellents in grocery stores. L.L. Bean, on the other hand, eschewed distributing to merchandisers. In short, everyone followed a different path except in one respect: Each was unorthodox for the time or for the industry.

Brand Preservation: Consistency, Secrecy, and Isolation

Having built a positive image and critical mass, these brand builders assiduously police the consistency and attractiveness of their brand. Think of the perennially consistent Levi's 501 jeans and Johnson's Wax, and the ever-tasteful Hallmark cards. Firms *treasure* the value of their brand. They know that once it has been established, it can be exploited only if it retains integrity in formulation, packaging, distribution, and promotion. So any changes to products and marketing campaigns begin as cautious experiments. In fact, brand leaders hardly ever change their recipes. Even L.L. Bean's Maine Hunting Shoes have rarely been altered since 1912. To protect these "children," firms ride herd over product quality, brand boundaries, and sales and distribution practices.

Setting the boundaries—the *limits* and *focus*—of the brand, is critical to its preservation. L.L. Bean keeps to a narrow range of styles for each of its kinds of merchandise: It stocks only goods of a quality, application, and image that are completely consistent with the brand. And Bean brand parameters are defined by a set of four categories that determine the kind of product that can be included in the catalogue: sporting goods, footwear, outerwear, and underwear. Said a corporate biographer, "The categories are to Bean what the kosher laws are to the orthodox Jews."[15] Despite the lure of much more rapid growth, Leon Gorman resists expanding into lines that might be incongruous with the quality, outdoors, preppie image of his firm.

Unlike other cosmetics firms that rely on advertising agencies, Estée Lauder itself formulates all the creative advertising for its brands—intent on being in complete control. It also specifies precisely how a product is to be sold. The following excerpt gives a good example of the explicit content of the 150-page basic-training manual for Estée Lauder "beauty advisers." In it, Estée sounds more like a cinematic director and choreographer than a boss:

- *Build a rapport:* Repeat what the customer says back in your own words to show her "you understood her needs." Advisers should make eye contact and hold a product "as if it were a rare jewel."
- *Link and bridge:* When a customer asks for red lipstick, show her several shades. If she is repurchasing a product, use "link selling" by showing her a companion item. Use "bridge selling" by asking what fragrances she prefers, then show her Estée Lauder perfumes.
- *Lay a foundation:* Hold each product the customer has viewed, explain it and hand it to her. She'll already feel like it is hers. Advisers should encourage the customer to return by mentioning other beauty concerns and scheduling an appointment.
- *Lead by the nose:* After trying a fragrance on a customer's hand, guide it toward her nose and say "Doesn't that smell wonderful?" The manual instructs, "Always have your customer acknowledge the scent."
- *Don't give up:* If a customer objects to a product's price, don't give up. "A customer objection is a sign of interest," the manual says. Advisers should "first empathize" and then list a product's benefits.[16]

Today, these manuals are scripted for all of EL's cosmetics lines, each with brand-tailored client dialogue, technique, and style of salesperson.

Levi Strauss was just as controlling, and was notorious for telling even its biggest clients how to display its jeans. According to Levi's former president, Philip Marineau: "We would try to tell people how our fixtures should look in their stores. We had a system that was very much: This is how we do business. You, Mr. Retailer, need to adjust to it."[17]

The brand is also protected via *secrecy* and *isolation*. Secrecy safeguards products that may not be hard to copy. Sam Johnson crows that because of family ownership he is able to preserve privacy about ad budgets, ingredients, sales breakdowns, and more—the kinds of facts he sometimes can get quite easily from the public reports of his competitors. Isolation, a more subtle protection, ensures that a firm's new offerings will not threaten existing brands. Leonard Lauder *separates* his brands, each targeted for a distinct audience, so that they do not undermine one another. Here is one observer's account of the contrasting layouts of EL's brands at Bloomingdale's flagship Manhattan store:

> *"Beauty advisers" for the original Estée Lauder brand, with its classic gold-and-blue packaging, are stationed front and center. Discreet, a little dull perhaps, the Estée Lauder brand seems best suited to the forty-nine-year-old woman active in the Junior League. Just behind, wearing white lab coats, are the Clinique "consultants" [for a dermatological image] hawking a simple beauty regimen perfect for the thirty-six-year-old mom with a GMC Suburban and no time to waste . . . To the right of Clinique, there's the counter for Bobbi Brown Essentials, a cult brand driven by one Bobbi Brown herself, a regular Connecticut mom/makeup artist who skillfully balances family and career and manages to look good too. Still farther back stands a row of M.A.C. makeup artists, all in basic black. M.A.C.'s spokesmodels [include] RuPaul, a six-foot-seven-inch drag queen . . .* [18]

Brand Leveraging

For all their conservatism, brand builders are not in any way stodgy. The best ones keep evolving and growing. They move into new countries, for example, or introduce complementary products. Levi Strauss expanded its men's Slates brand into a line of skirts and trousers for women; Dockers' khakis are being extended to a business-casual line named Dockers' Recode. Bob Haas, CEO from 1984 to 1999, also repositioned Levi's as a fashion product overseas, selling jeans at far higher than domestic prices. In 1984, foreign revenues were $500 million; in 1998, $3.5 billion—about half the company total. That's why foreign visitors to the United States shop so avidly for jeans; higher prices abroad create a profitable arbitrage opportunity.[19] S.C. Johnson too has never stopped diversifying and growing its brands—from floor wax to car wax to self-polishing wax to air freshener to Ziploc bags.

Even L.L. Bean has begun very selectively to leverage its brand by open-ing retail stores—three in the United States and twenty in Japan (ten completely owned by the firm, to maintain control).[20] It also launched llbean.com. Many kinds of leveraging, however, are taboo. The company refuses to let the major chains carry its merchandise because this might conflict with the character of the house, and because Bean feels it lacks an edge in that kind of retailing.

These stories are telling. But they don't explain how these family firms realize their strategic accomplishments when so many of their rivals do not. The answer lies in the four Cs.

The Major Priorities of Branding: Continuity and Cohesive Community

To create and implement their superior brand-building strategies, these FCBs emphasize continuity—a dream and commitment to build an endur-ing brand; and community—the cohesive culture that unites the organ-ization behind it. Continuity manifests in patient capital to build the brand; exceptionally long executive apprenticeships to convey its intan-gibles; and stable, hands-on brand management to preserve integrity and consistency. Community takes the form of a cohesive culture that polices the brand image and indoctrinates staff with highly tuned values and standards.

Pursuing the Dream: Patient Sacrifice and Brand Stewardship

Richard Salomon, who once owned Charles of the Ritz cosmetics, hated the last ten years of his business life. He had gone public and soon felt impris-oned by the shareholders—blocked from making the long-term decisions that would preserve his brand. Said Salomon: "It seemed to me I was under constant pressure for performance and not free to act totally in the interests of the business itself. The interests of the short-term shareowner too often were not parallel to those of the management . . . While a privately owned competitor might consider launching a risky product like [EL's] Clinique or Aramis, this is a luxury not permitted at a . . . company whose earnings had to increase not only annually but even quarterly."[21]

Contrast Salomon's predicament with the dictum of the late H. F. Johnson, Jr. of S.C. Johnson. H. F. stressed one rule that has sustained his firm for decades: "One should always plan in terms of twenty years hence, and nurture the firm today for the generations of tomorrow."[22] Brand leadership eludes the grasp of companies being pressed to produce quick returns. It is easier to achieve in a business whose managers are able to (1) embrace sublime patience and long investment horizons to build the brand, (2) commit to painstaking stewardship to nurture it, and (3) zealously control the brand to protect it.

Human and Capital Investments in the Brand

Brand builders are liberal investors. They are generous with their effort, money, and time, typically to a level well beyond the practical and emotional reach of their competitors.

Sweat and Blood. Some executives at these brand builders seemed superhuman—endowed with a level of energy and persistence that might be regarded as downright unhealthy. Unhealthy, perhaps, but probably also necessary, certainly in the early years of the business.

Nowhere was this more the case than for Estée Lauder. She began her business by selling skin creams, concocted by her chemist uncle, to beauty shops and resorts. At the time, no cosmetics vendors had been able to break into the major department stores. But Estée was simply more persistent than anyone else. "No," to her meant "call again." She stalked the bosses of New York City's biggest stores, repeatedly visiting the different managers, demonstrating her product, and talking about profit margins and the traffic to be drawn into their stores. Finally, in 1948, she was granted a few feet of counter space at Saks Fifth Avenue. There, Estée put into play her unique selling approach. She personally worked the sales counters, showing her clerks how to talk to clients, overcome resistance, apply makeup, and distribute free samples. Step by step she taught them, and they taught others. Via sheer will and by infusing conviction in those around her, the energy began to build. A revolution in cosmetics marketing had begun.[23]

Herbert Fiske Johnson Sr. was a kindred spirit to Estée, and his energy and tenacity were equally legendary. He traveled the world endlessly to sell his floor wax, wearing a white flannel suit even during the blistering heat. In the course of his hundreds of visits he would boast: "This product will not only shine your floor, it will polish it so shiny that you could drag me across the floor and not see any dirt on the seat of my pants." Once would-be clients took him up on his offer, he knew he was seconds away from making the sale.[24] His son and grandson were just as resolute in pushing themselves and their staff to come up with an ongoing stream of creative marketing ideas. The status quo was never good enough, and there was a climate of eternal challenge, debate, and stimulation. Letting up was not an option.

Such stories of personal chutzpah and "never surrender" selling abound in the histories of the brand builders. In fact, the protagonists sensed they were involved in something that really mattered, a mission to do something different and better. So, for all the pushiness, there was always a product to take pride in.

Money. If the human cost was steep, so was the investment in promotion; money that might only be recouped years later. Because of their devotion to the business's long-term future, families invest seemingly unreasonable amounts of money to generate critical mass for their brand. Estée Lauder spent a staggering 30 percent of sales on advertising and promotions—over a billion dollars annually. Rival Revlon, by comparison, had been spending about 17 percent, typical for the industry. Although EL sacrificed incalculable profits, it has catapulted itself into decisive market leadership. Promotion has also bestowed an aura that today allows EL to ask $15 for a tube of lipstick, in comparison to the $6 many of its competitors must charge.[25]

Hard as it may be to believe, our conservative friend from Maine, Mr. L. L. Bean was even more openhanded with his profits than Estée. Between 1912 and 1967—fifty-five years—he plowed back almost all of them into ads in hunting and fishing magazines. His descendants have only quickened the pace.[26]

Time. Investment may take yet other form: patient perfectionism—taking the time to do things exceptionally well. Hallmark has always insisted on the highest-quality ads. So the Halls, in striving for promotional excellence, undertook *years* of experimentation to design their subtle advertisements, making minuscule tweaks and testing a wide swath of audience reactions. They then waited years more for the ads to get noticed. Joyce Hall believed that the time spent reflected well not only on his brand, but on his taste and probity. Said Hall: "When you are selling what is basically a social custom, it must be on a high level. People want to reach up for a social custom, not down . . . [Thus] commercials had to be as tasteful as the [Hallmark Hall of Fame] show itself."[27] There were no singing commercials, or anything trite, and nothing loud or coarse. Ads were sophisticated, understated, warm, and to the point.

All of these investments—human, capital, temporal—were exceptional. They were creative, they were generous, and they required great persistence and patience.

Stewardship and Apprenticeship to Preserve the Brand

The managers at our winners are very conscious of the need to do two things: protect the brand and its reputation for later generations; and teach the new executives the business.

Stewardship. First comes stewardship. One bad product can torpedo a brand. So the typical family executive here is a control freak. Not only did Joyce Hall work compulsively to maintain the good taste and image of his greeting cards, he also stayed out of some of the faster-growing racier segments of the market, first, because they offended him, and second, because they did not make good business sense in the long run, given the firm's conservative, family-oriented clientele. Today, the members of the Hall family still personally inspect each and every card their company produces to ensure that they can be proud of the product, and that every new offering will complement the brand.[28]

Good stewardship also carries the onus of nurturing the business for coming generations. According to Sam Johnson, each generation since his great-grandfather has made a substantial and unique contribution to the company. Great-granddad was the founder, granddad the initial builder, dad the first diversifier into a broader line of waxes and polishes, and Sam himself the prime mover into international markets.[29] In all cases the contributions were substantial, but always the family "brand jewels" were preserved with great pride. Thus, when Estée Lauder introduced "rule-breaking" brands such as Origins, it introduced them under a new name to protect the more established brands.

Apprenticeship. One of the most important aspects of stewardship is to prepare the next generation for leadership; and given the subtleties of a brand, this demands long apprenticeships. So managerial "succession" at these companies was not a months-long search, but a twenty-plus-year odyssey, during which the mysteries behind the care and feeding of the brand were painstakingly communicated from one generation to the next. It was normal, for example, for upcoming family executives to labor for decades alongside the veteran generation, at home and at work, to witness firm values in action and to learn the subtleties of the brand and the business. Indeed, parents and close relatives have enviable advantages in teaching children: the luxuries of time and trust, the ability to instruct by revelatory and *self-critical* examples, and an openness in communicating ideas both simple and nuanced that, in many cases, would constitute an embarrassing interchange between unrelated adults. It is no surprise, then, that many members of the new generation learn their lessons so well.

Sam Johnson, his wife, and their four children met regularly to discuss all aspects of the business. Daughter Helen was already suggesting new products at the dinner table when she was in the fifth grade—one day it was "a toothbrush with toothpaste in the handle."[30] And the intergenerational teaching never stops. Estée Lauder's granddaughter Aerin says that cosmetics are in her blood: She grew up listening to product launches and hearing discussions of face creams at the dinner table. The whole family—father, uncle, brothers, grandparents—were in the business. The Lauder family, in fact, are still very close. All live near one another in midtown Manhattan and speak on the phone several times a day. It is as though everyone had not one coach but many highly qualified ones, twenty-four hours a day.[31]

EL has also done a great job bringing along non-family executives. Fred H. Langhammer, appointed CEO in 2000 (and to be succeeded by Estée's grandson William Lauder in July 2004), has been working closely with Chairman Leonard Lauder and following him around for decades. After joining EL in 1975, he became president of operations for Japan, then served as chief operating officer from 1985 to 1999, and as president from 1995 to 1999. He is today as much an insider as any family executive.[32]

Uniting the Tribe Behind the Brand: Values, Indoctrination, and Care

Brands attract by influencing perceptions. But understanding the precise source of attraction is not easy, and communicating it to others in an organization harder still. To do that, the brand builders have instituted richly textured community cultures. These make clear to all employees in a hundred ways the nature of the brand and what it stands for. They nurture the understanding and behavior that create a brand's appeal. And they treat people with a generosity that wins their hearts and makes them true brand ambassadors.

How the Family's Values Shape Organizational and Brand Identity

Brands, in essence, are cultural artifacts.[33] They are not simply products but purchasing experiences involving nuanced and subliminal associations. It must be made apparent to managers throughout the firm what those associations are. Otherwise, how would they be nurtured and replicated? The organizational community, therefore, and its leaders must reinforce the parameters of the brand at every turn. The values and identities that drive the brand get everyone thinking on the same page. They serve as road maps for product and promotional strategies, and are supported by elusive qualities that include physical surroundings, dress, jargon, stagy rituals, and, of course, work norms and ethics.

At L.L. Bean, the primary value is to enhance life's experiences by helping people commune with nature. This philosophy comes directly from the outdoorsy passions of founder Leon himself, and is still nurtured almost a hundred years later by his Gorman family descendents—true keepers of the flame. L.L. Bean strives to make useful, environmentally friendly products that put people in touch with their natural surroundings. So it keeps the headquarters where its heart is: the pristine state of Maine. Many products are made in Bean's own recycling-intensive plants, which also are located in sylvan northeastern settings. To make the brand more personal to staff, Bean, in the course of fun camping trips, instructs them in how best to enjoy the products they make. It teaches them hiking, fishing and camping, and about conservationist ways to enjoy nature. It holds "team days" and "outdoor experience days" to get its people closer to forests and wildlife, closer to Bean products, and closer to each other. Bean also makes available its nature camps for employee weekends and vacations. Staff get steep discounts on all company products that bring them outdoors, and are encouraged to wear casual clothing at work. The Bean catalogue, of course, celebrates nature not just in its products but its "woodsman-talk" and spectacular pictures. And most of the company's charitable donations go to local conservationist causes such as the National Park Foundation, the Appalachian Trail Conference, Ducks Unlimited, and Trout Unlimited. In short, Bean trumpets and enacts its values in its catalogues, physical locations, manufacturing policies, rituals, training, employee benefits, giving, and conservation programs. It is hard for employees or customers to miss that, and equally hard for rivals to imitate it.

At Hallmark the credo is: "Enriching people's lives and enhancing their relationships"—especially family relationships. The Hall family ensures that that is what the product does, *and* what the organizational community fosters among employees and through charitable works outside.[34] Hallmark encourages family harmony in programs like free childcare, free family and marriage counseling, part-time employment to facilitate child-rearing, staff sabbaticals, scholarships, and free take-home meals to reduce stress at supper time. Community giving and intensive volunteer programs target services for families and mothers. Indeed, "Hallmarkers" are suffused everyday in the company philosophy of family primacy and the centrality of harmonious human relationships. These ideals are reflected daily in the designs and delivery of Hallmark products.

Training and Socialization: Shaping Attitudes and Skills

Through socialization, brand builders communicate brand parameters— not only techniques and policies but image, symbolism, and ethics. Methods include frequent contact between an ever-vigilant family and their employees, lengthy training programs, and lots of meetings and rituals.

First are the personal family guidelines and tutoring. Estée Lauder would get up many Saturday mornings and go visit the Saks Fifth Avenue store in New York. Her purpose—to teach the representatives how to sell: how to dress; how to greet, understand, and charm the client; and how to close the sale. There were few better or more sincere instructors, and none who commanded more attention. Son Leonard has taken over that function, and through his constant travels, spreads his teaching around the globe. Now the third generation (William Lauder is COO) is helping to shoulder the load. The family, going back to Estée, also helped script those 150-page sales manuals for each brand—documents so encompassing as to shape not only how counter staff behave, but ultimately how they think about their clients, their products, and themselves. Guided by those manuals, 100 hours of initial training, and follow-up classes every year, staff members often become missionaries. They are convinced that with their superior products and "touch-a-face" makeup demonstrations, they will make a woman more beautiful and, more importantly, raise her self-esteem.

Socialization was equally central at Levi Strauss. During the 1990s, it trained virtually all its employees and managers in three required one-week courses: leadership, diversity, and ethical decision making. Diversity courses were tailored to each country; so, for example, in male-dominated Japan, classes grappled with the role of women. Ethics classes taught participants to consider decisions from every point of view. Involvement was intense as participants were confronted with feedback that rated them on qualities such as credibility and fairness. But what made the courses especially effective was one simple device at the end: a request for feedback on the gap between stated ideals and actual practice at the students' workplaces. That information was acted upon, changing profoundly processes such as compensation and appraisal (the bonus pool, for example, was expanded from 400 to 10,000 employees, and appraisals got directly coupled to objectives). Gradually, Levi's embedded its values by linking them to training, gap analysis, real corrective action, appraisal, and compensation.[35] The result was a satisfied, skilled workforce that could collaborate well.

The same integrity shines through at Hallmark. The Halls help craft meticulous guidelines about how to compose the messages and sentiments expressed in a greeting card: about the nuances of sentimental language, verse composition, matching cards to situations, and connecting messages to graphics. The guidelines make the elusive more concrete and show staff in all walks how to support and improve the brand and its delivery.[36] Socialization is also accomplished more broadly through internal publications and meetings. Hallmark's *Noon News* has, every weekday for forty-five years, featured articles on company values and achievements, successful new products and community projects, and events in employees' lives. It is rated nationally as one of the top ten employee publications. Then there is the Hallmark intranet with its subgroups to help creative people to share their ideas. There are quarterly "town hall" meetings to air opinions and allow Hallmark executives to interpret the business and its values. To make all this very personal, the CEO meets face-to-face with an astounding 5,000 employees per year.[37]

Of course, indoctrination only works with the right audience. Great brand builders reinforce their communal environment *by hiring and promoting only "people who fit."* The clear definition of what a firm believes in, stands for, and works toward makes it easier to identify and hire these people. An outside recruiter for one brand builder said, "We use a whole different set of screens [for these firms]. They want people who have shown evidence not just of sales ability but loyalty to their past employer, integrity, and service to the community." According to one CEO: "The sooner we get rid of someone who makes no effort to fit in and do a good job, the better." That same attitude prevailed among all our brand builders. But because renegades felt uncomfortable around all the brand hoopla and social philosophy, they usually departed of their own accord. How long could a cynical bachelor endure the pervasive "familiness" at Hallmark? Or what

New York couch potato would want to hang out in the Maine woods with his Bean colleagues learning how to hike and bait hooks?

Motivating Employees with Consideration

While designs and blueprints preserve the look of a product, only a gung-ho army of missionaries can keep a brand robust and evolving. Our firms treated their armies with a level of consideration and devotion that competitors not only failed to copy, but probably deemed unwise.

Judging from its human resources statistics, S.C. Johnson seems more like a warm nest than a business. The firm hasn't laid anyone off since its inception in 1886, and the employee retention rate is a stratospheric 92 percent—3 percent higher than the top rates on the Great Places to Work Institute's "Best Employers" list. Its *voluntary* turnover is a minuscule 2 percent, compared with 5 percent for *Built to Last* favorite and former FCB Procter & Gamble (P&G); and 34 percent of the workforce has been at the job for over twenty years.

Here are some of the reasons for those statistics. All staff have enjoyed profit sharing since 1917, a forty-hour week beginning in 1926, and a company pension plan initiated in 1934—during the depths of the Depression. Compensation is generous. The average entry salary for professionals is $74,000; for hourly jobs, $31,000 (versus $27,000 for P&G). SCJ provides its people with ample training—forty hours per year versus eighteen for P&G. Today it is ranked 23 on *Fortune's 100 Best Companies to Work For List* (P&G is ranked 81), the highest ranked of any firm in packaged consumer goods, and the only company to also appear on *Fortune's 50 Best Companies for Minorities*. It is also one of the *100 Fortune Best Companies for Working Mothers*—and has been for ten years running. Johnson seems almost *too* generous—until you look at its 115 years of success and its growing stable of powerhouse brands.[38]

Hallmark, listed as one of the ten best places to work in America, never stops surveying its employees, endlessly soliciting reactions to compensation, leadership, accountability, and voice. Former CEO Irvine Hockaday met with fifty different sets of managers ten times a year, without *their* managers being present. That way he got the inside scoop. He believed: "Companies can only be enduringly successful if they are committed to both excellence and brotherhood . . . As soon as people can no longer dream of . . . career progress, then [they] lose hope. What then happens, the quality of work, the inspiration necessary, particularly in a creative business, begins to diminish. We believe that we have to manage for the long term, protect our people from cyclical, changing markets; and if they know we're going to do that, they will help us solve the problem."[39]

Hockaday attributes the ninety-two-year no-layoff policy to the Hall family and the long-term view they have chosen to take. It helps too that employees own over 25 percent of the company. But the Halls believe that staff satisfaction and devotion derive mostly from intangibles—personal relationships with coworkers and managers, a climate of caring, and a shared sense of ethics and values. Founder Joyce Hall, in fact, believed that employee loyalty creates customer loyalty, that the *employees* build the relationship between the customer and the company. He might be right. Over the years, said Hockaday, Hallmark's returns on sales, assets, and equity were well up in the top quartile of *Fortune* 500 companies. Not bad for a nonagenarian.

Complementary Priorities of Branding: Connection and Command

Brand continuity and cohesive community, although invaluable, can lead to conservatism and insularity: Companies might stick too closely to a tradition or ignore the market. The firms in our study countered that threat by adopting practices associated with two complementary Cs, connection and command—connection to decipher and impress a changing market; command to reshape and renew the brand.

Being Good Neighbors to Elevate the Brand

Part and parcel of most brands is the public's "feeling" for the company. Brand Builders manage that impression first, with their leaders' visibility and dialogues with clients; and second, by displaying an unusual level of social responsibility.

Ambassadors and Antennae

Family leaders are corporate beacons, serving as role models to insiders and as brand representatives to outsiders. Their contacts with clients and the public also enable them to take the pulse of the market and discover how to tune the brand.

To the world, Estée Lauder embodied her company. Despite her humble origins, she moved with grace through high society. She invited the rich and famous to magnificent dinner parties at her New York apartment, where she served fabulous foods and wines on a dinner table that seated thirty. She also hung out with the likes of the Aga Khan and the Duke and Duchess of Windsor. Before long, actresses and socialites were wearing her cosmetics, and Estée was being photographed everywhere with members of the power elite and their wives. Certainly, the reflected glamour did not hurt sales, but as important was Estée's ability to solicit client reactions to her products. She received inspiration, too, from relationships with suppliers like Arnold von Ameringen, former head of the giant International Flavors and Fragrances.[40]

Chairman Leonard Lauder has inherited some of his mother's contacts, and all of her charm. In fact, he is said to be a "virtual clone" of Estée. He travels 165,000 miles a year visiting with the people behind the cosmetics counters in department stores that sell his company's products. "If you asked me what would I like to do on my vacation, I'd say, I'd like to go and visit stores."[41] One of his most important missions on these excursions is to talk directly with customers and retailers. Leonard comes away with a deep understanding of trends in the market that help him to update his brands, embrace new lines, and add value to clients.

Leonard is also there to put a face on the brand and inspire the troops. He knows how to make people feel important and build relationships, and he expects everyone to follow his lead. He said: "I'm the only person in the cosmetics industry that the retailers around the world know. *Because my competitors don't care. I care, personally* [our emphasis]."[42] No surprise. It's his business, his name, his family. Today, Estée's granddaughter, Aerin, has also become a figurehead for EL, whose publicists choreograph her moves from society lunches to charity balls—208 in the year 2000 alone. The enviable result: Ms. Lauder has appeared in every issue of *Vogue* that year, in unpaid news stories, not ads. She's also on *Harper's Bazaar's* best-dressed list.[43]

Sam Johnson has been an even more visible figurehead, appearing in many of his firm's television commercials. The ads make clear that this is a venerable business whose family owners stand behind their products. Sam provides a reassuring face and voice to the company that gives consumers confidence. He is also a founding member of the World Business Council for Sustainable Development, the adviser to world leaders at the historic Rio Earth Summit. Other leaders, although less public, were no less effective. What would the L.L.Bean catalogue have been without the familiar, friendly "voice" of Leon Bean? Where would Levi Strauss be without the social prominence and community contributions of Walter and Robert Haas? These leaders—and in virtually all cases, their progeny—humanized and personalized their brands, and in so doing served as focal points for the organization and its customers.[44]

Leaders are not the only market antennae here. We saw how EL "beauty advisers" collect cards on the needs and reactions of their hundred best clients. Bean staff compiled files on customer preferences that helped them to target marketing campaigns very precisely, long before the advent of computers. Hallmark, since 1910, has kept tabs on which cards sell, and studies the features of those cards in an ongoing effort to determine trends in customer tastes. These companies are truly in touch with the pulse of the market.

Social Contributions

Firms also connect to the market via the socially responsible image they create. Levi Strauss is the quintessential socially conscious corporation. When it went public (temporarily) in 1971, its prospectus made corporate history by warning that "profits might be affected by a commitment to social programs" (performance usually was outstanding). Levi's fought in Washington for desegregation—two decades before it came to pass; now it battles to protect workers in developing countries, and for women's rights. It also contributes lavishly, but quietly, to cultural and educational charities. And while companies like Coca Cola and Gillette rushed into China, Levi's withdrew to protest human rights abuses there.[45]

Hallmark, too, is a fine citizen. With its Community Involvement Program, it is a primary benefactor not only in its native Kansas City, but wherever its facilities are. Contributions are via charitable donations, intensive volunteer involvement in the community (40-plus percent of the staff!), and legislative advocacy to help the needy. Likewise, S.C. Johnson has made legendary contributions to all aspects of community life in Racine, Wisconsin. In the last five years, it gave more than $66 million to improve the quality of life of communities in the sixty countries in which it operates. Johnson's corporate giving, in fact, exceeds 5 percent of profits per year, versus less than 2 percent for the average corporation. And Leonard Lauder's wife Evelyn has raised over $100 million for causes ranging from breast cancer research to the Whitney Museum. Although there were few direct benefits to the firms from these gifts, they painted the picture of honest, caring organizations that people would like to work for and do business with.[46]

Freedom to Act Courageously in Shaping and Renewing the Brand

As we related in our strategy discussion, the independence of leaders from short-term financial targets and from conservative shareholders allows them to be courageous—innovative in shaping an original brand, and bold in renewing it. The Haas family, in the 1970s, took an increasingly troubled Levi Strauss private. They wanted the freedom to mobilize resources and turn the company around. So they borrowed $1.7 billion, some of it at 14.5 percent, to buy out the public's 63 percent share. The price was seven times cash flow, high for a troubled garment business. But the gamble paid off, and freshly unencumbered, the family was boldly able to renew Levi's with successful new offerings such as Dockers.[47]

EL too exhibited boldness, as when it bought edgy brands like the hip, urban M.A.C., suburban-targeted Bobbi Brown, and the youthful Stila. It also diversified into Aveda, a hair-care company that sells through salons; and Sassaby, owner of Jane, a cosmetics line for teens sold through mass merchants.[48] Recall that in the early years, independent command freed leaders to be original and unorthodox in first differentiating and building brands. Hallmark's pioneering radio broadcasts, Estée Lauder's striking investments in advertising and gifts, and L.L. Bean's catalogue marketing, all required courage and free thinking. These new approaches could take flight, in part, because there was no second-guessing from an uptight board.

Conclusion

Brand building is subtle, relying as much on public perception as objective outputs. Crucial to success, therefore, are seductive differentiation, captivating promotion, resolute consistency, and creative leveraging. Enter *continuity* in the form of (1) profound patience and effort to perfect and establish the brand, (2) record-shattering investments to promote it, and (3) intimate apprenticeships to imbue succeeding generations with brand parameters. A cohesive organizational *community* then indoctrinates staff with the values, attitudes, and knowledge needed to support the brand, and the inspiration to extend it. Profound consideration of employees brings not only loyalty, but dedication and creativity. *Connection* with clients keeps brands visible and relevant. It protects against any stodginess wrought by excessive continuity, while service to society puts a positive image on the company. Finally, independent *command* gives leaders the freedom to be unorthodox—which gets many brands noticed to begin with, and makes firms spry enough to renew brands as needed. Remember, brand building, like all our strategies, is a *configuration* that requires many elements to be in place and to complement one another. Thus, connection and command redress the gaps and offset the potential excesses of continuity and community.

Table 3-1 summarizes how the elements of the four Cs support the components of the brand-building strategy. The number of stars in the cells represents our estimate of how important those elements are.

Table 3-1

Relating the Four Cs to the Strategy of Brand Building

	COMPONENTS OF THE BRAND-BUILDING STRATEGY			
	Creation and Differentiation	Growth	Preservation	Leveraging
Continuity: Patient sacrifice and brand stewardship				
• Human and capital investments	**	**		*
• Stewardship and apprenticeship		*	**	*
Community: Uniting the tribe behind the brand				
• Identity and values	*	**	**	*
• Socialization and training		*	**	*
• Human consideration and motivation	*	**	**	*
Connection: Being good neighbors to elevate the brand				
• Ambassadors and antennae	*	*	*	*
• Social contributions		*	*	
Command: Acting freely to shape and renew the brand				
• Courage and originality	**	**		*

* facilitator; ** key facilitator

Chapter 4

Craftsmen

THE TWO OF US share a common strain of ancestor—the craftsman—specifically, a father and grandfather who were master machinists trained in France and Belgium, respectively. *Craftsmanship* to them meant, simply, that whatever device or machine they designed and built had to be perfect for its purpose. Not acceptable, perfect: an elegant configuration with just the right parts, materials, and connections, and the tightest tolerances the application demanded. One staple-making machine Dad was especially proud of, he named after his beloved daughter. Built at half the cost of its rivals, with far fewer parts and twice the output, ISA is still running after twenty years—every day. Thinking of the small size of his machine shop, we asked Dad what compromises he had to make in the design. "None that mattered," was the bold reply. Stupid question, to a craftsman. We came away with the same feeling while studying organizational craftsmen: Compromise, at least in the realm of quality, was not an option.

Coors, for example, made a beer so good that its fans were willing to break the law and cross state lines to consume it—and the brewery didn't advertise. Timken wanted the ball bearings it produced to be so perfect that it entered the steel industry to make them. Nordstrom turned client service into an art form. And the *New York Times*, despite recent lapses, is not only considered the best paper in America, it is also among the most sophisticated *and* widely circulating, a unique combination.

These craftsmen reside nowhere near the Aristotelian mean. They embrace exacting standards, are willing to wait years to get decent returns, and sacrifice untold sums to do things right. In large part, this is because the controlling families see quality as an intrinsic good, something that reflects their ethical, and sometimes even religious, values. In part, too, it is because quality represents a path for enhancing the reputation, professional opportunities, and economic well-being of the family—now and for generations to come.

But the creed of quality is not simply an indulgence; it is a competitive necessity. It means doing something better than anyone else—so much so that customers will pay extra and go out of their way to tell others about the product. And because companies operate in a competitive world, quality leadership demands not just competence but unyielding devotion and actions. Our FCBs, because their families were willing to go to such extremes, were for many decades able to fend off their public rivals whose "more reasonable" profit-driven managers found these companies not only tough to compete against, but hard to understand.

Family-Controlled Craftsmen

Adolph Coors Company

- Founder/Family: Adolph Coors/Coors
- Founding Year: 1873
- Revenues (2002): $3.78 billion
- Market Share: Number-two brewer in the United Kingdom; number three in the United States

Adolph Coors believed man is measured not by wealth or power but the quality of his work. Even today, executives are "all afraid old Adolph is going to rise up out of the grave and kick their ass" for any lapse in craftsmanship.[a] He—and, more recently, his fourth-generation descendants—obsessed with getting the best ingredients for their beer, and brewing them to a perfection never before sampled in North America. Their quality compulsion assured their watchful and ubiquitous presence on the brewery floor and in the testing labs. It drove them to develop their own ingredients and cans, and motivated a stream of process improvements that revolutionized the industry.

The New York Times Company

- Patriarch/Family: Adolph Ochs/Ochs and Sulzberger
- Founding Year: 1851; family purchase: 1896
- Revenues (2002): $3.08 billion
- Market Share: Most widely circulated newspaper in New York City, and number three nationwide; number-one newspaper site on the Web

When Adolph Ochs bought the *Times*, few foresaw that it would become "the mother ship of American journalism."[b] Ochs-Sulzberger family members for four generations have defined their relationship to the *Times* as guardians of a public trust rather than as owners of a business, and have demonstrated an abiding passion for prize-winning journalism.[c] Currently, the *Times* is considered to be the preeminent U.S. newspaper, with a weekday circulation of 1.2 million, and 1.7 million on Sunday. The publishing empire now includes twenty-three newspapers, nine magazines, and ten broadcasting operations.

Nordstrom, Inc.

- Founder/Family: John W. Nordstrom/Nordstrom
- Founding Year: 1901
- Revenues (2002): $5.98 billion
- Market Share: Number-two upscale department store in the United States

Centenarian Nordstrom is an upscale department store that was said to provide the most attentive, responsive, and friendly service in the business. For four generations the Nordstrom family has nourished this reputation by searching for the finest merchandise, spending generously on store environments, and copiously training and rewarding the best staff. Until its recent problems (see chapter 8) Nordstrom had for decades reaped among the highest margins in the industry.

The Timken Company

- Founder/Family: Henry Timken/Timken
- Founding Year: 1899
- Revenues (2002): $2.55 billion
- Market Share: Number-one roller bearing company in the United States; number three worldwide

Timken's revolutionary tapered roller bearings, invented in 1899 by Henry Timken and his nephew Reginald Heinzelman, had less friction and better durability than conventional ball or roller bearings. But they also required tremendous precision and peerless steel for their manufacture. Timken delivered on both counts. For five generations the Timken family has embraced utopian standards for their bearings and materials, and invested far more in process improvement than any of their rivals.[d]

a. Dan Baum, *Citizen Coors: A Grand Family Saga of Business, Politics, and Beer* (New York: William Morrow, 2000), 4; Russ Banham, *Coors: A Rocky Mountain Legend* (Lyme, CT: Greenwich Publishing Group, 1998).
b. Tony Case, "Publisher of the Year," *Brandweek* 41, no. 19 (May 8, 2000): N24–N29.
c. Chris Welles, "The Arthurian Legends: A Tale of the Times," *BusinessWeek*, October 4, 1999: 19–20.
d. Bettye H. Pruitt, Timken: *From Missouri to Mars—A Century of Leadership in Manufacturing* (Boston: Harvard Business School Press, 1998).

A Strategy of Quality Leadership

Quality at the great FCBs is all about creating client-relevant excellence unavailable elsewhere. A resolute focus on a core competency—such as a particular process, technology, or service—promotes cumulative quality enhancement. And to render the steep quality investments economical, competencies are leveraged across enough types of products and markets to pay the bills.

Thus, the craftsman strategy consists of four major elements:

- The design, production, and delivery of clearly superior offerings
- The perpetual improvement of offerings and processes
- A laserlike product-market focus tied directly to core capability
- The leveraging of capabilities across multiple products or markets to fund further quality development

Perfecting the Offering

The quest for quality and its results are nowhere better demonstrated than at the Adolph Coors Company, whose pursuit of brewing excellence has been described by a company biographer as an anachronism and odd-ball. For years, however, this extremism earned Coors a dominant market share in all fourteen states where it was sold, sometimes as much as 75 percent of the market—*sans* advertising. Coors achieved this under an arrogant but accurate founder's credo that stipulated: "The more we do ourselves, the more quality we have." The Coors family insisted on absolute control over anything affecting the beer that bore their name. To that end, they, unlike their rivals, bought and situated their brewery on the land that supplied pure spring water. They were also alone in making their own malt and developing their own strains of barley; and their quality control verged on the obsessive. Coors scientists—and generations of family members—were constantly to be seen crouching on hands and knees in the fields of the farms where the barley was grown, measuring starch and oil content against the most demanding standards. The efforts involved were enormous for the then small brewer, but the family insisted on a superior product. That's what they lived for.[1]

The *New York Times* has earned its reputation as America's journal of record through unstinting depth of coverage, analytical fastidiousness, and the courage to make gutsy publishing calls—all the way from revelations on Boss Tweed in the mid-1800s to self-critical accounts of its plagiarism problems and biased coverage of the Iraq conflict in 2004. Because the controlling Sulzberger family regards the *Times* as a public trust, the paper is the antithesis of "news lite." As noted earlier, it has more reporters and international news bureaus than any other U.S. news organization (let alone newspaper); and judging from its record number of Pulitzer Prizes, it has captured the finest journalists. To ensure accuracy, the paper has for most of its history maintained a pristine separation among news, editorial, and advertising functions. The *Times* has also insisted on clear attributions for every assertion. A city room joke for years went: "When a thunderstorm hits New York, the weather bureau must be named as the source." The solid, credible reporting that resulted from such policies enabled some journalists to change the course of public opinion—as did David Halberstam with his 1960's reportage about American involvement in Southeast Asia. In fact, for over a century now, beautifully crafted, painstakingly researched *Times* articles have constituted, in so many instances, the most authoritative journalism in the country.[2]

Quality, however, is important not for reaching abstract standards, but for *adding value* to the client. Certainly, Nordstrom provides its customers with quality goods and luxurious surroundings. But so do many far less successful chains of department stores. What makes it all worthwhile for the client is Nordstrom's service—the heart of its craftsmanship. According to Edward Meyer of *Direct Marketing Magazine*: "The thing that makes the Nordstrom emphasis on service so appealing is not the fuzzy warmth of personal pampering. Customers go there because terrific service makes Nordstrom incredibly convenient. Nordstrom helps customers save time."[3] There are myriad stories: the Nordstrom associate who ran out of the store to pick up a pair of Donna Karan slacks for a client—from a neighboring competitor; another who got customers tickets for shows, and seats at a favorite restaurant. Yet another associate, in outfitting lawyers from the same firm, always took care to avoid embarrassing wardrobe duplications. These extras are made possible by the detailed "customer book" all staff members keep on each of their client's dimensions, purchases, and tastes. Said one star salesman: "Ninety percent of new clients come from referrals from current clients who appreciate the job [we] have done." But service is costly: It requires Nordstrom to be especially liberal in its inventory management—in the amount and variety of goods it keeps on hand. Founder John Nordstrom pioneered the policy of being unsurpassed in the depth and breadth of inventory—the back-bone of great service. Even today, with computerization everywhere, Nordstrom carries 20 to 30 percent more inventory per square foot of selling space than any other specialty apparel retailer. Adding to the expense is the unconditional "no questions asked" returns policy. All of this makes some clients so loyal, that even after they move, they return to their hometown Nordstrom stores to shop.[4]

Constant Quality and Cost Improvement

Quality sometimes can be copied by rivals, but a trajectory of constant improvement is far more difficult to duplicate. Our winners not only built but kept enhancing quality. Coors turned somersaults trying to improve its beer. In the 1950s, it launched a campaign to do away with pasteurization, the universal process of heating the beer, which inevitably compromises its taste. After years of searching, Coors finally came up with a process called cold filtering that would do the trick—provided the beer was kept cold. The company had to completely redesign the production lines to implement the new process. But that was just step one. A bigger challenge was that no one along the distribution chain had refrigeration, and all were reluctant to pay the price of acquiring it. The Coors' reaction was simple: "It's a privilege to handle Coors beer, and you should be proud to be part of a leap forward in quality. If you want to distribute our beer, then refrigerate your trucks and warehouses now, and be sure your vendors store the beer in the coolbox with the milk. Otherwise, no deal."[5] The merchants were livid at being dictated to like that, but the Coors brothers insisted that the superior brew was worth the investment. When the first unpasteurized Coors was shipped, in 1959, the out-of-pocket distributors and grocers were skeptical, but it turned out the Coors were right: The public was delighted with the great taste of the new beer, and sales exploded.

This focus on quality improvement can even drive firms to vertical integration. Timken's tapered bearings demand not only precise machining but "perfect steel." At first the Timkens sat on their suppliers to get better steel; then they stationed their own most uncompromising employees at the steel mills to push for even better quality. But still they were unhappy. Finally, in the name of excellence, the family Timken built a small steel mill of their very own in 1917, initiating a mode of vertical integration unheard of in the industry. Now they could get what they wanted: the highest-quality steel made in America, steel that was later to be sold to finicky outside clients for the most exacting applications.[6] One of the main advantages of this move was that the bearings business's ever-increasing demands for quality would maintain the mill at the leading edge of electric-steel technology. Conversely, Timken's growing understanding of steel enabled it to create the alloys that supported better bearing designs.

We should mention that these craftsmen toil away not only on improving products and services but on the *processes* of creating, manufacturing, or delivering them. Timken so dedicated itself to discovering sounder and more economical manufacturing processes that, by the mid-1920s, it was by far the lowest-cost producer in the industry—remarkable, given that it was also the quality leader.[7] The Timkens realized that in order to sustain quality, they needed to invest constantly in plant and people. To support that investment, they kept searching for process and production economies. These brought lower prices and, therefore, larger volumes, which further enhanced efficiency, freeing resources for quality improvement. Here are some recent results from that virtuous circle:

- *Efficiency*: Timken's Faircrest steel plant in Canton, Ohio, by 1989, was the most efficient in the industry, with 25 percent of the standard manpower needs per ton. It was also ranked number one among all steel operations in computerization.[8]
- *Quality*: The life of a Timken bearing has increased sixteenfold since 1980. And Timken steel, said now to be the purest in the world, turned rivals into customers and drew Japanese clients from Japanese competitors. Most unusual.[9]
- *Speed and flexibility*: Timken's Altavista, Virginia, plant, a just-in-time factory with Timken-designed equipment, transformed parts into finished and packaged bearings in ten minutes. The industry standard was twenty-four hours. Timken also could fulfill an order for a customized bearing part it had never made before over a weekend.[10]

Fueled by its dedication to quality and constant improvement, Timken has gone a long way to achieving its goal of being the "best manufacturing company in the world." Both the Bucyrus, Ohio, bearing plant and the Faircrest steel plant have won *Industry Week*'s top award as U.S. Best Plant, Faircrest being the first steel plant ever to win that award.[11] The lesson: True craftsmen never stop chasing quality in materials, designs, processes— whatever it takes.

Stay Focused

Achievements as described above would have been impossible without dogged focus. Whereas other businesses move into assorted lines to grow more quickly, these craftsmen concentrated only on the products and markets that would benefit from their core capability.

At Timken, making any bearing not of the tapered roller variety was sacrilege. As far back as the early twentieth century, H. H. Timken was convinced of the advantages of tapered bearings: They had dramatically superior friction and wear-resistance properties than the cheaper ball bearings and conventional roller bearings. In fact, H. H. offered a guarantee *eight times* longer than that of his rivals. Although competitors such as Hyatt Roller Bearings (run by the legendary Alfred P. Sloan, later to become president of General Motors), were making inroads with their cheaper models, the Timkens never gave it a thought. H. H. believed that his resources were better spent improving a superior product than straying afield. Timken hasn't changed that philosophy in over 100 years.[12]

Focus also shows up in the product itself. Compare the *New York Times* to its New York City rivals. The *Times* is a superb newspaper not only because of what it is: thorough, factual, global, and with a unique sophistication in its coverage. It is also great because of what it is *not*: There are no tasteless ads, comics, sensational stories, slang, overemphasis on sports, racing results, cheesecake photos, or astrology columns. That kind of content would violate the *Times'* character.

Such enduring focus makes parsimonious use of resources to build on strength, it facilitates cumulative learning, and it avoids reputation erosion caused by straying beyond capability.

Leverage Core Capabilities to Fund Quality

Focus orchestrates resources to produce superior capability. An important way to exploit that capability, and get the returns needed to extend quality, is by leveraging it across different products or markets. Thus the firm amortizes its investments over larger revenues and is able to invest more in capability development to *sustain* advantage. Leverage also guards against narrow focus that might mire craftsmen in the past or blind them to opportunity.

The *New York Times*, for example, disseminates its authoritative journalism via national distribution and alliances with the ABC television network. The resulting audience enhancement provides a revenue base that the paper uses to maintain standards and extend coverage and reputation. Helping to push sales is a massive, multimarket ad blitz utilizing print, outdoor, broadcast, direct mail, and cross-media partnerships. The *Times* has also expanded its presence on the Web; it is the first newspaper company to take public its Internet unit, New York Times Digital.[13]

Other quality leaders leveraged to reduce their dependence on one type of customer or industry. By the mid-1920s, Timken had become too reliant on the automobile companies, Ford in particular; its bearings were being used in over 80 percent of the motor vehicles produced in the United States. The family could easily have sold out to one of the car companies and reaped a large fortune. But they wanted to keep the company sound for later generations. So they began to use their emerging metallurgical and manufacturing skills to make bearings for trains, medical equipment, and, ultimately, spaceships and computers. To this day, they have kept pushing out new models for emerging applications, from automobiles to the Mars Pathfinder, serving virtually every industry. Currently, the company produces bearings that range in weight from 0.5 ounces to 9 tons, and sells 300 grades of specialty steel. It has also expanded its steel-making capacity and operates in twenty-nine countries.[14]

The Major Priorities of Craftsmanship: Continuity of Craft and Community of Effort

From our descriptions so far, it would appear that there is a lot in common between the strategies of these craftsmen and other quality leaders. Quality leadership at our FCBs, however, is not only about standards of precision or durability, but commitment to excellence. It's about overcoming the temptation to cut corners, train less, be tolerant, and save hours and dollars. And it's about being extreme and stubborn—and marching to a different drum. The lengths that these companies go to achieve excellence and keep improving on it derive from the devotion of the controlling families, and their willingness to commit to the long-term future of the firm and its people. This is revealed most strikingly in the two C priorities of continuity and community.

Pursuing the Dream: A Mission of Excellence

The quality movement emphasizes "total" quality and statistical "Seven Sigma" standards. Our winners, however, pursue "eternal" quality—which is to say fretting and investing deeply today to ensure state-of-the-art quality *indefinitely*. First, of course, is the very personal quest at the top—never settling for good enough and making that clear in missions, policies, and attitudes. Second are the long-term investments, disproportionate resource commitments, and sacrifices to attain and boost quality. Third are the lengthy top management tenures and long apprenticeships that serve to build and institutionalize quality and pass craftsmanship from one generation to another.

The Mission, Passion, Policies, and Attitude Behind Quality

Quality is a product of a mission that surpasses technique to encompass moral attitude. It gives rise to inviolate policy priorities that spread the discipline of quality across the organization. These are not entries on some list but fundamental codes of conduct that everyone in the company must understand from day one. Four basic components lie at the heart of these firms' craftsmanship:

- A fundamental, substantive mission
- Passion for its pursuit
- Clear policies to institutionalize quality
- Organizational discontent, which drives eternal improvement

A Mission of Substance. Henry Timken had a dream: "The man who could devise something that would reduce friction *fundamentally* would achieve something of real value to the world [our emphasis]." That simple articulation became the corporate driving force and campaign for the next hundred years. Henry and his successors believed that increased mechanical efficiency was the critical element in the productivity revolution of the twentieth century, and they saw their company at the vanguard of that revolution. The Timkens were convinced—they *knew*—their tapered roller bearings beat all others in this war against friction.[15]

Now add to that the family concern for honorable reputation. For Henry's son, H. H., reverence for the family name drove corporate purpose, which was to make the Timken imprimatur the symbol of "reliability, great engineering, skill and accuracy, and excellence of workmanship." The company's products and scientific advances have won its members three Legions of Honour from France, positions in the Inventor's and Automotive Halls of Fame, and an unassailable reputation. The firm has also grown over a century to dominate its market and survive through the toughest economic times of the last hundred years.[16]

An Abiding Passion for Quality. Ambitious missions require passionate pursuit. Such passion is writ large in the intense personal involvement of family members and their disciples. They are always on the case, and their fingerprints are all over the business. The Coorses, for example, insisted on locating their facilities in a single plant so they could oversee operations on a daily, sometimes hourly, basis. Adolph Jr. and Bill situated themselves not in a remote office tower but in a tiny office a few feet away from what was happening in the brewery. More than just riding herd over processes and sourcing, they themselves, slowly and painstakingly, created many of the firm's products. In the1940s, Adolph and son Bill spent countless days and nights at the brewery lab competing with each other to develop a superior-tasting beer with less alcohol. The challenge was compounded by their refusing to use dry milled corn, which could give a stale taste. Instead, they innovated and used the far more costly rice. After much reformulation and testing with assorted yeasts and endless blends of malt and rice, they produced some promising concoctions. Although Bill was occasionally delighted with the result, his dad, known for his impossible standards, was not. Their product was still a little rough, Adolph Jr. would conclude, or the aroma was odd, or they had to slacken off on the rice. It was a case of a connoisseur trying to please a hyperconnoisseur. It took more than a year of this intense family effort to formulate Coors Light Beer, and then the company could not make enough of it. In fact, the Coors had succeeded in inventing a new kind of beer that became the industry standard.[17]

Bill continued to be the quality ayatollah throughout his career. In the 1970s, he had gotten wind that East Coast college students were helping to fund their education by driving west, stocking up a van full of Coors, and returning home, where they sold it at a decent profit. Although Bill was proud of the popularity of the beer, soon the thought occurred to him: Unrefrigerated beer is not going to be at its peak when it reaches the customer. So he took out costly full-page ads in numerous East Coast papers with the bold heading "Please don't drink Coors beer." The ads only served to elevate the Coors mystique in these contraband regions.

That same perfectionism persisted twenty years later, as an aging Bill patrolled the Denver supermarkets checking cases of Coors to make sure none had expired dates. Finding one, he would scurry to the parking lot and, from a pay phone, call the distributor and demand that the beer be pulled immediately. These are not examples of one man against the world, but of a family both symbolizing and policing quality, and imparting to hundreds of others what quality is all about. Such stories are enshrined forever in company lore, and replayed whenever quality-watchers begin to doze.[18]

Clear Quality Standards and Policies. The mission and passion for quality are institutionalized in part through inviolate organizational policies and standards. At the *New York Times*, the components of quality journalism were articulated eloquently and often, beginning with Adolph Ochs's "All the News That's Fit to Print" credo in 1896. But during the political turmoil of the 1960s, charged and biased journalism was upping the circulation of countless newspapers, nowhere more so than in New York. The Sulzbergers and their editors acted immediately to guard against any hint of such impulse on the part of their own journalists. They loudly reiterated their principles—circulation be damned:

> *Although total objectivity may be impossible because every story is written by a human being, the duty of every reporter and editor is to strive for as much objectivity as humanly possible.*
>
> *No matter how engaged the reporter is emotionally, he tries as best he can to disengage himself when he sits down at the typewriter.*
>
> *Expression of personal opinion should be excluded from the news columns.*
>
> *Pejorative phrases should be excluded, and so should anonymous charges against people or institutions.*
>
> *Every accused man or institution should have the immediate right of reply.*
>
> *Presenting both sides of the issue is not hedging but the essence of responsible journalism.*[19]

It's Never Good Enough! Mission, passion, and policies are kept fresh by these craftsmen because they are accompanied by a pervasive discontent.

For all their accomplishments, the executives here are never happy. They're forever haunted by an attitude of self-examination and self-criticism. It is an irony, for example, that at Nordstrom, people talk about customer service constantly, but in a paranoid rather than self-congratulatory way. The Nordstroms, as well as their employees, are reticent to talk to outsiders about their reputation for service, because, deep down, they feel that it is not good enough. "We know that at this moment, someone somewhere is getting bad service at Nordstrom," said Jamie Baugh, an executive vice president and general manager of the Southern California division. "It was never that we were so great, it was just that everyone else was so bad."[20]

The implication is that things are never satisfactory, that the firm can never rest on its laurels, and that vastly exceeding the standards of others is little consolation—it is just a starting point.

Long-Term Investment and Sacrifice for Quality

Passionate missions mean little without the resources to implement them. So craftsmen's standards are backed by intense commitment and investment.[21] In reading the following examples, imagine being in the shoes of a rival (they might just pinch a bit).

The Coors were convinced that steel cans, despite their ability to protect beer from the light, contaminated the taste. They believed that aluminum, which was far more inert, was the way to go. Sceptical managers at aluminum giant Alcoa told Bill Coors he was nuts even to think about making beverage cans from aluminum—it simply wasn't economical. The cans, they said, would cost many times more than the beer itself. And that was if Alcoa made them, let alone a small, ignorant brewery. But quality was at issue, and a family legacy of self-reliance at stake. After all, Bill's granddad had made his own malt and bottles while his rivals stuck to brewing. It would take five years and 10 million 1950s dollars for the first Coors canned beer to be produced, but the cans cost only a penny and a half apiece. Before long, the American Can Company and every other brewer came to buy the technology from Coors, ultimately *rendering obsolete the entire U.S. steel can business.*[22]

Investment continues at these craftsmen, even as rivals cut back. In the early 1980s, when steel plants worldwide were closing down due to recession in the long-declining steel industry, Timken, as usual, ignored the trend. It simply saw an opportunity to become the international quality leader. It invested $435 million, half of its market value and two-thirds of its equity, to build the first integrated steelworks in the United States since World War II. By 1988, the plant was producing at 45 percent above planned capacity and had become the most efficient in the world: two hours of labor per ingot ton versus the industry's seven hours. A unique fabrication process made the steel as close to perfect as possible.[23]

Investments could also take the form of deep personal sacrifice. After Adolf Ochs died in 1935, his family set up a trust that controlled all the Times Company stock. When the firm went public in 1969, family members, including some of the Ochs and Sulzberger "poorer cousins," unanimously agreed to a plan that would ensure their continued control of the paper. Then, in 1986, the Sulzberger family, again unanimously, signed an extraordinary pact barring any potential sale of the business for another *century*. In doing so, the family forfeited for their lifetimes potential capital gains of billions of dollars. To them, ensuring Americans an independent press of unforgiving excellence was more important than money. Every employee now knew that.[24]

Lengthy Executive Tenures and Apprenticeships to Preserve the Quality Tradition

Stable governance underlies continuity. Focused and sustained quality depends on executives who are there long enough to build and institutionalize their quality program and pass on the tradition of excellence to the next generation. It helped that executives enjoyed lengthy tenures, often more than twenty-five years. Adolph Coors ran his company for fifty-three years; his son Adolph Jr., for forty-seven. Adolph's children Bill and Joe Sr. started at Coors in the 1940s and retired only recently (a third son, Ad, was kidnapped and killed in 1960). Fourth-generation Peter and Jeff came on board in the 1970s.

At Nordstrom, in order to thoroughly learn the business, everyone begins their careers at the bottom, even the sons, grandchildren, and great-grandchildren of the founder. All the Nordstroms, in fact, had to perform similar housekeeping jobs—vacuuming carpets, washing windows, and sprucing up displays—before they were allowed to sell any merchandise and step onto the sales stage.[25]

At home too the families talked frequently about the business, imparting to the younger generation not only industry lore or strategic recipes but deep values, craft and traditions. This was not knowledge that could be garnered at business school. Here is Dan Baum's description of a lesson in the Coors legend:

As a boy, [Peter Coors] bathed in stories of travail his grandfather and immigrant great-grandfather had faced. The early orphaning of Adolph Coors, his intrepid ocean crossing and venture into the Wild West, the hewing of the brewery from great vision and toil, the sacrifices to keep workers employed during Prohibition and World War II—these were Genesis and Exodus, the Iliad *and the* Odyssey *for the Coors family . . . [P]ioneering the aluminum can, mastering cold-filtering . . . beer [that was] stylish and of peerless quality. The Coorses didn't need to flaunt their accomplishments. To carry the name Coors meant to possess not only personal wealth but the dedication and work ethic to make visionary dreams come true.*[26]

In short, the continuity priority embodies the passion and commitment to "eternal quality," and what this means for policy and resource allocation. But because quality must be the responsibility of *everyone,* it can be assured only by a vibrant organizational community.

Uniting the Tribe: Building a Community of Craftsmen

Nordstrom is nothing without its crack sales troops, nor is the *New York Times* in any way outstanding without its prize journalists. To reach their unmatched standards, these businesses pay unusual attention to creating a tightly knit organizational community that breeds not just slaves to quality but inventors of it. Indeed, the essence of many craftsmen is that they are like communities: driven by shared values and common beliefs and caring of their members. Families socialize with and initiate employees, and accord them exceptional consideration and loyalty. Employees, and especially executives, are in turn expected to devote themselves to quality—or else! In fact, community is even more exclusive among craftsmen than among brand builders—more elitist, more intolerant, and more reliant on the initiative of individual members. That exclusiveness starts among the executive ranks.

Executive Devotion to Quality

Our families ensure that their managers are true believers—that they are in tune not just with policies but the spirit of the owners and their values. These can be subtle. A 1996 episode at the *New York Times* shows what happens when even a very competent and high-performing executive misses these subtleties and seems to put quality second.

Lance Primis was in many ways a promising and dynamic president at the *Times*. He grew the business by paying attention to the bottom line and new opportunities. After four years at the helm, the stock price was at a seven-year high and headed up, while cash flow and earnings were at record levels, and the paper remained in good shape. Primis also had the support of such powerful board members as Lou Gerstner, CEO of IBM. On the day of a major board meeting, publisher Punch Sulzberger called Primis into his office. Primis was sure it was to learn of his selection as CEO. Instead, he was handed his walking papers. The problem: Primis simply had not fit in. First, he seemed more interested in the bottom line than the quality of the paper. He rarely talked about the news (some at the *Times* said he just read the ads). Second, he had visions for expansion into somewhat alien businesses such as cable television programming, broadcasting, CD-ROMS, and online products. He even delved into golf driving ranges and real estate, which, whatever their commercial merits, were simply not what the *Times* was about. Third, Primis's personal style was a bit too "grand" for the conservative, understated *Times*. He wore tight-fitting, obviously expensive suits, jetted off for golf vacations with executives from other firms, and drove a red Ferrari. To a growing cast of Sulzbergers, this grated. Finally, Primis did not have a sense of the importance of the Sulzberger family and its traditions. The hundredth anniversary of Adolph Ochs's purchase of the *Times* was to be celebrated by a gala reception for hundreds of luminaries in the Temple of Dendur wing of New York's Metropolitan Museum of Art. Primis said he was too busy to show up, and was true to his word. In family businesses such as the *Times*, symbolic actions speak loudly. Primis's days were numbered. Certainly earnings mattered at the paper, but a manifest interest in the content and quality of the newspaper was far more important. "What happened to Lance?" asked a fellow executive after hearing news of the ouster, "Did he think the *Times* was a public company?"[27]

Contrast Mr. Primis's predicament with the attitude of "hired hand" William Umstattd, who after a fifteen-year apprenticeship through the ranks at Timken became its president in 1934, at age thirty-nine (he lasted a "brief" twenty-five years in that role, then another fourteen as chairman). Umstattd had seen lots of action during the Great War and came away impressed with the ability of the Timken-equipped army trucks to outlast all others, and thereby save countless lives. So the Umstattd style became more Timken than Timken. Although he spent freely on new machinery, his office (like that of coexecutives Bob and Henry Timken) was Spartan: The top half of the walls were in glass and furnishings were seedy—this was at a time when profits were soaring every year. About decor, Umstattd cared nothing; about tapered bearing superiority, everything. Each piece of equipment that came into the plant, down to the printing press that stamped the outgoing boxes and crates, had to come equipped, or be refitted, with Timken bearings on all its moving parts. When Umstaddt bought a cane with a ball and socket joint at the base, he soon had it replaced with a specially designed tapered roller bearing. The personal frugality, honorable simplicity, and conviction of the people at the top could not be missed, either by their employees or their clients. In fact, every Timken employee, from the chairman on down, punched in and out. And no one, not a single one, drove a Timken-less GM car.[28]

The Making of a Craft Culture: Socialization and Indoctrination

The tone at the top needs to cascade throughout the company. The socializing influences here are shared values, imbued and institutionalized by executives "talking the talk" and "walking the walk"—and by extensive training.

Communicating Quality Expectations. The eternal message from the family is that quality is to be embraced, defended, and nourished. Nothing new there. But what stands out in these statements, what makes them credible, is that they are not invocations or lists so much as explicit prioritizations. Quality, almost inevitably, is *compared against* and *placed above* something else—revenues, growth, profits, costs.

In a corporate video for new employees, John Nordstrom said: "We are not committed to financial markets, we are not committed to real estate markets, we are not committed to a certain amount of profit. We are only committed to customer service. If we make a profit, that's great. But customer service is first. If I'm a salesperson on the floor and I know that the people that own this place are committed to customer service, then I am free to find new ways to give great customer service. I will only be criticized if I don't take care of the customer."[29]

Another aid to indoctrination was that quality was proselytized "up close and personal" by family members. The now hackneyed acronym MBWA, or "managing by walking around," reflected a core leadership role as family members manifested a ubiquitous presence to monitor operations and reinforce quality standards. A Nordstrom pacing the floors at one of the stores had a huge impact on service quality. There are indeed many Nordstroms "talking the talk": the firm is well into the fourth generation of the family, with six sons of brothers John, Bruce, and James Nordstrom in management positions and on the front line.

Modeling Craftsmanship. The business literature overflows with tomes on culture: tracts admonishing managers to call attention to firm values—moral guidelines, principles, something special a company stands for. Of course values only resonate if people see them in practice. There must be "proof" that those at the top are willing to hurt for their principles. Nowhere has this been more apparent than at the *New York Times,* where again and again the Sulzberger and Ochs clans staked their fortune and influence on doing the right thing.

Some decisions cannot help but serve as profound signals. For decades under Arthur Hays Sulzberger, the *Times* always gave in to labor right away to keep the presses rolling, to give the community "its chief defense weapon: the right to be fully informed." Staff and readers alike were impressed. Then there were the notorious Pentagon Papers, classified government documents that gave a thirty-year history and analysis of the U.S. policy and involvement in Vietnam. They disclosed that, for decades, the government had knowingly misled the American people about the conduct of the war—its range, casualties, and rationales. They were dynamite. The *Times'* lawyers made clear that the publication of such documents, which in effect had been illegally released by Daniel Ellsberg, could constitute treason. The *Times* would risk severe prosecution, steep fines, and perhaps even the imprisonment of some of its staff. Yet Punch Sulzberger approved publication of the documents in their entirety—devoting to them thirteen pages of Section 1 without advertisement. He continued publishing the papers in a series even after Attorney General John Mitchell had advised the paper that doing so was directly prohibited by the Espionage Act—that further disclosures would cause "irreparable injury to the defense interests of the U.S." The headline on the third installment read: "Mitchell Seeks to Halt Series on Vietnam But Times Refuses."[30] Even though editor A. M. Rosenthal knew this would give solace to the antiwar sources he detested, he told a colleague at the time: "[I realized publication would] hurt my view and the views of my friends. I don't want to see it published but it must be published."[31] Every journalist got the message: "Serve the public with truth."

The teachings of quiet Bill Coors too resided more in his legendary decisions than his words. At one point, after six months of persistent experimentation, a proud team of lab and marketing people came up with a stronger new beer they had code-named the "Bud Killer." With trepidation they brought it to Bill for approval. But first they presented a ream of super-impressive market taste-test data. Bill promptly pushed aside the data and said: "Let me see the beer." He peered intently through the glass, took several sips, then some long drafts, and finally said "It's good—but . . . " Then he got up poured a can of Coors Banquet, and added a dollop of Killian Irish Red ale. He tasted the blend and proclaimed, "This is better." One by one the team tasted the blend Bill had taken thirty seconds to devise, and they all had to agree. Back to the drawing board! Another brief lesson in craftsman standards had just been delivered by Uncle Bill: Quality is not determined by customers but something you pull them up to.[32]

At Timken, often, the *system itself* was the message. Take the unusual bonus program: Bonuses were paid to workers once they reached a certain defect-free quota—but no more if they exceeded it. The logic was simple: If you rush people, quality suffers, even if the problems can't be detected in the testing department.[33]

Training in the Craft. If talk defines values and actions prove their primacy, training imparts the how-to's. Timken trains incessantly. Since 1918, its apprenticeship program has enlisted high school grads with top marks and good math skills, and for four to five full years combines on-the-job training with extensive classroom instruction in a specialized area of operations. Workers become experts who understand the how *and* the why, so they can both create quality and figure out how to improve it. The learning is very broad. When a renowned German job design expert visited Timken's Faircrest steel plant in the 1990s, hoping to sell the company on the benefits of cross training, he randomly asked a nearby rolling mill operator how many functions he could perform. "All of them," the worker replied. That is true for most operators at the plant. The payoffs for the company have been great. Historically, 80 percent of the training program's graduates have stayed at Timken for their whole careers, and roughly 40 percent have joined the ranks of management. For the latter, and for university grads, there is also a supervisory training program to instruct staff in the technical and managerial aspects of the business.[34] Nordstrom has the same attitude as Timken. It spends three to four times the industry budget training its associates, and often family members themselves get into the act.

Getting Commitment by Giving Commitment

Indoctrination runs the danger of eliciting compliance and conformity rather than winning hearts and minds. Craftsmen therefore supplemented it with a rare commitment to employees. It is not simply that people were well paid and given incentive. It is that a family went beyond "normal concern" to display personal loyalty to people year after year, sometimes at uneconomic cost.

Said Elmer Nordstrom, a second-generation Nordstrom executive, "Some companies demand loyalty from personnel, but we felt that loyalty should come from us to them first."[35] This tradition has been carried on for generations. Here is what it looks like. Nordstrom employees earn about three times the average at other stores—their productivity warrants it. Profit-sharing benefits, which accrue to virtually everyone, vest 60 percent after five years and 100 percent after seven. Benefits increase with seniority, to reward loyalty. To propagate the service culture, all promotion is from within, and a no-layoff policy was in effect for decades. Elmer again: "We did everything we could to get the best people, and once we had them, we did everything we could to keep them. We wanted our people to know that they could work their way up, while also learning about the business on different levels." In fact, one of the drivers of expansion was to create more advancement opportunities for the best people. All the while, to give employees a voice in how they are treated, the Nordstroms make themselves very accessible. They answer their own phones and keep their office doors open (the company newsletter is called "The Open Door").[36] The outcomes of all this pampering: skilled and motivated associates and a loyalty that keeps their talent within the firm. Today, Nordstrom ranks among *Fortune*'s top 100 companies to work for.

Timken is not a sentimental company. But because it invests so much in hiring and training its employees it wants to keep them. It abhors layoffs, but when they were absolutely necessary, the Timkens made major donations to the local community to help the workers and their families, pending a recall to work. As at Nordstrom, to preserve the discipline of quality, all promotion is from within, the only hires being entry-level. As a result of these practices, quality and seniority are high and employee turnover is low. Approximately 30 percent of the workforce has more than twenty-five years of experience. Also, around 60 percent of employees are shareholders who own 13 percent of the firm (versus the family's

18 percent)—one reason why the firm has paid dividends every quarter for nearly 100 years.[37]

Successful craftsmen did not always treat their staff so well. Sometimes, as firms grew larger and more impersonal, they began to accord less attention to employees, particularly those whose jobs could be tightly controlled. So at one time or another, Coors and Timken did face problems with their unions. But these were lapses in the family attitude that represented departures from form, and from the modes of operation that for decades had made these businesses stars.

Getting (Only) the Right People to Stay. Notwithstanding this commitment to employees, these are not gratuitously charitable places to work. Craftsmen strive to recruit the right people, and quickly dismiss those who don't fit the demanding culture. Thus, in return for their investment in human resources, quality leaders insist on absolute conformity to core values. Nordstrom, for example, hired only one out of a hundred applicants. Yet if employees were not willing to do absolutely everything to serve difficult clients, they did not survive the month. Unlike some brand builders that want to convert everyone to their warm cultures, craftsmen simply expel those who do not clear the hurdles.

Van Mensah, who sells men's clothes in a suburban Washington, D.C., Nordstrom, always advises prospective employees: "If you're interested in retail, this is the best place to work. But you have to understand this is not for everybody." A general manager confirmed that opinion: "People who don't want to sell will never make it in our system because if you don't understand how important that is, and if you don't understand how important the relationship with the customer is, you just won't do well here."[38]

The result is a meritocracy in which employees are not by any means equal. The superstar salesperson stands head and shoulders above others; he or she is extremely well rewarded and accorded high and visible status. Conversely, the company is careful to prune its staff of low producers. This not only increases returns, it also enhances quality by having more customers served by the best people. According to Bruce Nordstrom, doing so will "result in better customer service and higher sales, and more income for superstars. We want *them* to be happy [emphasis ours]."[39]

Abe Rosenthal, another perfectionist, was for several decades the irascible news editor at the *New York Times*. There were many who disliked him and had been bruised by his "I don't want to hurt you, but . . . " attacks during the daily conferences. He could be taxing to anyone not upholding the *Times* standards of excellence. So, many journalists did not last because they were tempted to violate the paper's principles by editorializing in the news. They left for positions where they could express their sentiments. Although the *Times* lost some excellent people, it did not, during Abe's tenure, lose its reputation for being factual.[40]

Liberating Employee Initiative

There is an important difference between initiative and compliance, and these firms were mostly after the former. That came from a community culture rather than a set of bureaucratic controls. Given that firms are populated with those who buy into the quality mission, the main job of craftsmen is not so much to script people's actions to preserve quality as to get them to use their talents to improve it. The *Times* relies on the initiatives of editors and reporters to get good stories. Timken depends on the ingenuity of its engineers to come up with ideas for better alloys and designs, and on its plant craftsmen for insights into process improvement. At Nordstrom, service initiative in making a sale is everything.

The true test of community in a quality leader, then, is its ability to get people at all levels using their hearts and minds to do the best job, *and* to be creative in that capacity. Because people are "on board" and indoctrinated with firm values, they can be trusted to do the right thing and be freed to use their initiative.[41] According to longtime Nordstrom watchers Robert Spector and Patrick McCarthy:

> *Nordstrom expects, encourages, preaches, and demands individual initiative from the people who are on the front lines, people who have the freedom to generate their own ideas (rather than wait for an edict from above) and to promote fashion directions that are representative of their store and region . . . Giving salespeople and managers at all levels a wide range of operational and bottom-line responsibility (such as controlling costs) without shackling them with lots of bureaucratic guidelines . . . allows Nordstrom people to act like entrepreneurial shopkeepers rather than blocks in a retailing mammoth.*[42]

Bruce Nordstrom claims that what separates Nordstrom from its competitors is its army of "self-empowered people who have an entrepreneurial spirit . . . These salespeople have the opportunity to be successful because Nordstrom gives its employees the freedom to make decisions. Nordstrom management is willing to live with those decisions." At Nordstrom, there is only one rule for the employees: "Use your good judgment in all situations." And staff can sell merchandise from any department to their clients. This freedom is not, however, free of pressure: Employees have to confront an endless set of sales objectives, and they must do whatever is needed to satisfy the client. That is the source of the Nordstrom mystique. One star salesman built up a list of 6,000 client names, all the way from junior managers to senior executives and the Nordstrom brothers themselves, whom he advised on their wardrobe needs.[43]

Timken, too, fosters initiative, which reaps great quality and productivity. Although Timken's Bucyrus bearings plant uses the latest automation and computer technology, its top performance comes from its people and the way they are organized. There, self-directed work teams and project teams are charged with specific improvement initiatives. Team members rotate across six role positions in which they assume responsibilities formerly handled by supervisors—equipment, quality, cost, safety, and so on. Decision-making responsibility is all at the front line. So any associate with a good idea discusses it with his or her supervisor and implements it on the spot, without having to go through layers of approval. Said one worker: "It's not just warm bodies out there; people are thinking." By 1991, Bucyrus had already achieved seven-sigma performance. Its statistics were impressive: Schedules were met 98 percent of time; employee suggestions increased from 489 to 1,852 in two years; improvement in first-pass yields were up 72 percent; and changeover times were down by 65 percent.[44] The Faircrest plant also employs teams to tackle cross-departmental problems. In just a few years after its opening, the teams reduced costs by 25 percent, electrical consumption by 18 percent, customer rejects by 62 percent, and work-in-process by 15 percent. Production schedules were met 100 percent of the time, and downtime shrank from 600 to 175 hours per year. All told, the teams increased capacity by 38 percent without *any* capital investment. And because this was accomplished by empowering and challenging, rather than stressing, the workforce, labor turnover remained a minuscule 0.09 percent.[45] For both plants, these achievements were a product of the superb training and a recruitment effort that, as at Nordstrom, often hired only 1 of 100 applicants for a job.

Complementary Priorities of Craftsmanship: Connection and Command

The quest for craftsmanship can be dangerous, sometimes very dangerous. The risk is that companies will act in the pursuit of pure quality—a personal passion—rather than quality that is relevant and something clients are willing to pay extra for. Enter connection—relationships that firms form with suppliers or customers bring privileged, frank, and often stark information on what they are doing wrong and why quality, although perhaps superb, may be totally off the mark. Spry command, in the form of empowered and diverse top management teams, can also increase the relevance of quality, and help to renew it.[a]

a. That family heads are there for the long run, with the power to make enduring commitments, and the incentive to preserve their reputation, make them ideal relationship partners. Family executives are not apt to cut corners or renege to make short-term gains.

Connecting with the Customer to Ensure *Relevant* Quality

The Timkens learned a lot after they formed close relationships with Ford to supply automobile axle bearings. Ford's pressures and dissatisfaction caused Timken to redesign its manufacturing facilities to make them far more efficient. These efficiencies then allowed the firm to capture higher-margin customers that did not have Ford's immense bargaining power. Today, Timken sends out highly skilled teams of sales engineers to work directly with customers to address their particular friction problems and tailor a solution. This gives Timken ideas about where problems lie and about possible new products and applications. In short, Timken imbues an engineering culture with a customer orientation. It also has a long-standing policy, based on its encompassing attitude toward quality, of fixing not only its own mistakes but mistakes of its customers that it feels it might have been able to prevent with better advice.[46]

Nordstrom, too, forms relationships with its customers by keeping close tabs on their purchases and preferences and shaping offerings accordingly. Salespeople also engage in conversations with the more regular customers about things like products, styles, and services, and use the feedback to alter the merchandise mix, which is *their* decision. Because Nordstrom gives refunds on merchandise even years after it has been purchased, it engenders high expectations from customers, and thus solicits more of their reactions and complaints.

Spry Top Teams

Another powerful tool for offsetting excessive traditionalism and insularity is a diverse and cohesive top management team. Among the great families, an important asset has been the presence of a blend of relatives and outsiders on the team, typically from different functions. These members could be open and frank, honoring quality but also pressing to make it relevant and economical. That one sibling could be the quality representative while others advocated for marketing or finance created a richness of perspective and worked against going overboard to serve a single function.

Take Nordstrom. Like their predecessors, the third generation of Nordstroms encompassed a variety of personalities who shared a love of the business. John was the more analytical, the brother who questioned and prodded the others and set tough standards about how things should be done. Bruce mastered the shoe business, a key slice of revenues at 20 percent of sales; and Jim was the superb marketer and cheerleader. Jack MacMillan, another member of the top team, brought to bear a nonfamily perspective; he was mainly responsible for human resources. Bruce Nordstrom explains the intimate, smooth communication among these executives: "We were all raised the same and went through the same experience. [Our values] tend to be the same . . . We've worked together our whole lives and it's such a second nature to us, and we unconsciously lean on each other's strengths. There's no question that . . . the four of us, by being a cohesive committee, bring a much stronger single presence to the office of the CEO because we all have little things that we probably do better than [the other]."[47]

Conclusion

Some of the stories in this chapter are remarkable because these craftsmen are in many ways extreme specimens. They hold fast to their missions, give their all in the pursuit of quality, and make sure the people at the top are true believers in word and deed. Then they create a culture of like-minded, highly trained people who imbue the company with the craft and the creed of quality. The danger, of course, is that continuity can turn into stagnation or irrelevance, and community into insularity, as the firm loses sight of the changing needs of the marketplace. This makes it especially important for the companies to stay in close connection with the clients, and to have a command team diverse and spry enough to renew and redirect the product line. If not, quality becomes irrelevant perfectionism. It is this balanced combination of the Cs that makes it possible to *sustain* advantage. Table 4-1 shows how the policies and practices of craftsmen support the different components of their strategy.

Table 4-1

Relating the Four Cs to the Strategy of Craftsmanship

	COMPONENTS OF THE CRAFTSMANSHIP STRATEGY			
	Get It Right	Constant Improvement	Focus on Competencies	Leverage
Continuity: Pursuing a mission of excellence				
• Compelling mission and values	**	**	**	
• Long-term investment and sacrifice	**	**	*	*
• Stable governance	**	*	*	
• Long apprenticeships		**	*	
Community: Building a corps of craftsmen				
• Executive dedication to quality	**	*	**	
• Socialization and indoctrination	**	**	**	
• Commitment to and from employees	*	**		**
• Liberating employee initiative	*	**		**
Connection: Linking with the customer				
• Ensuring market relevance	*	**		**
Command: Acting and adapting freely				
• Spry top team		*	*	*

* facilitator; ** key facilitator

Chapter 5

Operators

D ANNY DID NOT ENJOY his visit to IKEA. Carless, he had prevailed on a friend to get to the store in the burbs. Together they ambled through a labyrinthine warehouse-showroom, with nary a sales rep in sight. Mission: to furnish a living room. The spare, utilitarian selection, six-week wait for couches, and do-it-yourself prospects for the rest of the pieces soon had the shoppers heading for the exit—which took ten minutes to find. Isabelle had a different experience outfitting her home office. She made a plan and took measurements, went through the IKEA catalogue to choose the pieces and style, and, with her dad in tow, headed for the store. Within minutes she was on her way to the checkout counter with various kits in her cart: for a desk, swivel chair, two shelves, and a CD rack. That evening, the office was assembled, and it looked lovely—indeed, for the price, amazingly so.

IKEA is the quintessential operator. It has shaped its operations to be highly efficient and economical, and both wants and attracts only those customers who fit its model. Suburban locations, restricted product range, few staff, catalogue shopping, and self-assembly are all part of a configuration for supplying good furniture at very reasonable prices for those willing to do some work.

As we will see, these operators are less romantic than our other types—less clanlike, less participative, more mechanical, sometimes less human. In fact, there is the temptation to view them as boring companies in boring industries, places that focus on efficiency and then just sleepwalk through the motions. For our FCB operators, nothing can be further from the truth. These companies are indeed efficient. And they do make much use of routines, standard procedures, and automation to do their business. But they are very different from their competitors: They embrace starkly unorthodox business models and execute on them in original ways.

Family-Controlled Operators

Cargill, Incorporated

- Founder/Families: Will W. Cargill/Cargill and MacMillan
- Founding Year: 1865
- Revenues (2002): $50.83 billion
- Market Share: World's number-one grain trader and grower of genetically modified foods

Juggernaut Cargill is the world's largest agricultural commodity middleman. Its grain-trading business grew quickly after the Civil War, with U.S. westward expansion. The founding families followed the railroad, setting up facilities to store grain and bring it to market. Over five generations, they built an unparalleled global infrastructure for trading and transporting commodities—and never stopped improving it. Cargill pioneered ingenious storage and processing systems that shaved expenses and waste to the bone. Today, it contracts with farmers and provides crop supplies, processes the output into food, and markets it to wholesale end users.

IKEA International A/S

- Founder/Family: Ingvar Kamprad/Kamprad
- Founding Year: 1943
- Revenues (2002): €10.98 billion
- Market Share: World's number-one furniture retailer

With almost 50,000 workers in thirty countries, IKEA of Sweden has evolved an ingenious strategy, offering a limited variety of goods, partnering with suppliers around the world, and building economical megastores in the suburbs. Its elegantly simple furniture-in-a-kit is cheap to manufacture, ship, and stock, and its catalogues make it unnecessary to have a large staff in the stores. IKEA has succeeded in its internationalization by adapting its offerings and sales techniques to local markets.

J.R. Simplot Company

- Founder: John R. "Jack" Simplot/Simplot
- Founding Year: 1929
- Revenues (2002): More than $3 billion
- Market Share: World's number-one processor of frozen potatoes; number two in frozen vegetables

Three generations of Simplots have reinvented the front end of the value chain, supplying processed potato and veggie products to massive clients like McDonald's and KFC. They have captured those clients with economy and convenience, delivering exactly the right quantity of goods to the right locations, just in time. They also add value by supplying almost ready-to-serve food tailored to client needs, and by working with customers to create new products. Much of the business is transacted automatically, and marketing costs are rock-bottom.

Tyson Foods, Inc.

- Founder/Family: John Tyson/Tyson
- Founding Year: 1935
- Revenues (2002): $23.37 billion
- Market Share: World's number-one meat processor and marketer

Ebullient ex-CEO Don Tyson of Tyson Foods claims, "We're dangerous." Between 1973 and 1996, Tyson's stock rose almost two-hundredfold. In 1993, Tyson was ranked number four in the *Fortune* 500 list in ten-year total shareholder returns. Awesomely efficient, the Springdale, Arkansas, enterprise is the world's largest fully integrated producer, processor, and marketer of meat and meat-based convenience foods. It is also a leading breeding stock supplier. Tyson has more than 120,000 employees, operates in 15 countries, and is recognized as the market leader in almost every retail and foodservice market it serves. Clients include more than 80 of the top 100 fast-food chains.

Wal-Mart Stores, Inc.

- Founder/Family: Samuel Moore "Sam" Walton/Walton
- Founding Year: 1945
- Revenues: $244.52 billion
- Market Share: World's number-one retailer and biggest company

Wal-Mart, by far the largest business employer in America, serves a staggering 100 million customers a week and hires 600,000 people per year just to stay at its current size. It has grown faster than any comparable retailer, and for decades reaped superior returns with a business model geared to low-cost operation. Wal-Mart leads the industry in cutting-edge technology to buy and deliver goods cheaply and track how people shop. Merchandise is wide in categories, but not deep, and suburban locations and lower wages hold down operating costs. Wal-Mart partners with major suppliers to manage shelf space and share the savings. Despite recent ethical and labor tribulations under Sam's son Rob (see chapter 8), 100 shares of Wal-Mart bought in 1970 for $1,650 traded at $8 million in 2003.

A Strategy of Operations Superiority

Operators have, in effect, rethought their industries to compete in a new way. They derive competitive advantage by adding value more efficiently than their rivals to one or more stages of the value chain, and optimize their business model by catering to a sharply defined price- and cost-sensitive target market. In order to implement and defend this model, operators evolve an elaborate, capital- and relationship-intensive infra-structure whose many interconnections and efficiencies are exceedingly difficult to imitate. Activities for which firms do not enjoy advantage are outsourced to upstream or downstream partners.[1]

The strategies of these operators are distinguished by four core objectives:

- Evolve an original business model that adds the most value to clients at the lowest cost.
- Cater only to price- and cost-sensitive clients.
- Build a sophisticated operations infrastructure that places a premium on efficiency.
- Specialize and partner along the value chain.

The division head of a textile firm we worked with summed it up nicely. He said, in effect, that his firm could compete because it worked smarter— it had a better business model, more efficient operations, and partnered to focus on what it did best. The company could achieve success only because its owners were willing to invest for the very long term in infra-structures and partnerships.

An Original, Economy-Driven Business Model

The business models of operators are not loose assemblages of elements, but complex, integrated systems. IKEA's business model, for example, is based on a simple idea: Furniture, if well designed, can be cheap with-out being ugly. The elements of the model include: attractive, low-cost, reasonable quality furnishings; limited variety; self-assembly; young-family-oriented suburban megastores with nurseries and plenty of parking space; catalogue-driven self-service; and no costly advertising. These elements all keep expenses and prices down, and they reinforce each other. Catalogue sales and limited variety, for example, make it easy to get along with fewer sales personnel. Standardization and focus in the product line make it possible to rely on suppliers that can be closely monitored and controlled by IKEA. Flat packages save space in transportation and warehousing. Suburban locations and large stores reduce expenses, self-select for young families with cars, and reduce delivery costs. And so it goes. Rivals hoping to imitate this business model would have to embrace all of it—and that would be hard and expensive to do.

Like IKEA, Wal-Mart employed an original business model, incorporating large stores in rural locations where competition was sparse and land cheap. Self-service cut staffing costs, while everyday low prices reduced advertising expenditures, and modest category depth limited inventory expenses. So did a state-of-the-art hub and spokes, computerized distribution system that delivered goods to stores faster and cheaper than anyone else. Third world suppliers, low corporate overheads, and rock-bottom labor costs complete the picture. Such models, however, do not emerge full-blown. They surface gradually from brave, persistent experiments.

Sam Walton was inspired by the notion of a discount store with a limited range of low-price merchandise and was the first to take it into severely underserved rural areas. He staffed his early stores with the nicest and most competent people he could find, and talked endlessly with them and with customers and suppliers about what to do next. He also used his thriving flagship Harrison, Arkansas, store as a model and training ground for the new stores. In 1970, Walton made a first public offering of $5 million, to build new stores and complete the first distribution center, always keeping family control. As Wal-Mart's buying power increased, economies of operation grew, and its reputation began to attract more and more people. The ascent had begun.[2] Then a crisis hit. The Arab oil embargo of 1973 forced Walton to rethink his distribution strategy to avoid becoming hostage to inflation in energy prices. Cleverly, he began to build all stores within a twelve-hour drive from the nearest distribution center, making a gradual march across America, one center at a time.[3]

Targeting Only Value-Sensitive Clients

Operators' business models alienate many kinds of customers. So these firms only go after those that want the lowest costs. IKEA seeks value-sensitive shoppers willing to do a little work to save money. Wal-Mart asks its customers to put up with limited variety, larger packages, and some driving time in exchange for its low prices. In the cases of Tyson and Simplot, the principle is the same: Target only those clients that are economical to serve. But here the clients are very large—major restaurant and fast-food chains, for instance, that purchase huge quantities, typically via automatic restocking. Because of the bargaining power of those customers, the only way to earn good margins is by doing more to the product—selling "food instead of animals" and "solutions instead of products." Thus, Tyson delivers its regionally adapted chicken formulations, just in time, daily, to each of a chain's outlets. It also helps clients such as McDonald's and KFC develop new dishes. Preprocessed food and timely delivery reduce these clients' labor costs, ensure consistency, and minimize inventory. Tyson benefits, too, from the additional processing, as the volatile prices of the grain used to feed the chickens now represent a much smaller fraction of the selling price.

High-Volume, Integrated Infrastructures

The business models of great operators rely on intelligent efficiency— adding more value, more cheaply. This is typically accomplished by building in scale, automation, and integration to extract all the extra cost from operations. Although any business can invest in infrastructure, these FCBs were extraordinarily generous in this regard because of their far-sighted family ownership.

Scale and Volume. The primary vehicle for increasing efficiencies is expanding the scale of operations—processing higher and higher volumes. Wal-Mart and IKEA, not surprisingly, have the largest stores in their industries, typically located in rural or suburban locations, to minimize both selling and overhead costs. The scale and concentration of the total operation and the limited variety offered also cut expenses, as people and facilities are spread across a large volume of product.

Sam Walton kept growing his chain, conferring upon it more and more buyer power to support the low-price strategy, which further fueled growth. Store sizes too were ramped up, from about 46,000 square feet in 1976, to 64,000 square feet in 1983, to a whopping 220,000 square feet today—so more products were offered and more shoppers kept coming in. It was all a virtuous circle that in some years produced revenue and profit growth of almost 50 percent.[4] After opening 39 stores in its first decade, Wal-Mart built 452 in the 1970s, and 1,237 in the 1980s; over 400 are planned for 2004 alone.[5] Under Rob Walton, Wal-Mart has continued to grow by moving into urban centers, incorporating groceries, introducing Sam's Club warehouse-style stores, and expanding abroad.

In the meat business, according to Don Tyson, size is everything as well: Economies of scale are essential for low costs, and market share is vital to get adequate prices from powerful clients. Greater demand means bigger facilities, which allow more automation and more shifts. One way to gain scale is to make acquisitions. Don strove to increase the company's chicken-processing capability by at least 6 percent per year (far more than rivals and far less than Tyson was used to before it had reached critical mass). He chides: "Do you want me to give you a list of the twenty top chicken producers? I call them every six months." Most are not for sale, he says, and those that are, are asking for too high a price. But judging from recent history, his persistence has paid off.

Acquisitions, of course, not only speed growth, they may remove competition and bring skills and clients. They also provide opportunities for rationalization and leverage know-how. In effect, they have allowed Tyson to become the "General Motors of meat," now processing over 50 million chickens a week in seventy large plants.[6] The lesson here is not to get as big as possible, but to grow to a feasible size that best leverages the business model and infrastructure.

Automation and Integration. At these operators, whatever can be simplified, standardized, or connected, is. There is little slack in the system, as standards and controls are exacting. Information and logistics systems are absolutely state of the art. And many activities are triggered automatically, governed largely by fluctuations in input costs and demand. Waste is a cardinal sin, and everything happens according to spec. Take Tyson's modern chicken processing plants, which are, in a sense, a microcosm of the rest of its operation. They are fully automated—over 200 birds per minute go in one end, and fully cooked and dressed fried-chicken pieces come out the other. These are then delivered to each and every client site, just in time, with the right seasoning. Human intervention is minimal.[7]

Scale and automation facilitate such process integration, both inside the firm and with value-chain partners, to further enhance efficiency. Indeed, some operators are so tightly linked to their partners in a continuous, real-time chain that they share the same information and logistics platforms for automatic purchasing and delivery. That integration is hard for rivals to imitate.

Perhaps the ultimate example of an integrated system is the one evolved across more than a century by Cargill, which now connects at every stage of the food supply chain, from seed to packaged end product. Here is what this looks like:

- A grain farmer buys all the Cargill inputs as a package: seeds, herbicide, and Cargill fertilizer. The farmer signs a contract, which determines the growing and handling conditions, to deliver the produce to Cargill at a specified price and quality.
- The farmer sells the harvest to a Cargill elevator (storage facility).
- Cargill processes the harvest into animal feed.
- Cargill ships the animal feed to Thailand.
- There it is fed to poultry, by a farmer under contract to Cargill.
- Cargill buys the poultry and processes, cooks, and packages it.
- Cargill ships the packaged product to Europe and sells it to a McDonald's or supermarket.[8]

The business model makes contract workers out of many farmers, and gives Cargill significant influence over the entire value chain. Yet Cargill remains very much anchored to its core competency: as a middleman that removes inefficiencies from the supply chain between producer and consumer. It rarely becomes involved in farming or selling to the final customer.

That same integration is in evidence at Wal-Mart, where sourcing, distribution, sales, and information functions are so tightly connected as to permit productive fine-tuning."[Wal-Mart's system gave] its executives a complete picture, at any point in time, of where goods were and how fast they were moving, all the way from the [supplier's] factory to the checkout counter . . . This made it easier to tailor the assortment of goods according to local tastes and to experiment . . . [It] also meant Wal-Mart could keep less inventory on hand." By 1983 the firm had already opened a major cost advantage, spending only 2 percent of sales on distribution costs in comparison with KMart's 5 percent. Then in 1988 Wal-Mart became one of the first firms to speed the entire system with its own satellites. So Sam Walton could personally communicate with all of his store managers, and any buyer could inform all department heads about forthcoming products.[9]

Leveraging. Leveraging the infrastructure extends the range and power of the system and cuts costs. Tyson, for example, leverages its unmatched computer, processing, and replenishment systems across different meats, countries, and acquisitions, pulling them all onto one efficient processing and logistical platform. Cargill uses its grain storage and trading expertise to move into a host of other commodities, such as cocoa, cotton, fertilizer, oil, salt, orange juice, and—via its financial products division—currency. This breadth lessens the impact on earnings of commodity price swings and makes maximum use of an infrastructure of ships, railway cars, storage facilities, and expertise around the world. The company is now moving up the food chain, with food processing accounting for more than half of revenues. It is also expanding globally by extending its network of foreign offices, thereby accessing better information on local markets.[10]

Value-Chain Specialization

The business model, we have seen, focuses on parts of the value chain where the firm has the deepest capabilities and economies, and where it can add the most value. Because of this specialization, it is necessary to partner with suppliers or distributors to complete the chain.

Sam Walton had an abiding belief that the only way he could get his business model to work was by driving down the costs of his suppliers. So he worked with them directly to help improve their production, logistics, and even sourcing operations, in some cases turning weaklings into efficient competitors. Walton was especially keen to work with American suppliers that had been beaten up by foreign competition and were hungry for work.[11]

Wal-Mart, however, formed the tightest relationships with its *major* suppliers, in part to get costs down but also to extract more value. Procter and Gamble (P&G) and Wal-Mart effected one of the closest associations ever between a mammoth supplier and an equally big client. Wal-Mart accounted for over 10 percent of P&G's global revenues, a figure that had kept on growing. So, at Sam's instigation, the two firms linked up. Wal-Mart pressed P&G to set up a client team of dozens (ultimately hundreds) of people from all its functions, product categories, and relevant geographies, and dedicate these resources exclusively to the Wal-Mart relationship. The job of the P&G team was to work with Wal-Mart to provide more economical and responsive service via improved computerized logistics and more exacting stocking strategies. Wal-Mart was, in effect, outsourcing a piece of its merchandise management. The two firms concocted automatic procedures to make ordering and deliveries more efficient and reduce inventory costs to the lowest levels in history. In the first few years of the relationship, these costs were slashed by more than 10 percent.[12]

Sometimes operators team up with suppliers out of sheer necessity. In its early days, IKEA's Swedish competitors boycotted any manufacturer that would sell to the troublesome discounter. This forced IKEA to look outside the country for suppliers. Ultimately, they stumbled on a Polish manufacturer, which, although willing, required significant training and investment from IKEA. But there seemed a real likelihood that the potential supplier could learn to make good furniture at extremely low costs. In time, that is what happened. IKEA, by forming alliances with such suppliers, controls its designs, its methods and materials, and even its costs and margins. This has proved a winning formula. Today, IKEA's real secret weapon is its network of over 2,400 suppliers in more than sixty-five countries that allows it to sell simple quality at the lowest possible prices.[13]

But outsourcing stopped where there was no cost advantage. When they could do the job better or more cheaply, operators actually took over the roles of their suppliers. To avoid exorbitant delivery costs, for example, Wal-Mart bought its own fleet of trucks to pick up merchandise from the factories and bring it to their "smart" distribution centers. Wal-Mart trucks were then routed to each of the 200 stores attached to a distribution center so they would never travel empty. The result: Wal-Mart has the lowest distribution costs of any retailer.[14]

The Major Priorities of Superior Operations: Continuity and Value Chain Connections

These strategic components of superior operations rely especially on continuity and connection: the former to build and improve daunting infrastructure, the latter to partner effectively to complete the value chain. Continuity fuels relentless focus and striking investments, while connections embrace synergetic alliances with clients and suppliers based on integrity, openness, and responsiveness.

Pursuing the Dream of the Perfect System—and the Biggest Business

Continuity among our brand builders, craftsmen, and innovators (these are discussed in chapter 6) is often linked to a larger social mission. That is rarer among operators. There is just as much resolve and dedication here, but it is directed more internally—to building better systems and infrastructure, and growing them into the biggest and the best. As before, leaders are willing to commit resources and wait ages for the payoff. They keep improving the system and carefully husband the resources to do so; then they stay in office until a big chunk of the master plan is in place.

Persistent Investment and Financial Sacrifice

Exceptional processes, as we have seen, come from sophisticated and constantly improving infrastructures, those beyond the reach of less determined rivals. These require *persistent investment*—an unusual plowing back of earnings into physical assets, and a willingness to grow and expand for the future while forgoing today's profits and dividends. Without this far-sighted, disciplined investment, it would have been impossible to build Wal-Mart's and IKEA's sophisticated retailing and warehousing systems, Cargill's grain infrastructure, and Tyson's and Simplot's integrated, automated plants.

The leaders behind these operators care so deeply about the business that they continue to make these infrastructure investments, decade after decade. And they are never satisfied with the result. When asked about the key to his success, Jack Simplot said, "The only thing I did smart . . . 99 percent of people would have sold out when they got their first $25 or $30 million. I didn't sell out. I just hung on."[15] He certainly did.

Simplot did not get to be the potato king of the world by accident. He invested in one long-term innovation and contract after another and just kept building, knowing full well that it would take years to get his money back. In 1928, he invested in the first electric potato sorter, and traveled the countryside to serve farmers. Then he began to open warehouses so he could buy and sell potatoes. Before a decade was up, he had thirty-three such warehouses, and was the largest shipper in the West. Having got wind of a process for drying onions, he promptly invested in a major dehydration plant, which he used to perfect the drying of potatoes. It became the biggest such plant in the world after Simplot landed the contract to supply the U.S. Army during World War II—again, thanks to lots of up-front investment. Still not content, he used the profits to buy potato farms, ranches, and lumber mills, so that by the end of the war he was growing his own potatoes, processing them himself, shipping them in boxes from his lumberyard, and feeding the waste to his cattle. He was just getting started. Because he was convinced of its potential, Simplot invested heavily in frozen food technology, hiring scientists and building labs and plants to make the first frozen fries. It took about seven years to perfect the product and another thirteen to land the first large client: McDonald's. How many companies would have been at once so persistent in their attempts to grow, yet so patient in waiting for the big payoff? [16]

At Cargill, too, time horizons were measured in decades, and capital requirements in the hundreds of millions. The payoffs could be glacially slow, but the family kept the faith and waited out the dry periods, which occurred not just during Cargill's early years as it built its storage and transportation infrastructure, but throughout its history as grain prices and economies gyrated and wars came and went. In fact, just to complete its system, Cargill would invest in grain-handling facilities that by them-selves produced notoriously low yields. It could then use these to take advantage of market opportunities when they arose, often years or even a decade later. The investments it made in the early 1960s, for example, reaped great profits—but only in the early 1970s with the explosion in Soviet and Chinese demand. Cargill was the only firm ready with the capacity to profit from this "first mover" investment strategy.[17] The same attitude prevails at IKEA as it enters the former Soviet bloc countries. Chairman Kamprad happily predicts that financial returns will begin to come only ten years hence.[18] But the octogenarian isn't worried.

Even once earnings were forthcoming, firms reinvested them to improve the infrastructure and add more value to outputs. In a typical example, from 1972 to 1976 Cargill invested an astounding 110 percent of its record earnings—$775 million—in capital expenditures to expand and globalize its network and to exploit its processing knowledge in more sta-ble commodity niches. In fact, the policy is almost cast in stone at Cargill that profits will be reinvested to keep building the system and so that the company will not have to take on large debts.[19]

Stewardship and Humble Parsimony

The danger in building a major system is to go too fast—to swallow too much too quickly. Many entrepreneurial firms perish in the process.[20] But for all its depth and generosity, family investment was rarely reckless. Bold expansion alternated with cautious consolidation. Indeed, investment embodied an orchestrated blend of venturing *and* conservatism.

The Cargill and MacMillan families, very clearly, were concerned with long-range survival, and were legendary for their parsimony. Although the level of investment is high, there remains a no-frills attitude and a tenacious insistence that whatever is purchased be strategically critical to the system. Said CEO Pete McVay: "We are productive, inventive, and efficient—Spartan, if you will—but good citizens. We are embarrassed by sloppiness, carelessness, indifference, lack of discipline. But we are equally embarrassed by extravagance, opulence, pretentiousness, and waste."[21] This parsimony extended to the top executives of the company. Whitney MacMillan, the founder's multibillionaire great-grandson, and Cargill CEO until 1995, drove to work in a station wagon, wore inexpensive, off-the-rack suits, and worked in a bare, drab office—a clone of Sam Walton in all these respects, except that Walton drove a beat-up pickup truck.

At Wal-Mart, a world pioneer in sourcing and distribution with a gargantuan computer center, Sam Walton was known as a hard sell on technology. He knew its great merits and was prepared to lead his rivals by years. But, as he noted looking back:

> *Everybody at Wal-Mart knows I fought all these technology expenditures as hard as I could. The truth is . . . it was important for me to make them think that maybe the technology wasn't as good as they thought it was . . . It seems to me they try just a little harder and check into things just a little bit closer if they think they might have a chance to prove me wrong.*[22]

Such strategic investments tended, at least ultimately, to pay off very well. According to Cargill's Pete McVay: "We bought more capacity with each capital dollar than our competition . . . musts, not wants. The result—we out-earned the competition by twice, measuring profit per bushel processed, and up to five times measuring profit on capital invested."[23] But when Cargill did expand into new lines or countries, it did so slowly, first investing in a tiny business it called a "scout," to test the waters.[24]

IKEA's Ingvar Kamprad is quick to point out the salutary discipline imposed on investment when one's family's money is being spent. He resisted suggestions from the executive board about going public to be able to expand quickly and have access to capital. Said Kamprad: "We want to grow at our own pace so that we keep up not just with what is new but also develop what we already have. IKEA's strategy has long been to take at least half our resources to improve what already exists—the other half to do what is in the future, if at a somewhat slower pace than if we had had access to unlimited money."[25]

Meliorism: The Philosophy of Operations Betterment

Continuity also showed up in the *meliorism* of family leaders—in their irrepressible desire to keep improving things. Even as firms grew large, family managers very carefully scrutinized operations for improvement opportunities. To ensure optimal use of resources, Sam Walton and Ingvar Kamprad were on the road up to 200 days per year visiting stores and suppliers. And Walton knew how to get employees to talk: He'd go into the back of a store and have everyone sit on the floor; then he'd get down on one knee and encourage people to express their ideas. The result: a constant stream of suggestions for bettering the system and extending its durability.[26] Today, son Rob Walton continues to exert Sam's cost-cutting pressures, albeit from a greater distance (see chapter 8), while Kamprad's sons help keep watch over IKEA.

Constant family pressure also kept Cargill inventive throughout its history. Here is a list of its firsts:

1920s: Among the first firms to use teletypes to link offices to communicate about crops and commodities

1930s: Radical new elevator designs to store grain more efficiently and safely

1940s: Revolutionary new ship designs using automatic welders

1950s: First use of linear programming to develop scientific feed formulations

1960s: First development of the unit train to efficiently move grain inland

1980s–present: Fermentation, steam pasteurization, and hybridization; also biotech discoveries that transformed the making of products ranging from citric acid to vitamin E[27]

Managerial Continuity

As with brand builders and craftsmen, these operators enjoy unshakable stability in their top management teams, now not so much to shape culture as to sustain the vision for building the system and its partnerships. Firms can best pursue the dream when there are no distracting changes in leadership. Having the same team in place allows efficient learning and focus and improves the ability to implement a complex, unified system.[28] Lengthy tenures are valuable in forming enduring relationships with suppliers and major clients, and they provide ample time for tutoring the new generation of managers and passing on contacts.

At IKEA, Ingvar Kamprad shared his intuitions with his sons. He took them to meetings and negotiations, dissected for them deals with suppliers and expansion plans, and brought them along on visits to distant parts of the empire. After these visits he would replay the conversations, citing exact prices, terms, rationales, pitfalls—everything. "Occasionally the sons interrupt, a question or two is given a long answer . . . [They] are absorbing [Ingvar's] experiences while he is still alive, while he is testing the limits of their knowledge, involvement, and attention . . ."[29]

Being Good Partners: Building Solid Connections

We saw that operators partner closely with others to complete the value chain—and that their gargantuan infrastructures and high volume operations favor large partners. Tyson and Simplot sell to massive customers such as McDonald's and Colonel Sanders's KFC, each of which purchases a large fraction of their output. The supply side too benefits from partnering. To nurture such partnerships, operators were exceptionally trustworthy and cooperative, thus reaping not only efficiencies and added business, but privileged information about techniques and markets. Operators, in short, placed greater emphasis on partnering and forming intimate, enduring outside connections than did most of our other winners.

Connection is all about pursuing lasting, win-win relationships with external parties rather than trying to optimize a fleeting transaction. These operators want to establish mutually beneficial associations that will spur growth and sustain the company during periods of economic stress. So they treat partners with *integrity, openness, responsiveness,* and *generosity.* This takes the form not of charity but of committing ample resources early in a relationship.

Integrity—and Handshake Megadeals

According to Wayne Broehl, a scholar of Cargill, the core belief and operating philosophy is that "honor and respect were the essence of the company." Said former CEO John MacMillan Jr. back in 1951: "Our reputation for integrity . . . has not only assured our receiving the preference from a host of customers, [it] is the backbone of our credit which makes it possible to borrow many times our working capital."[30]

A reputation for integrity can initiate profound relationships. On the basis of a single handshake over thirty years ago, J. R. Simplot agreed to supply Ray Kroc of McDonald's with frozen fries. Recalled Simplot: "I got them into the business of frozen French fries . . . Old man Kroc called me to his California ranch and I showed him what we could do . . . [Kroc responded:] 'Okay, Jack, build me a plant, and I'll put these stores on just as fast as you can deliver them.' We said, 'It's a deal,' and we shook hands. That's the only deal we ever made." Then Jack Simplot had to do what he did best: pour tons of money into building dedicated plants and the transportation and logistics infrastructure to supply a fast-food giant. Today, half of MacDonald's fries are still supplied by Simplot.[31]

Openness with Partners

If integrity helps initiate and sustain a relationship, openness can harvest its benefits. Relationships with major suppliers, for example, are especially beneficial when parties are able to work together—to pool talents, exchange information, couple logistics and other systems, and exploit complementarities. As noted, Wal-Mart linked tightly with vendor P&G—sharing intimate, online information as well as distribution and logistics systems for automatic purchasing and resupply. This demanded great openness. Specifically, Wal-Mart began to supply P&G with complete information on the sales of all items in each and every store. P&G could then use its own Nielsen and other market research information on demographics and purchasing trends to assume full responsibility for managing Wal-Mart shelf space, not only of P&G brands but of all *rival* brands in the same categories. The information exchange made it uniquely possible to match store needs with just-in-time supplies. P&G was then assessed and rewarded by Wal-Mart according to its ability to increase the yield on the shelf space.[32]

Tyson also enjoys a very open relationship with Wal-Mart. It uses its state-of-the-art computer and inventory replenishment systems to handle Wal-Mart's ordering and distribution, allowing Tyson to see which product is moving and where. This helps Tyson to develop and market new products.[33]

Generous Commitment and Responsiveness to Partners

The most fruitful and enduring partnerships flowed out of farsighted responsiveness and self-serving generosity. Great operators were willing to invest in their suppliers and wait for years for the payoff. As noted, IKEA forged particularly lasting relationships with its Eastern bloc suppliers by investing deeply in them and giving them very long-term contracts—which they kept active even when there was no demand.[34] IKEA, moreover, has served as a school and a bank, providing those suppliers with extensive training and capital. In return, it gains a level of cooperation that begets absolute adherence to IKEA design standards, as well as unbeatable economies. IKEA boss Ingvar Kamprad says that he pursues "good capitalism":

> IKEA did not wish to let anyone down. We wanted to be part of [their] development . . . I detest capitalists who go to underdeveloped factories and buy up everything they have—ten thousand bicycle baskets straight off—and then just leave. Our way is to return, build up a relationship, contribute with our knowledge, draw up long-term contracts, emphasize the importance of delivery on time, quality, and the environment [our emphasis]. That is what we did in Poland, in Yugoslavia, in Hungary, in the Czech Republic, and that is what we are doing in Taiwan, Thailand, Vietnam, and China.[35]

In fact, IKEA paid its suppliers within ten days, while its rivals took three or four months (and still claimed the 3 percent discount!). Part of what was on Kamprad's mind was doing the right thing—embracing fraternity. But just as important was the reciprocity that a long-term relationship with suppliers might bring in the form of quality goods, reliability, exclusivity, and favorable terms.[36]

Generosity also takes the form of investing significant resources in strong, enduring client relationships, in dedicating factories and logistics infrastructure to a single customer. The intent is to add more value to the customer and thereby improve loyalty and margins. Tyson and Simplot actually "organized around" their major fast-food customers, devoting immense resources such as entire plants, and creating staff accountabilities around a single client.

Catering daily to hundreds of one client's outlets often requires building special facilities and distribution centers near the client and setting up complex logistics, replenishment, and data-exchange systems. Without this generous investment and a spirit of cooperation, the big fish simply swim away. Here the line blurs between a client-supplier relationship and a true partnership in which both parties work together to help each other. Most operators favor the latter, with its steep early costs—and its ultimate benefits.

Even short of these investments, the desire for long-term connections led our FCBs to be unusually responsive to clients. According to Don Tyson: "Our customer's strategy, to be successful, keeps evolving . . . We try to know that customer, work with [him] through our technical people, and try to help him do well. Because he has to do well before we can do well."[37] He explains further:

> What we did was try follow our customers around and anticipate [their] needs . . . We work with the food service industry—our guys will visit with them, and if there is any kind of product they want, we come back and start trying to make it for them [in our R&D department]. As a producer of food goods, we are going to have to produce more and more complicated products. And we like that . . . We will be producing all those products up to the point where all the restaurant is doing is reconstituting the product.[38]

McDonald's Chicken McNugget and KFC's Rotisserie Gold brands are both Tyson creations and explain why the firm tended to earn gross margins of almost 20 percent, twice the industry average. Tyson is now following these large chains as they venture into Mexico.[39] To earn decent margins, even with tough supermarket giants like Wal-Mart, Tyson makes 2,500 different poultry meals, from chicken wings to chicken cordon bleu.

Viewed from the outside, then, many FCBs are desirable partners that, in addition to their integrity and generosity, enable business to be transacted with a family member whose capital is at stake, whose name is on the door, and who takes personal responsibility for decades.

Complementary Priorities of Superior Operations: Command and Sometimes Community

Original business models, and steep investments to create infrastructure and sustain partners, rely on a top manager's ability to make courageous decisions—decisions that impatient investors might feel uncomfortable with. Fortunately, our leaders were unusually free to exercise their prerogatives of command. A very different priority, community, could be a source of systems improvement and better service. But it appeared only sporadically among these operators.

Freedom to Act Boldly and Differently

Continuity with our operators did not spell lethargy or stagnation. These firms did not follow anyone in building their systems; they led the way. Majority family ownership gave their leaders the independence to boldly commit resources and embrace unorthodox ways of doing things.[40]

According to Terry Fisher, who worked for Tyson's advertising agency in the early 1980s, "It was very entrepreneurial. We'd throw something out there and see if it stuck." Although some ideas, such as tilapia farming, flopped, the duds were overwhelmed by winners. Don Tyson's freedom also allowed him to expand by buying companies his rivals were too afraid or too slow to go after, giving him the highest rate of growth in the industry.[41] Similarly, IKEA was among the first firms to contract in a major way with Eastern bloc countries; Simplot undertook major contracts before it had the facilities to fulfill them; and Cargill—and for that matter all of the operators—kept expanding and renewing its product lines to seize market opportunities. These were bold, courageous companies that never shied away from the need for change and renewal.

But firms rarely acted rashly, in part because they preserved diversity on their top management teams (TMTs). Over the course of Cargill's history, the firm shifted between two kinds of top teams: entrepreneurial opportunistic CEOs, reined in by relatives with internal financial and efficiency concerns, and internally focused consolidators, pushed to expand the business by more externally focused family members. This variety on the TMTs, both at a point in time and across time, ensured robustness and farsighted balance in the firm's strategy. This was especially true given the close and frank relationships among the family members at the top, and between those members and others executives.[42]

Community—Sometimes

For brand builders, craftsmen, and innovators, community is a major pillar of strategy. Here, however, it plays only a complementary role and is occasionally underemphasized. Where present, however, community can get people to work together more effectively. An absence of bureaucracy and spirit of participation, for example, had people volunteering ideas for how to make the system better.

IKEA's Kamprad sought out hundreds of his junior people, and frequently invited managers to his home for dinner to discuss the business and its problems into the wee hours—frequently after drink and fatigue had loosened their tongues. Emotional interchanges, which tended to be rare in Swedish firms, were very much in evidence as Kamprad worked his guests to determine what they felt in their hearts about IKEA. Status, rank, and formality had no place. Kamprad's philosophy was, "This business is a family, you are a family member—you have not only a right but a duty to speak to try to make things better." It was not uncommon for Kamprad to shed tears with the group, remembering the hard times of the company and its people, and the sacrifices that were made all around, by those living, and those long departed. Kamprad reflected: "It could be said that we simply transferred the family spirit from Elmtaryd [Sweden, IKEA's birthplace]: helpfulness, thrift, and a strong sense of responsibility."[43] But this was sentimentality with a purpose: to get everyone onboard and involved in creating a better company.

IKEA is steeped top to bottom in Ingvar Kamprad's bible, "A Furniture Dealer's Testament," and its summary, "The little word book." These serve to constantly reinforce maxims that, in a real sense, determine employee attitudes and accountability. A sampling of sections reads as follows: "The IKEA Way and Bureaucracy," Fear of Failure," "Doing It a Different Way," "Fellowship and Enthusiasm," and "Simplicity." People are encouraged to use their creativity and try new things, all in the interest of developing a better-functioning system. Rather than trying to get efficiency by turning people into robots, IKEA implores managers to use their imagination to improve things. The culture proclaims "you are part of our family—please pitch in your best ideas to make things better for everyone."[44]

Another aspect of community is the tight cadre of employees and managers who understand each other and work well together because of extensive common training, long job tenures, and promote-from-within policies. Cargill people, who are trained exhaustively in myriad aspects of the business, rise slowly in the company and often spend their entire careers at the firm. They also tend to rise in tandem with a stable cohort, who lends his or her support and cooperation throughout. Intimates of the firm attest that indoctrination is so thorough that "you're Cargill now and forever" and that "you come out of there with Cargill tattooed on your ass."[45]

Again, however, community was by no means *central* to all of these operators or all parts of those operators, especially those requiring minimal human intervention at the client interface, or those facing steep cost pressures and the temptation to export jobs. Wal-Mart has been accused recently of exploiting its workers and hiring illegal immigrants (see chapter 8). Tyson, Cargill, and Simplot can be highly structured and impersonal places to work, especially at operating levels. And because they rely on tight process routines and relentless automation to drive efficiency, jobs can be monotonous and sometimes dangerous. There tends to be a sharp distinction between managers and technocrats, who are charged with running and improving the system, and the less fortunate individuals who have to suffer the routines.

Table 5-1

Relating the Four Cs to the Strategy of Superior Operations

	COMPONENTS OF THE SUPERIOR OPERATIONS STRATEGY			
	Original Business Model	Price- and Cost- Driven Clients	Build and Develop Infrastructure	Value Chain Specialization
Continuity: Pursuing the perfect system				
• Persistent investment and sacrifice	*		**	*
• The philosophy of betterment	*		**	
• Stewardship and parsimony			*	*
• Managerial continuity	*		**	**
Connection: Building solid partnerships				
• Integrity		*		**
• Openness with partners		**	*	**
• Generous commitment to partners		**		*
Command: Acting boldly and distinctively				
• Courage to be original and bold	**	*	*	*
Community: Sometimes!				
• Folksy informality and simplicity	+		+	+

* facilitator; ** key facilitator; + sporadic facilitator

Conclusion

Superior operations rely on an intricate balancing act. Profound investment in infrastructure must be balanced by careful stewardship so as not
to overtax resources. Internal efficiency and operations integration must
be protected from irrelevance by partnering with suppliers and clients to
keep firms on the leading edge. And always, the firm must avoid becoming
a centralized, closed system. To achieve that, upper echelons have to stay
in touch with and develop a deep understanding of clients and emerging
technologies. They may also need to enlist their grassroots people to keep
offerings evolving and relevant. Finally, command is there to keep the firm
original, energized, and entrepreneurial. Table 5-1 shows how the elements of policy and practice support the operations strategy.

Chapter 6

Innovators

ONE OF OUR DEAREST friends is an unusual man. With degrees in physics and economics from Ivy League schools, he has been, for most of his colleagues, an enigma. For over twenty frustrating years he taught and researched at a university that rarely appreciated his formidable talents. Although he had completely mastered his field, he found much of its research uninteresting. He said his colleagues were publishing not because they had anything important to say but to keep their jobs.

He decided to take a different approach, working on the big problems others feared to broach. This was at considerable risk to his career, as there were many years when he had nothing to publish—the result of the inevitable false starts and blind alleys. The administration cut his research budget and boosted his teaching load. But he was willing to pay the price. Ultimately, he did succeed in making seminal contributions to the social sciences, and his work will be remembered long after his colleagues have gone to their just rewards.

Our friend is the quintessential innovator: one who takes risks, embraces projects of considerable scope and ambition, and searches endlessly on the frontiers of his discipline. Though his rewards were big, so too was the sacrifice he was willing to make. Our innovator companies, like our friend, don't just adorn their domains with marginalia, they revolutionize them with completely new ideas—in the form of technologies, products, or business models. They even reshape the world, sometimes more than once per generation. Such ambitious pioneering demands financial, time, and personal sacrifices that would frighten off most companies. One skeptic of the Corning way said, "There's nothing better they'd like than to find a cure for cancer, and if they happened to make money, that's fine."[1] But through such devotion and the collaborative, communal organizations it fosters, innovators make creation a way of life. By the time the competition reacts, these enterprises have moved on.

Family-Controlled Innovators

Corning Incorporated

- Founder/Family: Amory Houghton Sr./Houghton
- Founding Year: 1851
- Revenues (2002): $2.63 billion
- Market Share: World's number-one fiber-optics company

The Houghton family's zeal for innovation has kept Corning at the forefront of the glass industry for over a century. According to today's fifth-generation CEO James R. Houghton: "When I was growing up I was taught that investing in R&D was like a 'religion.'"[a] That research perseverance paid off in growth businesses such as lightbulbs, radio, picture tubes, Pyrex glass, and the massive fiber optics industry. Although it has recently floundered (see chapter 8), Corning's courage to continue investing in its future has kept it ahead of its rivals for most of a century.

Fidelity Investments

- Founder/Family: Edward C. Johnson II/Johnson
- Founding Year: 1946
- Revenues (2002): $8.90 billion
- Market Share: World's number-one mutual fund company

Fidelity has become number one by relentless pioneering. Three generations of Johnsons have poured far more money into experimentation and innovative infrastructure than their rivals. Major innovations include the first mutual funds sold directly to the public, the first money market funds with check-writing privileges, the first sector funds, and the first no-load funds.[b] As important were Fidelity's contributions to developing the client interfaces of the early twenty-first century: twenty-four-hour telephone access to accounts and representatives, Internet trading, and online research support.

Compagnie Générale des Établissements Michelin

- Founders/Family: Cousins Aristide Barbier and Nicolas Daubrée/ Michelin (Barbier descendants)
- Founding Year: 1832
- Revenues (2002): €15.65 billion
- Market Share: World's number-one or number-two tire maker

Michelin has been reinventing the wheel for decades: From the pneumatic tire in 1891 to the radial in 1946 to the indestructible tires devised for the Space Shuttle and the Concorde. Michelin is, according to sixth-generation CEO Édouard Michelin, the industry's technology leader. Its new, ecologically friendly tire reduces roll friction by a third. Michelin has, in good times and bad, invested 5 percent of sales in R&D, double the industry norm, and is the only tire manufacturer to create its own revolutionary production machinery.[c] It employs over 120,000 people.

Motorola, Inc.

- Founder/Family: Paul V. Galvin/Galvin
- Founding Year: 1928
- Revenues (2002): $26.68 billion
- Market Share: World's number-two mobile handset manufacturer

Although troubled of late, and now no longer family-controlled (see chapter 8), throughout its history Motorola has been a stellar innovator in several domains, beginning with the car radio and progressing through two-way radios, pagers, cell phone technologies, and semiconductors. Three generations of Galvins have made innovation and "constant evolution" core organizational values. Motorola has been able to pioneer a major new product every generation, as well as race down the cost curve to make those products attractive to a broad market—and win the coveted Baldrige Award for exceptional quality.

Tetra Pak AB

- Founder: Ruben Rausing/Rausing
- Founding Year: 1943
- Revenues (2002): €7.50 billion
- Market Share: World's number-one liquid food processing and packaging company

At Sweden's Tetra Pak, three generations of Rausings have pioneered aseptic packaging techniques that allow perishable food products such as milk and tofu to be packed into materials like coated cardboard and remain fresh for months without refrigeration. The high-temperature process sterilizes packaging materials, forms them into brick-like containers, and fills them with liquids. The Institute of Food Technologists ranks Tetra's innovation as one of the twentieth century's most important contributions to human nutrition.[d] Through continual research and improvement, the firm has grown to over 18,000 employees and is a "one-stop shop" for processing, packaging, and distribution.[e]

W.L. Gore & Associates, Inc.

- Founders: Wilbert L. and Genevieve Gore/Gore
- Founding Year: 1958
- Revenues (2002): $1.23 billion
- Market Share: Gore-Tex, world's number-one waterproof, windproof, breathable fabric

The creators of miracle fabrics such as Gore-Tex, as well as manmade human surgical membranes, sutures, biomaterials, dental floss, guitar strings, and dozens of other products made from polytetrafluoro-ethylene (PTFE), Gore has thrived by finding new applications for this versatile chemical. The family has put together a team with the unique capacity both to make discoveries and to quickly find commercial applications for them. Its "lattice" organization design splits the firm into innovative teams and gets people collaborating via an intensive program of socialization and mentorship, resulting in a culture of innovation.

a. Margaret B. Graham and Alec T. Shuldiner, *Corning and the Craft of Innovation* (New York: Oxford University Press, 2001), xx.
b. Alex Taylor III, "Why Fidelity Is the Master of Mutual Funds," *Fortune,* September 1, 1986, 57.
c. Claudia H. Deutsch, "In This Particular Tire Test, Failure Was Not an Option," *New York Times,* November 11, 2001, 2; Patrick Chabert, "Michelin: le grand secret" [Michelin: The Big Secret], *Les Echos,* January 13, 1998, 54; E.S. Browning, "On a Roll: Long-Term Thinking and Paternalistic Ways Carry Michelin to Top," *Wall Street Journal,* January 5, 1990, A1.
d. "Obituary: Gad Rausing," *The Economist,* February 5, 2000, 80.
e. "Gad Rausing," *The Times* (London), January 31, 2000, 19.

A Strategy of Innovation

Former CEO Robert Galvin of Motorola once said: "Renewal is the driving thrust of this company. My father never stopped renewing and nor have we . . . . Only those driven to [generate] a proliferation of new, creative ideas . . . and [who have] an unstinting dedication to committing to the risk and promise of those ideas will thrive."[2] That about sums up the competitive approach of our successful innovators. The elements of their strategy include:

- Pathbreaking innovation
- Incremental innovation and leveraging of discovery
- Commercialization of innovations tailored to key markets
- Creative destruction—a preemptive jettisoning of the old in favor of the new

Pathbreaking Innovation(s): Episodic "Craziness"

Corning and Motorola were built on pioneering innovations so advanced that competitors had little prospect of imitating them. Indeed, for many decades, Corning brought forth innovations that were life-changing and life-enhancing, from heat-resistant Pyrex to radio and television tubes to optic cable and photonics for gene manipulation. It invented new purposes for glass and opened new markets decades before these discoveries were even on the radar screens of rivals.

Michelin engineers spent years trying to get the flabby radial tire right, a pursuit that made them a not-so-private joke in the industry for longer than they care to remember. Today, their steel-belted radial has transformed the tire business as fundamentally as the transistor revolutionized electronics. So, as usual, Michelin got the last laugh—and a dominant market share. Fidelity Investments, too, attracted the skepticism, and ultimately the anger, of other financial institutions by inventing a new class of money market funds with checking; and, even more outrageously, a new way of selling and servicing them, not via personal representatives but through call centers, and with low or no sales fees. "How unprofessional," said the competition. "How nice," said the clients.

Though few people outside the food business have heard of Tetra Pak, everyone has benefited from its ingenious products. Tetra invented sterile packaging that increased exponentially the shelf life of foods; it also pioneered new food-processing techniques, economical packaging materials (read: cardboard and plastic), and assorted boxlike shapes, all of which dramatically added value to retailers and consumers. The Tetra Web site framed the early vision: "A package with the kind of shape that had so far only been seen in geometry lessons, manufactured by a machine that nobody could picture, and made of a material that didn't exist." It is hard now to suck on one of those juice cartons without evoking that image.

Such pathbreaking innovations are at the heart of the strategies of these family businesses. They command the bulk of managers' attention and the lion's share of resources and talent. But especially impressive is the regular *recurrence* of these innovations. By continually reinventing itself, Motorola progressed from jerry-built car radios to television sets to M68000 microprocessors to pagers, cell phones, handheld devices, and satellite systems. And as these innovators are eternally open to opportunity, some breakthroughs come via the back door. Motorola's move into semiconductors was an "afterthought" to support its television business—but it quickly became a mammoth business of its own once the Galvins realized its potential.

At first glance it seemed as if every generation of these families was bent on coming up with a significant new technology or product class. A closer look, however, revealed firms working *constantly* on innovations. But these were so ambitious, futuristic, and unorthodox as to take years, sometimes a generation, to come to fruition. Indeed, it was not uncommon for a long-term project seeded by one generation to be commercialized by the next.

Incremental Innovation and Leveraging of Discovery

Firms need to slow down sometimes to husband resources and exploit their discoveries. So they keep working on "surer things"—incremental, less grand innovations and ways of leveraging these across a broader set of markets. Such projects vastly enhanced the returns from any one discovery and made it possible to pursue the more ambitious ventures.

Our innovators, in fact, became masterful at using yesterday's discoveries to create tomorrow's. Motorola leveraged its radio capability in its pagers, then its pager technology in its cell phones. Corning employed its expertise making light bulbs in its radio tube business, which in turn gave it an early edge in the television picture tube business. It even has an engineering department dedicated to squeezing more value out of each technology. With similar focus, Michelin moved from bicycle tires to horse-drawn carriage tires to automobile tires to a vast range of radials for every kind of vehicle (1,500 models), each time making the product stronger and more puncture-resistant. And Fidelity used the knowledge gained in introducing money market funds to spawn, very efficiently, attractive new equity funds.

In short, proprietary knowledge is built on cumulatively to progress across succeeding generations of products and technologies. Old learning, in essence, is used—and augmented—in developing new offerings. The primary motivator here is recognition that eternal "exploration" and renewal are core missions and that the enterprise must not rest on its laurels. At the same time, firms want to get the most out of their discoveries. Thus, rare pathbreaking innovations must be spaced between projects more amenable to harvesting than seeding, and by processes that are more "exploitative" than explorative.

Firms also engage in *market*-driven leverage, which is not so much concerned with piggybacking on old inventions as employing current knowledge to respond to different market needs. Gore, for example, looks intently at end users to discover niches for its Gore-Tex fabrics. It has segmented the market into specialized domains such as garments, footwear, luggage, and the like, and works hard to tailor its approach and products to different segments.[3]

Fidelity has for years been leveraging its massive technology infrastructure. The company was already handling record-keeping for large clients such as pension plans, so CEO Ned Johnson thought it would be a great idea to take on processing for benefits plans, payroll, and human resources—all activities that are not value-adding for clients, hence attractive candidates for outsourcing. The strategy would not only leverage technology but extend service to customers. "Besides," Johnson noted, "the history of equities is highly cyclical. Processing you do every day." Said an aide: "Markets come and go. This is a big diversification play. The future is technology-based service."[4] Such service also complements the investment business by effectively tracking data on the situation and actions of a huge number of potential clients, which Fidelity could attract as customers.[5] Again, it is only by spreading broadly the results of major innovations that a firm can build up the resources needed for pioneering.

Commercialization of Innovation

According to Roger Ackerman, Corning's ex-chairman, "We used to be like a casino—invent something and then roll the dice. But now we realize that if you don't understand market dynamics, you'll crash."[6] Thus, innovators "work forward" to adapt technology to market needs; they also "work backward," taking market needs into the labs. In both instances, the object is to render a discovery more attractive to the end user. This often takes the form of making an innovation more functional and economical, which also keeps the firm ahead of its potential imitators.

Cost-Reduction Targets and Process Innovation. At Corning and Motorola, a fundamental source of advantage is the ability to race down the cost curve and manufacture new products very efficiently. From light bulbs to picture tubes to fiber optics, Corning was able to reduce its costs of manufacture very steeply and steadily, essentially diffusing any temptation rivals (or large clients) might have had to get into the business. Decreases in costs and prices of over 50 percent in the first two years of a new product's life were not uncommon. In fact, for decades, Corning doubled the median 3 percent productivity increases in its industry with inventions like the ribbon machine and all-electric glass furnace, not to mention myriad technological tweaks.[7] Happily, innovation and low costs sometimes went together, as with Fidelity's electronic client interface, which decimated overhead and transactions costs. The savings generated were shared with existing clients and used to market to new ones.

Much cost reduction and quality improvement comes from process innovation. Michelin systematically monitored product performance data from dealers and customers to enhance its production and quality control configurations. As a result, during the 1960s and 1970s, it was the only company that had perfected the manufacture of steel-belted radials: No rival could get high quality and high volume simultaneously. So even thirty years back, Michelin was able to offer a 40,000-mile guarantee on its tires—the only one in the business to do so.[8]

At Motorola, Bob Galvin realized that to become a great global competitor, he had to break into the closed Japanese market. That meant beating out fierce competitors like NEC and Matsushita, and meeting their impossible quality specifications. Galvin set about revolutionizing his organization through the philosophy of "total quality." He realized that processes could be improved only if Motorola got the design of the product and process exactly right; then the quality would follow. The company set out in 1987 to reach, within five years, a defect rate of three parts per million (in quality parlance, "Six Sigma"). With its extensive training program, it came close. Quality was improved 150-fold during the period, and Motorola went on to breach the Japanese market *and* win the prestigious Malcolm Baldrige Quality Award.[9]

Client Partnering. Another reason these innovators have such high "hit" rates in commercialization is their closeness to customers. At Tetra Pak, for example, customers play a pivotal role in all R&D endeavors. For every major project, the company selects a "lead customer" to be intimately involved in project development. "The customer already has a need for the specific product we are going to be developing, and we further specify the product together," says Anders Olsson, Tetra Pak's American representative. "We have been very successful in new product development because we stay extremely close to the customer before, during, and after the process."[10]

The benefit here is that Tetra Pak makes a captive market for itself by leasing its thousands of machines, at little profit, to customers that must buy Tetra's packaging material—which yields a far higher return (about 80 percent of company profits). The machines don't work with any other material. In exchange for this allegiance, however, Tetra Pak offers customers a wide range of marketing and technical support. For one of its big customers, Hong Kong's Vita Soy International Holdings, Tetra Pak took the client's new products back to a laboratory in Sweden to test them again and again to ensure continuing quality. According to Eric Yu, Vita Soy's operations director, "We work hand in hand together to develop the market."[11] Michelin made customers comfortable with its product in a different way. It encouraged automobile use with its famous travel and gourmet bibles, the *Guides Michelin*, and its symbol of security: the ubiquitous man of rubber or "bibendum."[12]

Creative Destruction: A Pre-Emptive Jettisoning of the Old in Favor of the New

One way to keep innovation alive and immediate is to continually question the status quo. A policy of early shifting to new products and technologies makes it that much more urgent to fund and improve innovation, and thereby keep the firm ahead of potential imitators. Thus innovators exhibited an unparalleled willingness to engage in "creative destruction," to jettison yesterday's ways or outputs before their time.

Because of Corning's desire to stay at the cutting edge and reap innovator's profits, it began in the late 1980s to quickly get rid of its old businesses: lighting in 1989, medical testing in 1996, and housewares in 1998 (as we will see in chapter 8, this divestment may have gone too far). It turned instead to high-tech fiber optics for telecommunications, the glass threads that are replacing copper telephone wires, and whose escalating demand in 1999 and 2000 mushroomed sales from $2 to $5 billion in two years.[13] Similarly, Michelin pulled resources away from its traditional tire lines as it embraced the new radial design. Motorola moved from car radios to TVs, away from TVs to semiconductors, from semiconductors to pagers and cellular phones, and onward, always getting out of yesterday's products early to go into tomorrow's.[14] And Fidelity Investments kept up its service pioneering, all the while abandoning computerized client interfaces that were still the envy of the industry.[15]

The Major Priorities of Innovation: Courageous Command and Creative Community

All of these innovative capabilities—pioneering, improvement, commercialization, and creative destruction—rely profoundly on the priorities of command and community. Command liberates family leaders from the short-term constraints of financial markets. It promotes generous, farsighted investments in conceiving and exploiting innovation to renew the firm and its products. At the same time, innovation is complex, requiring creativity from experts and teamwork among diverse functions. This happens in a clanlike organizational community, with strong values, excellent treatment of employees, and a climate of initiative and collaboration.

Freedom to Innovate Boldly

Innovation demands a rare blend of risk taking, unorthodox thinking, speed, and, paradoxically, foresight—qualities our FCBs possessed in part because of the independence of their leaders. As at so many FCBs, the often-heard refrain at Fidelity is, "We're different, because we're private." Managers say the company can remain generously dedicated to developing new technologies for its 16 million-plus customers because the Johnsons cannot be pressured by shortsighted shareholders or analysts to cut back on R&D when times are tight. Said one journalist during the recent stock market slump: "When I visited Fidelity earlier this month, it was like stepping into some parallel universe: Few companies can afford to spend this lavishly on innovation."[16]

The same independence exists at Michelin. François Michelin and his family own the majority of voting shares; and the family, which is large, votes its shares en bloc. So François, and now son Édouard, can make major decisions "just by picking up the phone."[17]

Thus, a pillar of advantage for great innovators is command, or the freedom of leaders to pursue audacious projects—to bet heavily on the future, react quickly to opportunities, and embrace approaches so unconventional that they would be career-enders elsewhere. This independence gives rise to several strategic strengths:

- Courageous venturing, which confers a *commitment advantage*
- Idiosyncrasy and risk tolerance, which provide an *originality advantage*

- First-mover decisiveness, which creates a *speed advantage*
- A spry, empowered top management team, which makes it all work

Courageous Venturing: The Commitment Advantage

Whereas most investment for our other strategies went to support stable core competencies, at innovators, venturing was primarily for renewal—new technologies, products, processes, and facilities. This has required particular courage. After World War II, the Michelin family almost bet the company on the radial tire, aggressively transferring key human and physical resources to its daring new product.[18] Michelin's annual expenditures on business renewal for years equaled Goodyear's—when the latter was *twice* Michelin's size.[19] Indeed, Michelin has advanced to its preeminence in the tire industry by out-innovating the competition and building the scale that could support such mammoth innovation. In the three decades following 1960, Michelin expanded at the pace of a new factory every nine months—so its plants have long been the most modern in the industry. This deep commitment was simply beyond the emotional and intellectual grasp of Michelin's rivals, particularly its more earnings-obsessed American ones. After a debt-financed $1.5 billion acquisition of Uniroyal Goodrich in the early 1990s, Michelin became the biggest tire maker in the world.[20]

The Johnsons at Fidelity, too, courageously outspent competitors on pioneering ventures such as sector funds, twenty-four-hour customer lines, and computerized client interfaces. In fact, during the 1970s, they drained record profits for five years to set up the extensive customer service operation that spurred the firm's growth. So in 1995, Fidelity became the first mutual company to launch a Web site. Its spending plans continue to be a challenge to its rivals. The technology budget rose about 20 percent in the dismal year of 2001, to $2.3 billion—more than three times the fiscal 2000 profits of Charles Schwab, E*Trade, and Ameritrade combined. Expenditure on Internet development increased more than 30 percent, to $350 million, while another $350 million was spent on telephone support staff, a 35 percent increase.[21]

Such ventures have kept innovators ahead of the pack during good times and bad. But they required immense fortitude. At Tetra Pak, for example, the Rausing family had to support the company during *ten years* of red ink as they revolutionized packaging. Then, once Tetra became profitable, they plowed all their profits back into the business. At a time when after-tax profit was just over $50 million, less than $1 million was paid out in dividends to the family: "We take out only enough each year to pay the Swedish wealth tax." The same year, the company laid out $111 million in new capital investment.[22]

In a very real way, the scale and constancy of these ventures signal the commitment of these enterprises, and serve to discourage would-be imitators. They also make it more likely that these companies will keep moving forward and be tough for competitors to catch off guard.

Idiosyncratic and Risk-Tolerant: The Originality Advantage

These innovators do not simply make larger commitments to research and innovation; they make far more unconventional and original ones. They go after inventions that might change the world and have a massive payoff, but that are also risky and demand thinking outside the box. Family executives, it appears, are less subject to pressures to conform to industry norms.

We know the Michelins risked much to create radical tire innovations such as the radial—a product skeptics called an impossible dream. But even more unorthodox was the extension of their idiosyncratic approaches to a total recasting of the manufacturing process. It took the company thirteen years (1988 to 2001) of intense effort to develop the C3M machine, a project that consumed immense resources but that now allows Michelin—with unequaled simplicity—to make any tire it wants, whenever it wants, anywhere in the world. The machine sharply reduces the labor and stock requirements of tire making while dramatically shortening the process: It cuts the number of manufacturing steps from seven to one. It also quadruples the output of the last generation of machines. The equipment can be packed up easily and transported, even to developing regions where it is desperately needed—representing, in effect, a floating tire plant that can be set up within twenty-four hours.[23]

By ignoring the ways of its rivals in the fund business, Fidelity Investments has beaten them all. The company prefers Boston to New York, private ownership to public, and simple mail-order coupons to high-concept promotion. According to Michael Lipper, who tracks the mutual funds business, "The big difference about Fidelity is that they aren't afraid to be wrong."[24] Said Stanley Egener, head of the No-load Mutual Fund Association, "They are willing to throw money at a lot of things, even if they don't work out at first."[25]

Unlike more established firms such as Merrill Lynch and Dean Witter, Fidelity rarely talked to its customers in person. To bring Wall Street to the millions of new investors on Main Street, Johnson opened massive phone centers and asked customers to send checks to a post office drop. It was a new way of doing business: less expensive than setting up brokerage offices throughout the country and perfectly suited to capturing a commanding share of middle-class investors. The five phone centers, which one employee compared to NORAD, have the most sophisticated terminals in the business, while the computer center in Dallas that handles market data going to traders is the most advanced in existence. Fidelity uses such systems to minimize labor costs at the client interface and to do its outsourcing business.[26] The result of this maverick behavior? Fidelity has become the largest manager of mutual funds by growing faster than any other.

First-Mover Decisiveness: The Speed Advantage

The advantages of originality and a generous commitment to innovation can be neutralized by delays and vacillation. Innovators, however, act with speed, to which there are two aspects. The first is to act *proactively*, well ahead of the industry, laboring today for rewards that will only come after many patient tomorrows. The second, paradoxically, is to be decisive and get things done *rapidly*. In a competitive context, many innovations become irrelevant if they are slow to emerge or be updated. Both aspects of speed were aided by top managers' discretion to take initiative.

According to CEO James Houghton, Corning has innovated in *anticipation* of opportunity in emerging industries, rather than investing only after the payoff is more assured. He told us: "We did the first lightbulbs for Edison, the first radio tubes for Marconi, the first picture tubes for RCA." In the process, Corning has helped to shape new industries. Thus, as noted, the Houghtons began work on fiber optics more than three decades before the technology became profitable. But even by Corning's standards, its recent pursuits are highly futuristic. The company intends to create glass chips that can be used to detect which genes are active in the body at any precise time. Although scientists are excited at the possibility of using these chips to understand the roles played by particular genes in various disease processes, the technology is still precariously emergent, and its utility more theoretical than proven.[27] Should there be a payoff, however, it will be a huge one—like so many in Corning's long history.

To beat competitors to the punch, these innovators also make decisions quickly. At Tetra Pak, although there was an administrative center in

Lausanne, Switzerland, the command center was wherever the Rausing family happened to be. The brothers boasted that major decisions could be made with a couple of phone calls.[28] When Lars G. Andersson, a Tetra Pak veteran who opened the company's China operations, decided it was time to build a factory there, he telephoned headquarters in Sweden. He was transferred to Hans Rausing, who was out moose hunting. After a short talk, he got his approval. "We could take the biggest of decisions over a lunch break," he said.[29]

Spry and Empowered Top Teams

Because innovation can be so complex and hazardous, innovators avoid relying on a single top executive. They are run instead by tiny top management teams or "offices." Advantage comes from the closeness of the members of the team. At Michelin, top manager François was a co-*gérant*, or coboss, with his solicitous uncle and another comanager for four years. Then he brought in his friend and cousin Rollier to help out. The two ran the business in tandem, acting, as François characterized it, as "the same brain in two heads."[30] Well, not exactly. Having multiple leadership perspectives prevented the errors and excesses of a single entrepreneur, and the co-*gérant* policy continues today under Édouard Michelin. There is complementarity too between Fidelity's Ned Johnson and daughter Abigail, with the former pushing on technology and the business model, and the latter the management of the mutual funds portfolio.

At Motorola, there was a "chief executive *office*," usually occupied by three team members. The office not only provided an excellent training ground for young family leaders, it ensured that the toughest decisions would benefit from inputs by multiple Galvins and other executives. The intensive interaction did not slow things down, however. Personal closeness enabled team members to understand each other so well that they could make decisions quickly—whether about a full-fledged embrace of total quality management (TQM) or a bold move into semiconductors and cellular telecom. Moreover, where speed was of the essence, people trusted each other well enough to allow independent action.[31] Involving multiple generations of a family, as at Michelin, Fidelity, Motorola, and Tetra Pak, also helped balance new perspectives with old. Not only did the oldsters teach the kids, but vice versa—often in a bracing encounter with the shock of the new. This ability of close relatives with different viewpoints to interact frankly mitigated the chances of taking too much risk.

In short, independence of command gave these executives the freedom to lead the way. They could invest and commit deeply and quickly, ignore for years the financial consequences, and enter virgin areas where rivals feared to tread. Meanwhile, a cohesive, multifaceted TMT kept decisions on track.

Uniting the Tribe in Creative Collaboration

If bold, independent leadership is the spark of innovation, then an energized, collaborative corporate culture is the engine of research and commercialization. Effective innovation requires especially talented, creative people who are keen to develop their ideas and to work alongside those with the expertise to implement them. By fostering cohesive organizations, innovators motivate employees both to use their initiative to spawn inventions, and to collaborate to commercialize them.

First, firms establish and live exacting values of discovery, often girded by important social concerns. Second, they educate and connect their people by incessant training and mentoring. Third, they hang on to their critical human resources by treating them well and giving wide berth to their talents of discovery. Finally, they painstakingly choreograph collaboration across functions to make innovations more relevant. So lateral interactions and networking, wherever possible, displace the vertical hierarchy.

Although equally vital, community at these innovators differs from that at craftsmen and brand builders. As at the latter, emphasis remains on inculcating values, training, and consideration. But there is among innovators an even stronger drive to compel people to use initiative to make discoveries and to work across departmental boundaries to commercialize those discoveries. Here, therefore, individualism serves as a stronger counterpoint to collectivism.

Inspiring Values: The Noble Quest for Discovery

The typical driver of innovation is the family social mission to develop products and technologies that will change the world and make life better. From childhood, the Houghtons at Corning were reared to believe that innovation was an honorable mission and the foundation of family pride. Succeeding generations imposed that mission on the company, making R&D not so much an element of strategy, but, as noted, a religion—a way of ensuring a social contribution that would make the family proud. These beliefs were espoused publicly by the family leaders at every occasion, and communicated by them in the course of forty to fifty trips per year throughout the Corning "empire."

In that same spirit, to rouse his minions at innumerable encounters, François Michelin endlessly invoked the story of Sir Alexander Fleming and his discovery of penicillin through acute observation and dogged inquiry. Fleming toiled in systematic search of that rare spore that by chance had floated into his lab and eradicated his bacterial cultures. He realized that the spore was not simply a nuisance to his experiments, but a potential savior to those with deadly infections—and he went in relentless pursuit of it. These qualities of alertness, ceaseless inquiry, and tireless experimentation were, Michelin felt, the essence of discovery and innovation. They reflected the primary values his family had been infusing into their organization since the 1800s through their parade of engineer-CEOs. The Michelin family also made it clear that their innovations, like Fleming's, served critical purposes: making the world safer, more accessible, more ecologically friendly.[32]

But more than being spoken, values were enacted, often at great sacrifice. Upon testing the radial tire, Michelin managers were terror-struck by its performance. The tire lasted three times as long as conventional designs and would clearly cannibalize Michelin's other models and vastly cut sales volumes. It was also a faster, more comfortable, and more fuel-efficient product. In other words, a potential commercial disaster! To make matters worse, manufacturing the radial would require a total redesign of plants and equipment and an arduous process of training and getting production economy and reliability up to par. To fend off this monster, Michelin's American rivals bought the rights to the patent and proceeded to put the design on the shelf for *twenty years*: Their investors were afraid to embark upon what they felt would be a costly misadventure. But François Michelin, despite vigorous protests from his more conservative managers, decided to go with the radical invention immediately. The company, he said, *had* to do this for the customer; ethically, it was that simple.[33]

Values were made salient by a whole array of such convincing actions, especially in the form of resource allocation decisions. The Michelin family worked in drab, utilitarian offices, as did all their executives; theirs was very much a no-fringe operation. But when it came to research, labs, and equipment, only the best was good enough. Even in the early 1990s, when market slowdowns forced Michelin to slash its workforce by 10 percent and its investments by 75 percent, the Michelins refused to take a penny out of R&D. Market analysts and bankers complained, but the family persisted, ultimately coming up with dramatically improved tires and processes. To employees, these trade-offs spoke volumes about Michelin's priorities.[34]

Training and Mentoring: For Skills and Discovery

Whereas brand builders and craftsmen emphasized training in functional skills, innovators add to that mentorship to foster creativity and networking. First, take training. Bob Galvin at Motorola realized that the only way he could maintain cellular telephone production in the United States was by improving the working practices of all his staff. To keep boosting quality and efficiency, and to encourage process innovation, he organized people into self-directed teams in which line workers would take immediate responsibility for quality and processes. To enhance flexibility, he also insisted that employees master multiple skills and jobs. So he established the legendary "Motorola University," and committed every one of his 100,000-plus employees to continuous and universal training. The teaching staff consisted of 230 full-timers and 450 contract teachers. Besides specific technical skills, the curriculum embraced problem solving, teamwork, communications, and computational and managerial skills. This was no charitable gesture on Galvin's part. His calculations told him that the ratio of gain to cost of training was about 30 to 1. He also believed, given Motorola's philosophy of lifetime employment, that regular training was the only way to keep people at the cutting edge.[35]

Training, however, is not enough. When it comes to supporting innovation, mentorship may be even more important, as it imparts values and priorities that target discovery, and it makes for quick introductions that build the social networks that convert an idea into a product. At W.L. Gore, all employees must find a mentor within the first few weeks of employment, or be assigned one. Mentoring, or "sponsorship," as it is called there, connects one-on-one new hires with talented veterans—and thus with Gore's traditions and pioneering ethic. Because of the very personal and individual nature of the socialization, subtleties of the Gore culture are conveyed very early, privately, and frankly. Lessons may be about which people and teams get the most respect and why, what makes for a successful project, where to get resources, and who are the people one must know to get specific things done. Sponsors also share their web of connections and initiate the necessary introductions. This allows entrants to quickly get into the loop, making for a highly networked workplace where it is easy to get a team together to chase a new venture.

The Gore family retains direct control of the critical human resources function—Gore's mentoring center. In fact, sponsorship is effective at Gore because the firm hires only those who have superior social skills. Recruiters are known to contact as many as ten references for each hire and to put applicants through a rigorous interview process that probes their social capabilities.[36]

So effective at social and technical indoctrination was the paternalistic (and antiunion) Michelin that when it started building plants in the United States, it wouldn't hire anyone who had worked for a tire company before—lest they have to unlearn bad habits. Indeed, many new hires were sent to Michelin headquarters in Clermont-Ferrand for twelve months of training.[37] These programs enabled people to become more proficient at their jobs and, just as important, put them on the same wavelength. They also got everyone thinking about how to improve things, and gave them personal contacts in other departments to call on to put new ideas into play.

Jobs with Latitude

Like brand builders and craftsmen, innovators take care of their staff; but they encourage much more freedom. Especially important "perks" here are three types of latitude given to employees: in job scope, in career path, and to fail. All promote self-actualization at work, all support initiative and innovation, and all run counter to bureaucracy and hierarchy. All rely on the strong values and intensive indoctrination that allow a company to trust its people to make the best use of their efforts.

Job Scope. Special among these innovators is the unusual freedom they give to employees, particularly "knowledge workers," to use all their talents and follow their ideas free from bureaucratic constraints. Gore nurtures a famously egalitarian culture: Everyone is an "associate"; no one is or has a boss or title; and anyone has the ability to talk with anyone else. Education and seniority do not count, and positions carry no rank. People are not locked into particular tasks or hierarchies, but are expected to follow their passion and fulfill general expectations in a functional area. For instance,

Gore employees define their own jobs and commit to specific targets, with the help of their sponsors. Then it is their job to attain those targets by enlisting the help of others. The result? More than 50 percent of employees consider themselves leaders.

To foster a communal ambience, no Gore facility is allowed to house more than 200 employees, and all functions are represented in each: marketing, R&D, manufacturing, finance.[38] That way people all have closer, more diverse contacts and bigger, more varied jobs—jobs that compel initiative and creativity. Although there is a lot of respect for people, much is expected in return. Great responsibility is placed on individuals to be personally successful and to work toward business success in their part of the firm. This diligence, in fact, is the sole assessment criterion—and the primary source of innovation.

Flexible Career Paths. Because it takes time for people to find their talents and passions at work, and because innovators want to get the most from their people, career paths are flexible, and lateral job changes are common. At Michelin, even family members could instigate such changes. The inventor of the radial tire was not an engineer or scientist but a clerk in the export sales department, where he had devised an ingenious slide rule for making foreign exchange calculations. One day, CEO Édouard Michelin Sr., there on another matter, noticed the device and exclaimed, "But this man is a genius—he should be working on the technical side," whereupon with characteristic freedom from red tape, the man, Marius Mignol, was transferred to the "product experimental department." There the staff of experts treated him not as an outsider, but as a godsend whose talents needed nurturing and whose ideas demanded attention. Together, they changed the destiny of the company and the industry.[39]

At Michelin, status and roles are based not on rules but talent. People are not permitted to entrench themselves in formal positions or titles, and can move easily from one job to another. Similarly, at Corning, scientists are accorded the same status as managers: There is a dual ladder for promotion, making it possible for scientists to achieve the highest level of pay and prestige without becoming managers.[40]

Permission to Bomb. Unlike at craftsmen, where most errors are unacceptable, innovators give their people the freedom to make mistakes—at least when it comes to invention and discovery. Many years ago, a Michelin team endeavored at great expense to develop a rubber "rail-tire" for rail-ways. The idea was to build the car structure light enough to make this feasible. During the test, the flimsy locomotive sagged so badly that its belly almost touched the rails. Boss Édouard Michelin Sr. immediately summoned the hapless development team to his office. They fully expected a reprimand. Instead they were effusively congratulated for their daring. Édouard gave the team more funds to perfect their system, and now, decades later, the "Michelin locomotive" is still used in third-world countries.[41] As at Michelin, researchers at Corning and Gore singled out as one of the firm's biggest pluses the right to pursue an ambitious project and have it fail. The reasoning is always the same: Any one major success is impossible without many failures.

Consideration. To get people to make the best use of the latitude they are given, innovators treat them generously—with superior compensation and benefits, job security, and profit sharing. Here, in no particular order, is a short medley of feats and practices. Gore was listed by *Fortune* magazine as the seventh best place to work in America in 1998; in 2004, it was still number twelve. Its turnover is minuscule, and it is one of the healthiest workplaces in America, with 70 percent of the average health costs per worker and half the growth in medical costs.[42] Generous stock option and profit-sharing plans exist for all employees, who own over 25 percent of the company. At Fidelity, Ned Johnson distributed *51 percent* of the company to his executives and money managers.[43]

Even when things get tough, firms remain generous. When Corning had to effect layoffs, it asked the employees themselves to decide how to reengineer the work and "distribute the pain." The process was very gradual, and designed to affect managers as much as workers.[44] Gore uses an ingenious strategy to avoid layoffs: It locates its plants in clusters so that if work falls off for one venue, employees can be relocated to a neighboring plant instead of being laid off.[45] We've got dozens more examples in our files.

Collaboration Within and Across Departments and Units

If individual latitude and initiative are important in generating ideas and getting the best work out of people, collaboration within and across business units is necessary to develop those ideas into usable products and technologies.

Whereas innovators such as Intel are known for their individualistic cultures, these family businesses embraced *collaborative cultures* in which people from different functions teamed up to develop ideas and commercialize innovations. Corning's success was based on "independent thinkers who are also team players."[46] Gore and Motorola, as we discussed, demanded two qualities of new hires: technical expertise *and* social ability. So although "star" innovators were well rewarded and made into role models, there was little tolerance for "loner geniuses." Employees absolutely had to work well in teams.

At Gore, there are no predetermined channels of communication. This is strictly a superflat, team-based organization. An employee will identify a technological or market opportunity and then try to interest the people he or she needs to pursue it based on the merits of the project; for example, using Gore-Tex in shoes or in Army sleeping bags. A team may then be formed based on the overall requirements of the project and the skills and interests of the team members. Personal face-to-face communication is the norm; e-mails are discouraged. And, because people are both technically and socially skilled and work in small offices, interactions are smooth. The mentors, moreover, ensure that everyone has a good network of contacts starting almost immediately, which greatly facilitates collaboration.[47]

The most successful innovators are able to prioritize their projects and compose teams accordingly. Corning uses incentives to get its best employees to join teams working on the most promising technologies. It has set up a system whereby researchers attached to specific businesses receive extra compensation for applying their acumen to hotter technologies in other product lines. For example, the company wants to encourage scientists working on flat-panel displays to apply their knowledge of glass to photonics products. Several key scientific breakthroughs have already materialized from this cross-fertilization. Corning's new optical switch was made from inputs developed by its advanced materials unit. Its new DNA Microarray is a package of slides made of nondistorting glass for use in drug testing in genetic research. The product emerged from research done on Pyrex glass, catalytic converters, and photonics.[48]

Clearly, teams form most readily when departmental boundaries are amorphous. François Michelin always said a company must be a team because collaboration is the heart of innovation.[49] So Michelin's organization blurs the lines between departments, designating them by letters rather than functional names. As there is little territoriality, units share people and ideas and cooperate on joint projects. For example, those working at the Michelin research center to invent tire designs and materials collaborate closely and often colocate with people developing new production processes and equipment.[50] Interaction is also stimulated by the policy that problems be addressed jointly at the level at which they crop up—thereby speeding decision making, and avoiding political games. This policy also ensures that those with the most knowledge have the power to meet and decide.[51]

Finally, these innovators make productive use of the conflict that inevitably arises when people from different backgrounds are brought together in multidisciplinary teams. At Motorola, the Galvins actually *fostered* a climate of contention. To keep everyone thinking freshly, they encouraged arguments over policies, projects, and methods so that the new order would be constantly challenged and informed by the old. According to George Fisher, who succeeded Bob Galvin as CEO, "Meetings were contentious—not particularly polite, not particularly orderly. But they did get a lot of different views on the table, somewhat in a raucous way."[52]

When collaboration begins to flag, these companies act. From 1995 to 1996, the Fidelity culture became divisive as incentives drove fund managers to compete more and collaborate less. The results: redundant technology and marketing expenses, inferior investment decisions, and turf battles over customers. To repair the damage, the Johnsons revamped the culture to promote people-sharing and collaboration across funds, and to tone down the decentralized, gunslinging climate. Power, once spread among twelve senior managers, was consolidated among five. All the top players were then given 20 percent of their bonuses based on "their success in cooperating with one another"—a policy unheard of in an investment business notorious for its individualism.[53]

Company Towns. One reason collaboration is so effective at Gore, Corning, and Michelin is their company towns. Here, employees socialize, grow to understand one another, and become part of the same team. Living in such close quarters, they begin to share the same values, and so collaborate better. To reinforce this sense of community, firms and their owners contribute significant social infrastructure to the towns—schools, clubs, gyms, and even housing.

Complementary Priorities of Innovation: Continuity and Connection

There are natural dangers confronting innovators. Independent command can issue in too much risk taking and unrealistically ambitious projects. Cohesive community may homogenize worldviews, create insularity, and spur a tendency to do research "just for the joy of it." Innovators counter both of these dangers by employing two complementary priorities: continuity and connection. Specifically, managers act as careful stewards to manage risk. And they build close connections, especially with clients and alliance partners, to make innovations relevant and get a better view of the market.

Managing the Risks of Innovation

Concern for the continuity of the enterprise manifests in attention to controlling risks and adopting a long enough time horizon to ensure a robust business for years to come.

New Product-Market Risk Management and Stewardship

The families in this group curb innovative recklessness. First, they adhere to core competencies: Corning stuck to glass, Gore to discoveries around a complex chemical, Tetra Pak to sterile packaging technologies. These companies take risks, but generally in focused areas that they understand well. They also exploit each innovation to the maximum, as exemplified by Fidelity's dozens of funds, and Motorola's diverse uses of its wireless technology. This was possible because, notwithstanding its focus, the scope of innovation was broad enough to be leveraged across multiple markets and products. So firms get the best of both worlds: technological focus to reduce project risk and product-market diversity to reduce market risk.

Stewardship also takes the form of mother-hen family executives sweating not just the big picture but the telling details. The Michelins practically lived in their plant and knew every nook and cranny of their operation. The Galvins were hands-on managers who thrived on daily face-to-face interaction with people at all levels. Ned Johnson was a perfectionist— "a bear for every detail," said Caleb Loring, a longtime family friend and Fidelity executive. "It can drive you nuts."[54] Johnson was a relentless visitor to the computer room for updates on technology, and kept a quote machine to follow stocks and funds. A former employee remembers: "If he sees a computer problem, he'll call the programmer—if he cannot break the code himself." Every month, Johnson descended into Fidelity's basement to inspect the generators he installed to keep the company's computers running in event of a blackout.[55]

Investing in Long-Run Projects

As James Houghton told us, "The most important effect of family owner sentiments is that you're in it for the long run. You don't focus on the next quarter. So Corning invested in fiber optics for eighteen years before realizing any returns." And he told two corporate biographers:

> [R&D] was something you did on faith, in good times and in bad, whether you could see the immediate results of it or whether you couldn't . . . My father and his cousin supported the practice of this "religion" during the hard times of the Depression, and it paid off in Corning's huge television bulb business after World War II. My brother Amo and his colleagues kept this faith alive during some of the darkest days of this company, in the 1970s when many other companies curtailed their R&D.[56]

Michelin consistently sacrifices short-term concerns for the pursuit of just two objectives: quality and market share. Number one is the customer, whose comfort and safety are everything. So Michelin plows virtually all its profits back into the business, depreciating capital to the maximum and setting up all kinds of reserves to invest in product improvement.[57]

Secrecy

To extend the life of their discoveries, most innovators are secretive. Gore refused to patent hundreds of its inventions, fearing they would be copied. The process for manufacturing Gore-Tex, in fact, is so secret that even the chairman pleads ignorance of the details. Michelin took secrecy to a higher level still of obsession. It was one of the very few businesses the Nazis could not penetrate during the war. When General Charles de Gaulle visited a plant in 1959, he was allowed to enter just *one* of the research labs, and only without his entourage. Even representatives from the village fire department are not allowed to enter: The plants have their own sanitation and fire brigade and their own phone system and mail service. No waste materials leave the plant in a state that would allow competitors to analyze any aspect of tire construction. What cannot be recycled is destroyed.[58] According to François Michelin, the smallest indiscretion could put into jeopardy years of research and advanced technology—the two advantages Michelin had repeatedly cited as primary in winning over clients and markets.[59] Extreme as it was, the secrecy requirement highlighted very poignantly to employees the value placed on their discretion and research. It also made them feel part of a privileged group that was leading the field and a true object of envy and imitation.

Partnering to Assure Relevance

To avoid too closed an organizational community, innovators embrace connection—forming alliances and joint ventures with *external* clients and research partners. This is done not only to generate great ideas, but to keep innovation efforts market-relevant. Again, family reputations helped form these relationships.

CEO James Houghton notes that Corning's alliances have greatly expanded the company's reach—enabling it to leverage its research skills, develop new products, and move into new markets more quickly and cheaply than if it had gone it alone. Some partnerships provided a ready-made market for Corning's inventions; others permitted the company to concentrate on innovation while outsourcing production. Indeed, since its first alliance in 1924, Corning has embarked upon more than fifty joint ventures related to everything from the development of television tubes and food enzymes to fiber-optic cable and fiberglass. It has formed alliances with the Dow Chemical Company (based on an early family friendship) and Owens-Illinois, as well as cross-border ventures in Japan, Korea, India, Germany, and China. Today, Corning is engaged in about two dozen ventures, which, in a typical year, bring a third of earnings and revenues.[60]

What has given Corning such a high batting average in an area where many companies so often strike out? Corning Vice Chairman Van Campbell will tell you it's a decades-old culture of collaboration: "We don't view joint ventures as one-off situations like many companies. We view them as an essential way of doing business." However trite, the truth is that Corning is always on the lookout for partners. "We regard every company in any related industry as a potential partner," says Campbell.[61]

We have seen also how Tetra Pak works closely with its clients to create new packaging materials, processes, and solutions to fit their products. It becomes deeply involved in all of the details of a client's operations, from every phase of actual processing and manufacture to product testing and quality control. The aim is to make the company indispensable to the customer. That closeness also gives Tetra's engineers lots of ideas for perfecting and testing their own technologies.

Support for company towns is another aspect of connection that helps a firm gain respect and political clout from its community. For over a hundred years, the paternalistic and often controlling Michelin family have nurtured Clermont-Ferrand, France—often called "Michelinville." It is the geographic seat of the company's heart and mind, and an insular and cohesive society. The Michelins have built houses, hospitals, schools, churches, and industrial development centers to support small businesses in the area; and for years they were preeminent patrons in health care, education, and sports.[62]

Similarly, the soul of Corning resides in Corning, New York, a 2,150-square-mile, three-county region. The firm devotes about 2 percent of pretax profits to charity, approximately half of which go to its hometown. Professor Mike Beer, an ex-Corning executive now at the Harvard Business School, recalled for us the terrible flood of 1972. Then-CEO Amory Houghton went on the air at once "and gave an inspiring and Churchill-like speech to the community that provided hope and inspiration at a devastating time. He committed the resources of the company to the community. And he made good on this both in money and people resources."[63]

Conclusion

Some striking patterns emerge in the broad relief of our findings about innovators. First, the strategy of innovation among these firms is at once multifaceted and balanced. It relies as much on incremental improvements as big discoveries, on process improvements as new products, on leveraging as pioneering, on destruction of the old as creation of the new. So it delicately equilibrates all four C priorities. Independent command bestows the courage to make the leap forward and embrace original approaches and products. But continuity concerns counter excessive risk. Cohesive community focuses people on making discoveries. But connection with partners prevents clannishness and ensures the relevance of those discoveries.

As we will see in chapter 8, when this balancing act is flawed, even once-stellar FCBs like Corning and Motorola can get into trouble. Table 6-1 relates the elements of the innovation strategy to their supporting priorities and practices.

Table 6-1

Relating the Four Cs to the Strategy of Innovation

	COMPONENTS OF THE INNOVATION STRATEGY			
	Path-breaking innovation	Improvement and leverage	Commercialization	Creative destruction
Command: Freedom to innovate boldly				
• Courageous venturing: Commitment advantage	**	*	*	
• Idiosyncratic and risk tolerant: Originality advantage	**			*
• Proactive and decisive: Speed advantage	*			**
• Spry and empowered top team		*	**	
Community: Uniting the tribe in creation				
• Inspiring values	**			*
• Training and mentorship	*	*	*	
• Jobs with latitude	**	*	*	*
• Collaboration	*	*	**	
Continuity: Managing innovation risk				
• Stewardship, patience, core competency, secrecy	*	*	*	
Connection: Partnering to assure relevance				
• Forming alliances with clients, partners, and the community		*	**	

* facilitator; ** key facilitator

Chapter 7

Deal Makers

A CLOSE FRIEND works for an international FCB in the natural resources sector. When his company boldly sold off a part of its operations to the public and to a competitor, we thought this might be a nice opportunity to buy some shares. As the months went by, our investment began to melt—to about half of what we put in. When next we saw our friend we kidded him about his company having been fortunate to unload when they did. Luck, he remarked, was only a part of the story. The family running his firm knew a good deal more than we did about supply-and-demand patterns, about what rivals and major clients were planning, and about government policy. What looked to us outsiders like "a lucky deal" was the result of concerted study and a great network of savvy international contacts. The FCB also knew much more about running its business than the competitor, which purchased the operations and then let go some excellent executives. That edge is what our great deal makers are all about: inspired entrepreneurial moves, profound knowledge of the business, and the long-standing relationships needed to make smart and effective deals.

A Strategy of Deal Making

Our winning deal makers combine the bold cunning of a speed chess player with the contacts of a socialite. They are driven by a desire for brisk growth and impact, one major deal or project at a time. But they stick to what they know best and enlist the support of expert partners. The deal-making strategy rests on four unshakable pillars:

- Spotting opportunities early and creatively
- Capturing deals by making and "reading" contacts

- Executing intricate projects via superior knowledge and partnering skills
- Cumulative learning across projects to become ever more competitive in burgeoning niches of the market

Family-Controlled Deal Makers

Bechtel Group, Inc.

- Founder/Family: Warren A. Bechtel/Bechtel
- Founding Year: 1898
- Revenues (2002): $11.6 billion
- Market Share: Number-two construction group in the world; number-one contractor in the United States

Bechtel, with its fourth-generation leader at the helm, is one of the world's largest construction and engineering enterprises. Its 50,000 employees build everything from dams and refineries to power plants and entire cities. In 2001, they worked on 900 projects in 60 countries. The Bechtel family, who control the firm, are noted for their web of international connections with the rich and powerful, and their ability to organize and finance, at the drop of a hat, construction consortia for complex mega-projects. Landmark jobs include the Hoover Dam in Colorado; Jubail Industrial City, Saudi Arabia; Hong Kong's International Airport, built on an artificial island; and the first nuclear power plant.

Bombardier Inc.

- Founder/Families: Joseph-Armand Bombardier/Bombardier and Beaudoin
- Founding Year: 1937
- Revenues (2002): $13.78 billion
- Market Share: World's number-one regional jet and number-three civil aircraft manufacturer; number-one rail-gear maker

In 1942, mechanic Joseph-Armand Bombardier incorporated a tiny firm to manufacture his invention: a snowmobile, which could travel at great speed and open up the Quebec countryside during its long winters. After the energy crisis of the 1970s, son-in-law Laurent Beaudoin, the new CEO, initiated Bombardier's monumental deal-making phase, moving into mass transit to build railcars, first for Montreal's subway and then for

Chicago, Mexico City, and New York. In 1986, the company went into aerospace manufacture with the acquisition of Canadair. Bombardier has, for the last thirty years, kept growing by landing large contracts and, where advantageous, acquiring firms such as Learjet, Pullman, and Adtranz. From 1990 to 1997, it outperformed all firms traded on the Toronto Stock Exchange.

J.P. Morgan & Co., Inc.

- Founder (of founding firm)/Family: Junius Spencer Morgan/Morgan
- Founding Year: 1838 (family-run until 1943; family presence into 1980s)
- Revenues of JPMorgan Chase 2002: $43.4 billion
- Market Share: 1910–1930: Number-one security underwriter in the United States; 2002: number-one private bank in the United states; number two in financial services

By 1910, J.P. Morgan & Co. was the most powerful investment bank in the United States—perhaps even its most influential financial institution. Morgan controlled the railroad and steel industries through its voting trusts and bailed out France, New York City, and the New York Stock Exchange during their respective crises. Although the fearsome Pierpont Morgan brought the bank to its apex of power, it was his determined father Junius who put him in position to do so; and subsequently it was his diplomatic son Jack who modernized Morgan. The bank formed connections with the highest levels of international banking, industry, and government, and could tap into a limitless stream of capital based on reputation alone. The investment banking arm of today's JPMorgan Chase & Co. still enjoys the 100-year family legacy of ethics, philosophy, reputation, and even clients.

Olympia & York Developments Ltd.

- Founders/Family: Paul, Albert, and Ralph Reichmann/Reichmann
- Founding Year: 1955; Receivership 1992
- Assets (1989): $20 to 25 billion, controlled by three Reichmann brothers, world's fourth wealthiest family in 1991 at $12.8 billion[a]
- Market Share (1992): World's number-one private-property developer[b]

The Reichmann brothers built Olympia & York (O&Y) into one of the most successful real estate development and management firms in history. Projects included the World Financial Center in New York City and First

Canadian Place in Toronto, the tallest building in Canada. Specialization among the brothers had Paul Reichmann spotting propitious opportunities and assembling resources to execute deals, while Albert supervised the internal workings of the projects, pioneering new construction techniques along the way. Family reputation and influence enabled the Reichmanns to make massive deals on the strength of a handshake. Today, family connections are being leveraged by a subsequent generation of Reichmanns and helping to build a new empire following O&Y's 1992 collapse (see chapter 8).

a. "The Reichmann Brothers: King of Officeland," *The Economist* 312, no. 7612 (July 22, 1989): 17–19.
b. Walter Stewart, *Too Big to Fail: Olympia & York, The Story Behind the Headlines* (Toronto: McClelland and Stewart, 1993); Peter Temple, "An Empire Built on Property," *Accountancy* 104, no. 1152 (August 1989): 107–109; "The Billionaires of 1991," *Fortune* 124, no. 6 (September 9, 1991): 59+.

Ability to Spot Opportunities Early and Creatively

Most firms try to spot deals, but our deal makers do it for a living and take it to an art form. In fact, they discover opportunities where their rivals never even look. According to CEO Riley Bechtel: "If you're really in the game, you've got to understand what's happening in governments and markets and can see a deal before they put it out to bid. If the first time I hear about a big project is when the proposal is on The Street, then I don't have a good win plan."[1]

An endless stream of new projects is the very lifeblood of these firms: investment banking deals, construction projects, or orders to produce a fleet of aircraft or subway cars. There is little "stable" ongoing business here, just an ever-changing episodic mix of major contracts; "business-getting" is central. The challenge, however, is to identify projects the firm can do better than its rivals.

Bechtel's aggressive intelligence-gathering missions all over the world enabled it to spot opportunities before anyone else. Through government contacts, it learned precious information on U.S. projections on Middle East oil reserves and tips on upcoming government projects. It formed an especially close association with the CIA, even hiring ex-director Richard Helms as an "international consultant." Using such privileged sources and their own watchful people on the ground, the Bechtel staff compiled weekly international intelligence reports, which detailed global developments in political, military, economic, and technological categories. Circulated to key Bechtel executives, these reports drove the battle plan for business development that repeatedly put Bechtel in the right place at the right time.[2]

The Bechtels were as adept at creating opportunities as spotting them. Steve Bechtel Sr., for example, often recognized a promising venture even before his clients did. In 1949, he and the head of Socony, Mobil Oil's West Coast subsidiary, were chatting at a luncheon when the conversation came around to some large oil discoveries in Alberta. Said the oil man, "If they could ever run a pipeline from that field to the West Coast, I'd build a refinery up north, and I should think some other companies would want to do the same." By late the next year, Bechtel had commissioned economic studies of the pipeline, surveyed a route, and drawn up a plan. With its early lead and convincing cost-benefit statistics, Bechtel soon landed the contract to manage construction of the Trans Mountain Pipe Line—plus subsequent related contracts to build three refineries in the Northwest.[3]

Bombardier saw opportunities even where others saw potential disasters. In 1986, the company bought money-losing Canadair from the Canadian government for $120 million, after the former had written off over $2 billion developing the Challenger corporate jet (the liquidation value was estimated at $300 million). CEO Laurent Beaudoin and President Robert Brown knew the plane had potential and that the Challenger technology was beginning to take shape. They anticipated that the twelve-seat Challenger could be expanded into a more economical and attractive fifty-seat regional jet—one with real market potential. They also knew the government wanted to preserve jobs at Canadair and so would sell cheap.[4] A more recent coup for the company was its purchase, in 1989, of Short Brothers PLC ("Shorts") of Belfast, Ireland, for $58 million. There, the government, before the purchase, had invested $1.4 billion to modernize the plants and had relieved Shorts of $800 million of debt—but to little avail. Only Bombardier, it seems, saw how it could convert Shorts' operations into highly profitable plants. The Shorts deal would gain Bombardier access to the European Economic Community, help it produce orders already on the books, and take away a potential competitor.[5]

Deals are in the eyes and imaginations of the beholder, and Bombardier's vision was very sharp indeed. The company often could foresee what the deal would garner *after* it revamped facilities, retargeted product lines, or leveraged an acquired technology. What seemed to outsiders like risky ventures often turned out to be near-sure things for Bombardier. All these deal makers had this talent: not to see a project as it was, but as it could be.

Ability to Capture Deals: Making and Reading Influential Contacts

Having identified opportunities, deal makers were ingenious at capturing them, primarily because they did the scutwork to deeply understand the intricacies of the deal and, perhaps more important, the very local interests of the various parties to it. A part of that preparation was getting in touch with the right people in order to snap up information and assess the lay of the land.

Bombardier was an underdog when it went after a massive $1 billion contract to supply 825 subway cars for the New York City subway system. Rather than putting in a blind bid based on the New York Metropolitan Transportation Agency's (MTA) specs, Bombardier staff pushed to work closely with the MTA; that way they could get a read of the client and probe for acceptable ways to cut costs before the bidding began. In early 1982, they held a series of about thirty meetings with the MTA, during which teams of managers, lawyers, and engineers from both parties worked on the contract specifications. Armed with their insights, the Bombardier team then set up a "war room" in the New York Hilton, a few blocks away from MTA headquarters, in the final push to prepare the bid. To buy some insurance, CEO Laurent Beaudoin went to his contacts at the Canadian federal government. He understood these were economically challenging times for Canada, and that its politicians were under fire. They needed to do something to create jobs in a struggling Quebec to offset a growing independence movement. Beaudoin saw how federal financing of the contract would further the government's social and economic objectives. Ultimately, what clinched the deal was Bombardier's ability to procure from the government's Export Development Corporation a loan for 85 percent of the contract at 4 percent below the best rate the MTA could get anywhere else. Beaudoin also got his government contacts to help negotiate favorable terms with Kawasaki for the railcar technology. Typical of great deal makers, Bombardier was able to get close enough to the client to understand its needs, and then pull together the resources and contacts needed to land the big fish.[6]

Sometimes insight and homework could even overcome the superior political connections of rivals. One reason the Reichmanns at O&Y could capture such huge projects was their daring and brilliantly informed proposals. To land the massive contract for the World Financial Center from

New York's Battery Park City Authority (BPCA), the Canadian Reichmanns went up against New York's biggest and most politically connected developers—developers who had gone in with detailed plans and teams of architects. Paul Reichmann went alone and with one sheet of paper. His thorough study of the agency's financial situation convinced him that a primary concern of the BPCA was to pay off its debt. So he proposed to guarantee that his own company, O&Y, would do exactly that. He had calculated that O&Y could in fact meet these obligations comfortably, given BPCA's ten-year tax abatement on the property. No other developer had the insight that guaranteeing the debt would land the contract. Nor did they have the foresight or courage to assume the risk.[7]

Knowledge and Partners to Execute the Deals

If knowledge of the client and influential contacts are necessary to land major contracts, these very same resources must be built on to *execute* the contracts. Deal makers are typically viewed as being strong on action and instinct and shaky on knowledge and facts. Nothing could be further from the truth for our companies. True, the firms had adventurous spirits, but many also had the cautious practicality of greengrocers. So they developed a profound knowledge not just of their market environments, but of operating capabilities as well. And they built a web of close relationships with external parties that would help them execute their bold projects and grapple with the obstacles that inevitably crop up.

Knowledge of the Business and the Market. When we think of the bank that bears J. P. Morgan's name, we think of daring entrepreneurship and vision. But the only way Morgan made its deals pay off was by sweating the details—by knowing more about the industries and companies it financed and restructured than even the executives within those industries. This was essential given the scope of the deals and the speed with which many had to be executed. Thus, Pierpont Morgan took pride that he could do any job in his bank. Like his father who taught him, he wanted to see the fine print on the major projects and was said to have "a deadeye for fake figures in scanning a ledger." And unlike their rivals of the day, the Morgan dynasty, from Junius to Pierpont to Jack, chose their key executives based on talent and brains, not wealth. They made only the best-informed people into partners—and kept down to a small set of them to focus talent and maintain excellence. Partner Samuel Spencer, for example, was said to know more about railroads than anyone else in the country, "from the cost of a car brake to the estimate for a terminal." Most Morgan partners sat on the boards of many companies, making sure that the bank's financial stake was secure. This also gave Morgan an unusually broad vantage point from which to view an industry and economy.[8]

The Reichmanns too were ingenious at execution and famous for pioneering new construction techniques for their major buildings. First Canadian Place in Toronto was typical of O&Y's grand skyscraper projects, featuring acres of beautiful white marble and a rich, luxurious look. Certainly, O&Y was renowned for the beauty and quality of its buildings and its ability to attract blue-ribbon tenants. But its real secret was its immaculately economical construction techniques. Virtually all building took place inside the structure. Trucks loaded with materials would drive into the structure, be lowered by elevator onto a giant turntable, and be pointed to the spot where their cargo was required. Other elevators lifted people and materials to the floors under construction. Nowhere was there a ladder in sight. It is estimated that two and a half hours per worker day were saved using such techniques. Another advantage was that the lower floors could be finished and rented out to tenants while the upper ones were still being built. All it took was to sign one prestigious tenant, using loss-leader rents, to soon attract others who would pay more.[9]

The Reichmanns also used pioneering techniques in finance to stack the deck in their favor. Together with Lewis Ranieri, Salomon Brothers' resident genius of real estate financing, they floated a $1 billion issue that was the first bond to securitize a parcel of buildings. In addition, O&Y became the first developer to issue commercial paper in the United States and to sell eurobonds, enabling the Reichmanns to borrow very cheaply. These issues also insulated O&Y from the need to supply hobbling guarantees of repayment. By the mid-1980s, the builder had replaced about $3 billion of recourse debt with nonrecourse debt.[10]

Partnering. Deal makers rarely go it alone. As central as their expertise is their ability to partner to access the knowledge or resources they lack. Inevitably, large projects require collaboration with subcontractors, banks, and sometimes government agencies. Such associations can multiply corporate reach.

Bechtel strongly favored partnering, and it began that practice very early. In 1931, Warren Bechtel helped create one of the power industry's first joint ventures, the Six Companies consortium that built Hoover Dam.[11] Today, through such partnering, Bechtel drums up business by commissioning a project itself. It usually takes on a partner such as Pacific Gas and Electric (PG&E) or Shell Oil, antes up about half of the 20-to-40 percent equity, and finances the balance with nonrecourse bank debt, government guarantees, and the like.[12] In fact, Bechtel is partnering more than ever as it focuses on the higher-margin parts of its business and specializes in its areas of expertise. For example, it is expanding a previous venture with Royal Dutch/Shell Group, called InterGen, to go after power plant projects in the United States and abroad. Bechtel has the proven infrastructure capability to keep Shell state of the art. And in turn, Shell's $100 billion balance sheet helps capture the big deals. By 1999, the alliance had six projects either operating or under construction, including, in China, the nation's largest privatized coal-fired power plant.[13]

Cumulative Learning

The project nature of the deal maker's business makes learning across jobs essential. It's the only way firms can gain a competitive advantage in cost and quality over less experienced rivals still working on a "one-off" basis.

Start Early. It helps sometimes to be the first to scale the learning curve. Bechtel was not afraid to get in early and invest if it believed there was potential. That was certainly the case when it came to atomic power. Steve Bechtel Sr. had helped build several heavy-water projects at the dawn of the atomic age in the 1940s. He had also carried out a number of projects for the Atomic Energy Commission (AEC), and so was able in 1949 to get an AEC contract for an experimental breeder reactor. These early projects gave his firm its entrée into what was to become a high-stakes race to move the United States to nuclear energy. Because it invested in this early learning, Bechtel ultimately became the world's largest developer of nuclear power.[14]

Transfer Learning Across Projects. The Reichmanns at O&Y stunned their rivals as they augmented their capabilities from one project to the next and slid down the cost curve. One of the most able and profitable developers in Canada had been Toronto Industrial Leaseholds, owned by the Rubin brothers. The brothers had thrived by pioneering assembly-line techniques for the construction of hundreds of lookalike buildings. But by the early 1960s, the Reichmanns had them crying uncle. Said the defeated firm's senior manager Bud Andrews, "It got so we just couldn't compete. When it came to pricing a bid, there was no one in the same league as the

Reichmanns."[15] In fact, Paul Reichmann and his brothers learned so fast they became known in Toronto as the "Einsteins of building." In the early years of the company, the brothers had taken on similar projects that facilitated learning and its transfer across jobs. Soon, they began to cut their engineers and subcontractors less and less slack. It got so they could complete the typical job in three to six months, half the average, on time and on budget. This would have been remarkable for any builder, but it was doubly so for the Reichmanns with their screw-tight bids. To add to their competitive edge, O&Y's buildings were superior in functionality and appearance. Even for their warehouses the company would use brick instead of the usual concrete, and do a full landscaping, so the properties were that much easier to rent.[16] With a skeleton staff of a dozen people, O&Y would in its first decade erect more than 100 buildings.

Bechtel actually codified its project learning in its modular designs. "If left to their own devices, engineers will engineer something into perpetuity," said Riley Bechtel. "But an owner wants to minimize unnecessary costs of a plant, and maximize returns." By putting the financial people together with the engineers, Bechtel developed a series of standardized power plant designs that shortened the time spent on plant configurations and other details to hours rather than months. This modularization approach, which builds on Bechtel's industry focus, "has been so successful, our biggest challenge is finding enough capital to do all the projects on our plate," claims Paul Unruh, group president.[17]

Bombardier's managers had quite a different learning strategy. They entered industry niches by buying companies with promising technologies. Then they analyzed, adapted, and applied those technologies to the other businesses and plants they operated in a sector. They did this in rail and aerospace, leveraging not only process knowledge but product innovations from one acquisition and from the core business to the rest of the company.[18] When Bombardier acquired Short Brothers, it knew it could use the knowledge it had gained from its Canadair purchase to set up a more efficient production system. It proceeded to apply its Bombardier Manufacturing System, which emphasized incremental moves into full-scale production, responsive engineering-manufacturing interfaces, and task simplicity. The company kept perfecting the system from plant to plant and leveraged it across acquisitions. Bombardier was also adept at transferring knowledge from partners like Kawasaki, footing the bill to send not four or five but seventy people to Japan, both to learn state-of-the-art methods and to see what they were up against from potential Japanese rivals.[19]

The Magic. We should confess that this strategy story would not be complete without mentioning the "magic"—the nose that key deal-making executives have for ripe opportunities. These are people who are the only ones to sniff out the good deals or partners even when they are there for everyone to see. It is they who can price a bid low enough to attract business but high enough to make money. No one, for example, could beat Bombardier's Laurent Beaudoin at finding gold in acquisitions his rivals viewed as dross. Likewise, Paul Reichmann, it is said, "[h]ad the nerve of a poker player and the mental ability of a card sharp, who knew exactly how many tens, aces, and kings had been dealt from a four-deck stack."[20] No less an authority than legendary financier Bernard Baruch called the barrel-chested Pierpont Morgan "the greatest financial genius this country has ever known."[21] Theirs is an art few can master and that cannot be entirely imparted. It demands uncanny business intuition and risk assessment and, often, superb networking skills. What allows these deal makers to thrive is that they surface and empower those possessed of these talents, and build terrific teams around them. They also learn how to recognize these skills in their staff, and bring along the gifted ones by apprenticeship and promotion to where they will add the most value to the company.

The Major Priorities of Deal Making: Entrepreneurial Command and Extensive Connections

If the strategies of these deal makers were special, so were their foundations. For one, firms accorded extraordinary independence to their leaders—the broad discretion to make deals, take risks, and dedicate resources with speed and originality. But to mitigate these risks, deep continuity and stewardship guidelines were established. Deal making also relied on superb connections and relationships, based in part on firm and family stability and reputation. Such associations with clients and partners helped to snag promising deals and execute them in the best manner possible. Meanwhile, a collaborative organizational community linked different departments and business units together to carry out the projects. Again there is a symphony of counterbalancing priorities and practices that make the system work—a harmonious configuration.

Freedom to Act: Relentless Opportunity Seeking

The ability of deal makers to capture opportunities was enhanced by their leaders' control over company capital and their power to rapidly commit resources without having to go through approval hoops or worry about second-guessing. As emerging deals were at the core of the business, this capacity to seize opportunities and make bold decisions was vital.

Courageous Ambition

Family deal makers are not your typical entrepreneurs. Although they love growth, their ambition often extends beyond the financial, and that can be a source of boldness. Indeed, some wish to leave, by their definitions, a positive mark on the world. This sharpens strategic direction and provides the necessary conviction to be courageous and build memorable projects.

For Pierpont Morgan, like his father Junius and his son Jack, the real passion was not money but the chance to set straight the country's economy, rescuing banks, stock exchanges, railways, or the federal treasury as the occasion demanded. According to biographer Ron Chernow, Pierpont wanted the "power to take what he saw as a topsy-turvy financial world and set it right."[22] Similarly, the Bechtels, although financially driven, were proud of their work to modernize the world's energy and transportation infrastructures. They pioneered myriad techniques and technologies to do that in the fastest, most economical ways possible. The Bombardiers' more local aims were to build a great manufacturing company for French Canadians and an enduring "monument to the family."[23]

The Reichmanns of Olympia & York wanted their massive building complexes to enhance the skylines of major cities and make them more inspiring. But just as important, they strove to be Jewish Robin Hoods, reaping from their corporate tenants and redistributing wealth to revive the orthodox community and its faith. In straddling the contrasting provinces of bold capitalism and Jewish fundamentalism, the Reichmanns labored to balance faith and fortune: serving God and their community by serving Mammon.[24]

Speed and Decisiveness

Although these deal makers were not in the game to make a fast buck, they were, like our innovators, incredibly speedy decision makers. Their independence and sense of purpose spurred their decisiveness. No less a figure than President Grover Cleveland praised Pierpont Morgan for his "lightening-like rapidity," after the latter teamed up with the Rothschild banking family in 1895 to shore up the gold reserves of the country and, in effect, function as America's central bank.[25] This was the start of a long pattern of Morgan helping to strengthen America's economic system in the face of financial panics and crashes. Within a two-week period in 1907, Morgan, through his bank's timely infusions of cash, saved from ruin several trust companies and a major brokerage house, while also bailing out New York City from near-bankruptcy and rescuing the stock exchange. Morgan, along with fellow bankers George F. Baker and James Stillman, saved the Trust Company of America by investing $3 million, and lent $30 million to the City of New York to cover its obligations. At the same time, Morgan organized a number of bank presidents to come up with another $25 million to keep the stock market open. For his favors, he got Teddy Roosevelt to override the Sherman Antitrust Act so he could buy Tennessee Coals, making a handsome profit along the way.[26]

The Reichmanns were just as quick, sometimes betting fortunes based on their analyses of what Paul liked to call "unproven facts." And acting fast gave them a real advantage. The Uris package, as it was known, consisted of eight New York City skyscrapers put up for sale by Steve Ross's National Kinney Company. Paul quickly determined that the price of $46 million in cash and $300 million in outstanding mortgages would work out to $30 a square foot—or one-third of replacement cost. Although rents at the buildings were low in the mid-1970s, and the city was in a financial crisis, Paul figured that O&Y could hold out and service the debt for at least five years, even in a highly unfavorable rental market. He believed that the market would turn well before that. On September 19, 1977, O&Y signed the purchase contract. Over the next eighteen months, the Reichmanns invested another $80 million to improve the properties; as the market recovered, the average rent paid rose from $7 to $10, and then to $30 per square foot in a few years' time. By 1981, many of the buildings were fetching $60 a foot; and by the late 1980s, the properties were valued conservatively at $300 a foot. New York Governor Mario Cuomo heralded this real estate coup as one of the two great deals of New York history—the other being the purchase by the Dutch of Manhattan Island.[27]

What is especially notable here is that the Reichmanns were not alone in recognizing the deal. Canada's Cadillac Fairview Corporation, too, was very interested. But it failed to go forward with a bid, worried, the company's executive vice president said, that its public shareholders might become impatient waiting for a turnaround in the New York market. Said he: "If you are too conscious of the pressure to show quarterly increases on your income statement . . . you don't take a chance on assets that may be lucrative in the long term but are problematic today."[28] The Reichmanns, by contrast, showed the strength of all great deal makers: the speed and decisiveness to make a quick bid and the willingness to take a risk and be patient in waiting for a payoff.[29]

The fact that O&Y was a very lean, understaffed business, unfettered by assistants and lawyers, further speeded action. During a five-minute meeting, and at the drop of a hat, family members could commit $100 million. "While hammering out the deal that brought them a 50 percent interest in Trizec, a Calgary developer, Paul and Albert would periodically duck into the hallway and then reappear seconds later to up their bid by $50 million to $100 million. 'We just had a board meeting,' Albert would announce."[30]

Contrarianism

These deal makers didn't just do deals, they did inspired, contrarian deals: deals that stood out, enhanced family reputation, *and* made money. They went after such deals because these often represented terrific opportunities and bargains, which their independence from conservative shareholders left them uniquely free to pursue.

Bechtel would venture forth where few others dared—if the payoff were big enough. That was surely the case with nuclear power in the 1950s. Bechtel and a few brave utility companies put up $1 million apiece to build several prototype reactors; they wanted to determine the feasibility of atomic power. That was a massive amount to spend on highly speculative research, and Bechtel's advisers thought its chances were slim. But the early learning proved useful. When the going got too slow, however, Steve Bechtel Sr. approached General Electric's CEO Ralph Cordiner and suggested: "Enough with the prototypes; why not get beyond the debate about which type of reactor is best and move forward with a full-scale power plant that runs on atomic energy?"[31] The age of atomic power generation had begun—in earnest. By partnering with GE, Bechtel went from a regional, not very important, builder of power plants to a leading global contractor in the field.

Another contrarian was Laurent Beaudoin at Bombardier. He remained in Quebec, never an industrial hub. He diversified into hazardous and declining businesses like rail equipment and aircraft. And he expanded by buying companies with crippled balance sheets. He also tended to bid on the firms during weak markets and looked for niche players others were not interested in. That is how he got into the aerospace industry—buying smaller firms one at a time to acquire technology and build critical mass, ultimately becoming the world's number-three civil aircraft manufacturer.[32] Bombardier was contrarian as well when it pioneered regional jets at a time when air traffic was entering its slowdown. Although no one recognized it then, smaller planes were exactly what the industry was beginning to require, and today Bombardier is the global leader in that market. The firm also surprised observers when it moved to buy Adtranz, an electric locomotive business with half the margins of aircraft. Bombardier's intention was to reduce the cyclical nature of its business and couple Adtranz with its own railcar business. It has become the number-one maker of passenger-rail gear, ahead of Alsthom and Siemens.[33]

Complementarity and Trust on the Top Management Team

One of the striking contrasts between individual entrepreneurs and these deal makers is that very often multiple family members are involved at the top of the company, each with enough influence to curb the others' excesses and produce more balanced decisions. Because these family members have the long-run reputation and health of the firm at heart, trust is high and dialogue open and frank. That not only makes for better decisions, but quicker ones. The generations of Bechtels, Morgans, and Bomdardier-Beaudoins learned a great deal from one another and, given their differing temperaments, could bring complementary perspectives to their decisions.

Paul and Albert Reichmann were equal in their authority at O&Y, thus in part interchangeable. But their capabilities were complementary. Paul, a cerebral and sometimes aloof man, was the grand visionary, the one who scouted building sites, dreamed up projects, and made development deals. He was able also to convert his dreams into ingenious "pro formas" that detailed the economics of a project. Moreover, he was a superb salesman for his projects, very polite and calm, but persistent and with a command of financial and commercial details that inspired confidence among potential clients. Albert, in contrast, was the general manager who oversaw the construction work and administered the staff. He had an even more incredible command of detail, and a memory like a trap, and made sure that every aspect of Paul's dreams became reality. He was, moreover, a warmer person, whose deep religiosity did not distance him from his people.[34]

Trust among the brothers was complete, and eventually each would specialize in his own kinds of projects, with Paul doing the bigger ones with few outside partners, and Albert doing the more routine projects, often with partners and a much smaller commitment of capital. But for years, the brothers consulted each other frequently on every project. Again, this diversity of focus and skill promoted better decisions and a more balanced portfolio of work.

Being Good Partners: Leveraging Contacts and Building Networks

Family connections typically bring political influence and enduring business alliances that make it especially easy for FCBs to unearth and capture opportunities. These relationships, which frequently rely on a family's reputation and sway, may attract capital, clients, and influential partners. Deal makers went out of their way to develop *high-trust, enduring* associations by being worthy and generous partners—good neighbors—to those with whom they did business.

The Family Role in Connection

There are several reasons why many families are ideal builders of advantageous connections. First, because they are preoccupied with preserving the honor of their forebears and the reputations of their children, they behave in a *trustworthy* way. Second, they tend to be *stable*—the same managers stay in place long enough to form deep relationships with outsiders. They can be counted on as honest partners who are in it for the long run. Third, family leaders make sure to *pass on* their contacts to later generations, sometimes even sending offspring to different parts of the business to extend the network. Finally, they can keep *secrets*; in cases of private ownership, they do not have to inform the public about their deals or partners.

The Honor of the Family and Reputation. Deal-maker FCBs have to be concerned with their honor. It is their stock in trade—the basis for their reputation, which is so central to those having to look constantly for large new clients and capital.[35] During investment banking's baronial age of the nineteenth century, a company's probity was everything. So it was understandable that Junius Morgan would tell his son Pierpont, "Never under any circumstances do an action which could be called into question if known to the world."[36]

That said, honesty blooms in FCBs not only because it is good for business, but because it is a family value—because it preserves the honor and dignity of humanity's most pivotal social group. And some of these deal makers had exceptionally close families.

When reminded that their honesty had been a source of competitive advantage, the Reichmanns protested that this was not a business tactic but a pillar of the Jewish religion. According to Maimonides, the righteous Jew must act in his commercial activity in truth and faith. Here is the passage: "His yes is to be yes, his no, no; he forces himself to be exact in his calculations when he is paying, but is willing to be lenient when others are his debtors . . . He should keep his obligations in commerce, even where the law allows him to withdraw or retract, so that his word is his bond."[37]

Honor among the Reichmanns was reinforced by family rituals. Even at the height of their business careers, brothers Albert, Paul, and Ralph were expected every evening to drop by their parents home for a few hours of discussion about family and business—a practice that lasted until their mother's death in 1990.[38] Taking the business home every day to a religious family meant that integrity was not a tactical choice for the Reichmanns, it was an ethical *and* social imperative.

Thus, during the 1980s, all those doing business with the Reichmanns came away with a single impression: that the family was the "epitome of old-fashioned integrity in a corrupt, mercenary era." Said their architect Bill Minuk: "The Reichmanns very early on developed a high degree of respect as being very honest. We developed a lot of business just on that basis. If they shook on a deal, that was it."[39]

Family Stability. Reputation carries furthest when those who have it, or members of their immediate family, stay on the job for a long time. That is exactly what happens at these deal makers, where, often, contacts deepen into relationships. Executive tenures for the Reichmanns, Bechtels, Bombardier-Beaudoins, and Morgans typically exceeded twenty years and might exceed thirty. Over such tenures, leaders could strengthen their partnerships, proving time and again that they were trustworthy, meriting bigger contracts. They could also use their growing reputation to generate referrals. Thus, clients and partners came to know that these FCB leaders were there for good, that they were reliable, and that they had everyone's long-term interests at heart.

Passing on Contacts. Another family source of connection is the ability to pass contacts across the generations. Reputation attached to succeeding generations because of the family bond—and the inclination of partners to believe that later generations would honor the commitments and business philosophies of their predecessors. Junius Morgan introduced son Pierpont to the Drexel brothers of Philadelphia, who helped put the Morgan scion in business. Steve Bechtel Jr. benefited from many of his dad's introductions to the rich and powerful, sometimes at venues like the Bohemian Grove, a secluded retreat where the U.S. military, government, and industrial elite meet. The Reichmann brothers were able to get credit from families their father knew back in Europe and Morocco.

Secrecy. Deal partners place a high premium on privacy, as it conceals their intentions from adversarial interests. Private FCBs can *assure* such confidentiality to their clients. Take Steve Bechtel Jr., who had a passion for anonymity, and no patience with the public or press. "There's no reason for the public to hear of us," he told a reporter. "We're not selling anything to the public."[40] Bechtel was very much a business-to-business enterprise. It did its selling to companies and to governments quietly and out of public view: in boardrooms, on golf courses, in kings' palaces and prime ministers' residences, or at the Bohemian Grove. The Bechtels for generations favored family ownership in part because it provided an extra measure of privacy. They could deal discreetly with clients and respond flexibly to opportunities.[41]

The Result. Because of all of the above—family contacts, reputation, stability, and privacy—the deal makers found themselves in an enviable position. Pierpont Morgan, for example, because of his probity, financial contacts, and the great reputation of his father, was able to buy anything he wanted. Financing was never a problem. According to one partner of the day, a Morgan issue "from the desert of Sahara" would find buyers. Over the years, as its reputation grew, Morgan kept expanding its web of relationships in government, industry, and banking so that it could amass the capital and approvals to do its deals at will.[42]

Cultivate Contacts

Clearly, a family's reputation helps some FCBs amass a web of trusting partners. But such beneficial ties are not just legacies from the past. These firms work hard every day to build contacts and connections. Sometimes these are initiated in the informal atmosphere of an exclusive business or social group. Let's revisit the Bohemian Grove, where the Bechtels made so many contacts:

> The Grove membership included numerous governors and senators, three former presidents and a whole battalion of cabinet members, past and present . . . But the real business of the Grove, where a favorite pastime was figuring out the corporate connections and interlocking directorates of incoming members, was just that: business. Not business by contract or by deal—both of which were barred on the Grove's grounds—but business by sheer association, by men spending time with, getting to know and like each other. "Once you've spent three days with someone in an informal situation," explained John D. Ehrlichman, who attended Grove encampments while a chief aide to Richard Nixon, "you have a relationship—a relationship that open doors and makes it easier to pick up the phone."[43]

The Bechtels did not stop there. Through the Business Council, an elite association of 160 business and government leaders, Steve Bechtel Sr. met Pan American Airways founder and chairman Juan Trippe, for whom he was to build a global chain of Inter-Continental Hotels. There, too, he befriended IBM founder Thomas Watson and his son, Tom Jr. Bechtel was to construct several major facilities for both these men, and Steve Jr. would eventually serve on IBM's board.[44] According to Steve Bechtel Sr., "In this business . . . you get to know people, sit on their boards, and one day when something comes up, they ask you to take on a project. One thing leads to another."[45] It was the Bechtel organization's avid cultivation of friends in high places that had made so much possible.

But useful contacts are not the exclusive preserve of those with access to the movers and shakers. The Reichmanns, at first, worked to deepen their connections with acquaintances from the orthodox Jewish community—Peter Munk, from the prewar Hungarian banking family, or the Stone family, observant Jews who owned American Greeting Cards.[46] The Reichmanns teamed up time and again with these and other families to exchange capital and expertise. As time passed, the roster of partners and backers grew in size and stature. Ultimately, their biggest partners became the Bronfmans of Edper, a holding company that, by the mid-1980s, controlled 152 companies with assets of over $120 billion.[47]

Make Relationships Last

Even more important than the breadth of the web of contacts was the longevity of many of its connections. Always, deal makers invested in creating *solid, lasting* relationships. The rationale was that, over time, business-getting costs drop, trust grows, knowledge of the client expands, and learning from one project with a client can be used in a later project.

Bechtel went after only key clients—the most important names in world commerce and government—and it kept them coming back. More than 75 percent of Bechtel's volume has been repeat business. Because it enjoys close relationships with these "sweetheart clients," it gets lots of work without having to bid for it.[48] Bechtel executives achieved these benefits by forming long-standing personal relationships with the bosses of these customers. They worked hard to stay in touch and informed about the clients, *whether or not* they were doing business with them at the time. And, as noted, they kept clients and potential clients abreast of important technological and international developments that they unearthed through a finely tuned intelligence system and unparalleled access.[49]

Pierpont Morgan also wanted to form close bonds with his best clients. His object was to do much more than provide money. His firm strove to become the adviser, lawyer, confidant, and "high priest" of companies. To that end, he made J. P. Morgan & Co. into a true private bank, forming long-standing, encompassing relationships with clients, and typically winning positions on their boards. By 1910, seventy-eight major corporations banked at Morgan's, including the country's most powerful holding companies. Pierpont and his partners held directorships in 112 corporations in finance, rail, utilities, and transportation. As this was relationship banking, a board seat meant, basically, a monopoly on a company's business. In fact, during the first ten years of the century, Morgan floated $2 billion in securities, an astronomical sum for the times.[50]

Help the Powerful

Big deals often involve big government, which must help not only with financing but negotiations with foreign parties. Because large numbers of jobs, major infrastructure, and even the future of an industry may be at stake, government industrial policies loom large in key decisions. No one worked harder than these deal makers to understand and accommodate these priorities, or to form relationships with the key ministers and civil servants who established them.

Bombardier, recall, was masterful at constructing its proposals around the political needs and policies of multiple levels of government. It is no accident that it has on its staff exceptionally well-connected people, those with insight into and access to the power elite: Ex-CEO Robert Brown was a former top-level mandarin in the Canadian federal government; Pierre Lortie, president of the aircraft division, had been chair of the Montreal Stock Exchange and of Canada's Royal Commission on Electoral Reform; former Prime Minister Jean Chrétien's son-in-law serves on the Bombardier board. Based on such contacts and a deep knowledge of the government's agenda, Bombardier has landed itself prize jobs. In 1997, it was awarded a twenty-year contract from the federal government worth almost $3 billion for the training of NATO military pilots in Canada.[51]

Bechtel also avidly cultivated associations with the highest levels of government and tailored its sales pitches to government and political priorities. The family developed personal, first-name relationships with Presidents Eisenhower, Ford, Nixon, and Reagan, most of whom appointed the Bechtels to prestigious government posts and gave them access to government secrets, particularly relating to nuclear technology. Ties were especially close with Richard Nixon, whom Steve Sr. had backed politically and financially ever since Nixon was a California congressman. And the door swung both ways: The firm hired former senior government officials such as George Shultz, Caspar Weinberger, ex-CIA chief Richard Helms, and State Department official Philip Habib.[52]

After World War I, the "House of Morgan" was described by biographer Sir Harold Nicholson as being so influential that it was "almost a department of government." Jack Morgan's response to Nicholson was amusing: He was aghast at his firm's being "*reduced* to the status of a department subordinate to the government [our emphasis]." His bank, he asserted, was inferior to no organization, least of all a bunch of Washington bureaucrats.[53] The much-discussed downside of these connections, of course, is that firms such as Morgan, Bechtel, and even Bombardier may sometimes have had unfair advantage over their less influential rivals, to the detriment of the market and evenhanded competition.

Complementary Priorities of Deal Making: Continuity and Community

Because of the risks and complexities inherent in deal making, complementary priorities of continuity and community are especially important. Continuity interposes consideration for long-term survival and caution to offset risk taking. Community makes it possible to pull together the many resources, departments, and skills needed to pursue complex mega-projects.

Managing Risk and Accumulating Learning to Assure Continuity

The hazards of deal making are reduced by especially careful stewardship, a focus on areas of core expertise, and the lengthy apprenticeships of key executives.

Organizational Stewardship

These FCBs were not entrepreneurs out to make a quick buck, but businessmen who wanted a long and healthy future for their companies and families. So Morgan reduced risk by dealing only with the soundest clients and avoiding the more speculative ventures. Said biographer Ron Chernow, "Pierpont decided to limit his . . . dealing to elite companies. He became the sort of tycoon who hated risk and wanted only sure things . . . " Morgan clarified his policy as follows: "Neither my firm nor myself will have anything to do . . . with the negotiation of securities . . . whose status, by experience, would not prove it entitled to a credit in every respect unassailable."[54]

Notwithstanding their ultimate fate, the Reichmanns for most of their years at O&Y were exceptionally cautious. Whereas many developers need all their rent money to service the debt, the Reichmanns were so conservatively leveraged that they could carry many of their buildings half-empty. In fact, during the first half of the 1980s, they could have sold off their assets, paid off their debts, and been left with $5 billion in cash.[55] And for property developers, the Reichmanns were atypically hands-on. Most companies simply selected a site and an architect, arranged financing, and sought tenants. The Reichmanns got much more deeply involved. They picked and supervised the subcontractors who employed the tradesmen, then oversaw every aspect of the work with relentless intensity. It helped that O&Y never did projects on spec, always waiting for a roster of tenants before breaking ground. And they avoided speculating on land prices by having in inventory large tracts of property. They also pared corporate overhead to the bone, adding staff "only under duress."[56]

To further reduce risks, firms used the capital of their partners. Thus, O&Y got most of its capital for its early projects from other wealthy Jewish families. Bechtel now does less building of its own and more engineering and project management, consulting, and general contracting—higher-margin businesses that require less risk capital. Bombardier cut its outlays by getting lots of government subsidies and buying companies cheaply. Hugo Uyterhoeven, a professor at the Harvard Business School who sat on Bombardier's board, said of CEO Laurent Beaudoin: "He is a disciplined entrepreneur . . . In his heart and soul he is an entrepreneur, but he was trained as an accountant. These two conflicting traits have worked to Bombardier's benefit . . . Bombardier has always blended risk taking with an accountant's prudence." For example, before making acquisitions, crack teams visited facilities. They pored over technologies, products, and processes; probed into the company's values and culture; and gauged complementarity with the Bombardier business model and competitive plan. Bombardier was willing to buy firms with flaws—as long as it knew it had the capabilities to correct them. And it was happy to wait for years to get the right price.[57] The firm also expanded into niche markets where it could emerge as the dominant player.[58] Currently, in developing its new Global Express aircraft, Bombardier is reducing its risk by obtaining the financing and expertise of three able partners: Mitsubishi Heavy Industries, Honeywell, and Sextant Avionics, which are collectively picking up half of the $550 million development cost.[59]

Thematic Focus—with Scope

Many entrepreneurs stray from areas of expertise; in contrast, these deal makers were extremely selective in the projects they undertook. They adopted a two-pronged policy. First they stuck to domains that made the best use of their capabilities. Bechtel pushed hard on energy and transportation, focusing during different decades on dams, power plants, oil production, and atomic energy as global needs and technologies evolved. Morgan specialized for many years in railroad and steel financing. Bombardier had a firm policy of sticking to areas such as rail and air transportation. And O&Y concentrated on downtown skyscrapers in major metropolitan centers. This focus allowed companies to undertake major projects that might be risky for rivals, but manageable for a firm with deep experience and expertise. Focus also enabled the transfer of learning across projects, reducing risk, and increasing economies and margins. But scope was ample, and expertise leveraged broadly, especially across geographies. Bechtel operated all over the world, taking on oil projects in the United States, Saudi Arabia, and elsewhere. O&Y built in many different cities, while Bombardier undertook a diversity of subway, rail, and recreational vehicle contracts all over the world.

Managerial Apprenticeships

Few experiences teach the business as effectively as working side by side with a frank and open boss. The long apprenticeships of many executives at these firms allowed that. These privileged "courses" of instruction lasted many years and transferred to the next generation not only the skills of the trade but its craft, ethics, and intuitions. Through personal tutoring about subjects grand and small, and a vast correspondence, Pierpont learned from Junius and taught Jack. The minutiae of risk management were often topics of the many letters exchanged between Junius in London and Pierpont in New York.

A key wrinkle in these organizations is, as noted, the magical talents of top deal makers. There is every effort to ensure that their successors have those abilities. However, in the case of Morgan, son Jack (despite the tutoring) was not in temperament or cognitive endowment a great "deal man." Pierpont's contacts could be passed on to Jack, but not his brilliance. So other key Morgan partners, like Tom Lamont, had to take over much of the top-level deal making. Fortunately, Pierpont had had the foresight to hire and work closely with people whose talents matched his own to ensure his company survived him. Similarly, at Bombardier, Laurent Beaudoin had been giving his son increasing responsibilities for years to determine whether he could amply develop his operating and strategic skills. But non-family executives at the company were being developed as well.

Uniting the Tribe: Creating a Lean, Entrepreneurial Culture

Deal makers do two things that demand a robust internal community. First, they act fast, and so must be able to quickly coordinate people from different specialties to bid and do a deal. Second, they undertake complex projects that require intense and on-the-fly collaboration among different functions and business units. Therefore, they create organizations that are flat, decentralized, meritocratic, networked, and project-based. Compared with most other great FCBs, however, deal makers embrace a less considerate, more bottom-line-driven culture, where entrepreneur-managers can thrive.

Initiative Through Decentralization

High-end managers are encouraged to use their initiative to find opportunities and develop profitable proposals. As Bechtel grew, it moved the culture of entrepreneurship from the top of the firm down to its middle levels. Due to its scope, the firm was organized into eight divisions, specialized by lines such as power plants and pipelines. Each was a profit center that functioned as an individual company.[60] Today, Riley Bechtel has been pushing power even further down the ranks, moving away from an industry group structure to one that embraces a regional approach. He also opened up Bechtel's secret books to another 113 vice presidents and directors, to encourage these managers to think more about the global picture and the use of capital.[61]

To promote entrepreneurship at Bombardier, managers' incentives are tied to the growth of their divisions, which operate by and large as independent companies.[62] Bombardier was highly decentralized, with five operating groups of aerospace, rail, recreational, finance, and international markets, each headed by a president in charge of manufacture, marketing, and product development.[63] The head office was extremely lean, with a staff of only 150 controlling a global enterprise of 75,000 employees.

Such minimalist staffs were part and parcel of the entrepreneurial culture. O&Y was said to be chronically understaffed. Although it was twice as big in assets as major competitors such as Cadillac Fairview and Trizec, it employed only half as many people; and those rivals did not do their own general contracting, as did O&Y.[64] This ensured that people had challenging responsibilities and the authority to act. As in so many FCBs, there was a job to do and no room for ritualistic formalities or political games.

High-Pressure Meritocracy

Deal-maker companies are high-energy places to work and strict meritocracies. People are well paid—at Bechtel and Morgan, unbelievably so.[65] In the 1920s, Morgan partners took home bonuses of a million dollars a year, and Jack Morgan was said to take $5 million. But much was expected of these people. Because decisions were momentous and required speed, carelessness could be fatal. Thus job pressures were immense. The Morgan bank became known as a "partner killer" after several principals died in their forties and fifties from the seventy-plus-hour workweeks.[66] Although most family owners were considerate of their people in times of trouble, these were not usually "warm and fuzzy" places to work. And even where there was an extended family atmosphere, it tended not to extend very deeply into the organization. A positive aspect of the meritocracy system, however, was that promotion and succession would go only to the most competent executive. At Bombardier, Laurent Beaudoin's son Pierre has been passed over as CEO, at least for awhile, first in favor of Robert Brown, a veteran non-family executive, and now Paul Tellier, a turnaround maestro with superb government contacts.

Networked Project Organizations

Deal makers face a complex organizing task. As these are, in essence, project organizations, with every project different, staff constantly have to be assigned to new jobs according to their abilities. Moreover, the team composition for each project varies, so people must learn to work together quickly. Finally, any one project often requires many skills.

At Morgan, sector and financial specialists had to coordinate with lawyers and engineers to do the more complex deals. At Bechtel, industry, functional, and regional specialists and external partners collaborate on complicated mega-projects. Every few months or years, teams have to reconfigure and move, say, from a refinery project in the United States to a petroleum depot in Saudi Arabia. The trick is to be able to get the more experienced people to codify their knowledge so that best practices can be transferred across teams and projects.

Such organizational versatility and collaboration is compelled by leaders who get people to commit to the firm rather than the business unit. For example, incentives tend to be linked to how well a project or even the entire company does, not to the success of a unit or function. People selected for hire are often unattached and mobile workaholics. They also work well in teams. The inducements, as mentioned, are excellent pay and bonuses, and chances for rapid advancement. Organizational versatility and collaboration are also helped by deal makers moving from functional or product-based organizations to those structured around types of projects—incorporating all of the functions, products, and services required.[67]

Conclusion

Through an astute use of the levers of command and connection, these firms became consummate deal makers. They had the advantage over many of their non-FCB rivals of being able to ignore short-term results, take unorthodox action, and mobilize capital very quickly. They also had family honor, reputation, confidentiality, and stability to support their contacts, which often grew into highly profitable connections. Another edge these firms enjoyed over non-FCB entrepreneurs was that their concern for the future, the family, and reputation caused them to be more cautious and take more of a long-term view, thereby offsetting the dangers of unbridled command. This made them fine stewards of resources and managers of risk. Last, the decentralized meritocracy freed many levels of managers to use their initiative, while the networked structure enhanced complex collaboration and effective execution (see table 7-1).

Table 7-1

Relating the Four Cs to the Strategy of Deal Making

	Deal Spotting	Capture	Execution	Learning
Command: Freedom to seek opportunity				
• Courageous ambition		**	*	
• Speed and decisiveness		**	**	
• Contrarianism	*	**		
• Complementarity and trust on the TMT		*	**	*
Connection: Leveraging contacts and building networks				
• Family role in connections	**	**	*	
• Cultivate contacts	*	**	**	
• Make relationships last	**	**	*	*
• Help the powerful	*	*		
Continuity: Managing risk and accumulating learning				
• Organizational stewardship			**	*
• Thematic focus	*			**
• Managerial apprenticeship	*	*	*	*
Community: Creating a lean, entrepreneurial culture				
• Decentralized meritocracy	**	**	*	
• Networked project organization		*	**	**

* facilitator; ** key facilitator

Chapter 8

When Family-Controlled Businesses Stumble

S O FAR WE HAVE focused on the stellar periods of our FCBs to show how these firms attained competitive advantage. But even the great FCBs stumble, sometimes fatally, and their mistakes provide lessons on what all companies must do to *sustain* advantage. Olympia & York (O&Y) is a prototypical example of what can befall a deal maker when it mismanages the Cs.

By 1987, O&Y had become the most successful property developer in the world, amassing for the Reichmann family a fortune estimated at about $10 billion. But Paul Reichmann was convinced that the best was yet to come. Although always venturesome, he became reckless as his brother Albert's role diminished. A major component of O&Y's Waterloo was Paul's magnificent obsession: London's gargantuan Canary Wharf project. At twenty-four office towers totalling 12 million square feet, it was far grander, more speculative, and more complex than anything O&Y had previously contemplated. Certainly, Canary's size was daunting. But so was its proposed location: the shabby Docklands section, far away from London's central business district and with virtually no public transportation available or promised. This was hardly a venue to attract the elite banking and corporate clients O&Y was seeking. Indeed, with the flagging market of the time, there were no such clients in sight. After spending $3.8 billion on Canary's partial construction, followed by a year of desperate struggle for more credit, O&Y declared bankruptcy in 1992. The giant of corporate real estate had collapsed, diminishing the Reichmann family fortune by an estimated 99 percent.

Why did this happen? Chapters 3 to 7 revealed how each strategy was supported by a complementary blend of C priorities and related practices (table 8-1 summarizes these for each strategy). But sometimes, as at O&Y, managers begin to get the blend wrong, going too far in some directions and not far enough in others. This chapter examines how and why that can occur for each of our strategies. Indeed, some of the best evidence we have about the importance of the individual Cs, as well as their configuration, comes by examining what happens when things go wrong.

Most of the businesses in our study did well for many decades and continue to thrive. But some hit significant rough patches, while others are languishing after moving away from family control. Our analysis suggests that their problems came as a result of mismanaging the four C priorities—the *majors,* or focal organizational priorities, and the *complementary* priorities that offset excess and ensure resilience and balance. We found three types of problems, or "errors," to be by far the most common.

Type 1: Some elements of a major priority become dangerously excessive. As we noted in chapter 2, the four Cs are all subject to extremes. Too much continuity in the form of obsessive conservatism, for example, can lead to stagnation. Extreme homogeneity in a corporate community can cause insularity and intolerance—with everyone thinking the same way and blind to alternative approaches. Or too much independence of command may allow leaders, buoyed by success, to become reckless. And when tight and exclusive connections or bonds are made with a few key outsiders, especially governments or business cronies, these can tempt companies to take the easy way out and lobby for business instead of competing for it. In short, there is a dark side to each of the four priorities that is apt to manifest when they are distorted or taken to extreme.

Type 2: Some elements of a major C priority weaken. When this occurs, a firm loses its edge. Community in an innovator may erode as values begin to ring hollow and people fail to buy into the culture; causing the organization to fragment and creative collaboration to flag. Or continuity at a craftsman may wither as time perspectives contract in a rush toward profits.

Type 3: A complementary priority erodes. This error often accompanies type 1, as extremes along a major C draw attention away from a complementary priority. Or, conversely, deterioration in the complement may foster excesses within a major. At a brand builder, for example, erosion of client connection—a complementary priority—may invite brand ossification; that is, excessive continuity. In short, faltering complements provoke imbalances that sap resilience.

Table 8-1

Highlights from the Five Strategies

	Brand Building	Craftsmanship	Superior Operations	Innovation	Deal Making
Representative firms in study	Estée Lauder Hallmark Levi Strauss L.L. Bean S.C. Johnson	Coors New York Times Nordstrom Timken	Cargill IKEA J.R. Simplot Tyson Wal-Mart	Corning Fidelity Michelin Motorola Tetra Pak W.L. Gore	Bechtel Bombardier J.P. Morgan Olympia & York
Competitive advantage based on	Brand and image management	Quality capabilities and designs	Superior business model, operations and partnering	Pioneering skills and products	Prospecting, networking, and project execution skills
Major organizational priorities	*Continuity:* Patient investment, stewardship > build and protect brand *Community:* Shared values and textured, caring culture > define and teach brand	*Continuity:* Substantive mission, apprenticeship, sacrifice > excellence and improvement *Community:* Socialization and training > commitment and culture of perfectionism	*Continuity:* Longterm focus and investment, meliorism > superior business model and infrastructure *Connection:* Integrity and generosity in relationships > superior alliances with clients and partners	*Command:* Originality, speed, venturesome, creative courage > projects *Community:* Mentoring, job latitude, collaborative culture > more viable and frequent innovations	*Command:* Bold, complementary TMTs > entrepreneurial, contrarian deal making *Connection:* Nurturing of contacts and networks > opportunity-finding and execution

continues

> denotes connection between the C elements(s) and intended outcome(s).

Table 8-1

Highlights from the Five Strategies (continued)

	Brand Building	Craftsmanship	Superior Operations	Innovation	Deal Making
Complementary organizational priorities	*Connection:* Visibility, attentiveness, honesty > image and relevance	*Connection:* Reputation and relationships > alliances to keep quality attractive	*Command:* Independence, courage > original, evolving business model	*Continuity:* Focus and stewardship > learning and risk reduction	*Continuity:* Business focus; stewardship > synergy among deals and skills to reduce risk
	Command: Originality, courage > brand distinctiveness and renewal	*Command:* Top team diversity > product line relevance	*Community:* Meliorist culture > improving system	*Connection:* Client partnering > relevant innnovations	*Community:* Decentralization > networked meritocracy

Let's examine what happened to some firms when they lost their way. We will present cases and draw brief generalizations by strategy, before going on to look at the overall error patterns, or syndromes, that all businesses need to watch out for.

Brand-Builder Blues

Levi's still has great brands. But not such a great product line. Preoccupied with internal matters such as reengineering and employee surveys, it failed to look outside. While competitors are getting most of their sales from recently introduced hipper styles, Levi's is still trying to "get with it."

Levi Strauss: Losing Touch

Levi's has been losing market share, from 31 percent in 1990 to about 17 percent recently, with most of the decline since 1997. Profits have fallen to nothing, and sales are down to under $5 billion in 2003, from $7.1 billion in 1996. For most of that time, Levi's has been too slow to introduce new products—lines such as baggy or low-cut jeans that appeal to a younger, faster-growing niche. It stuck to the traditional classics, while competitor VF Corporation, maker of Lee and Wrangler brands, now gets 50 percent of revenues from the new designs. Philip Marineau, the CEO appointed to succeed Bob Haas in 1999 admits, "We were walking away from the merchandise."[1] Levi's, moreover, has marketed primarily to staid outlets such as J.C. Penney, which are tied to declining markets. And it has ignored young women as a key segment. Add to that operations plagued by diseconomies and untimely delivery—forty-five days late for the critical back-to-school season, for example.[2] Said a chastened Bob Haas, "There's nothing as blinding as success. It's easy to get inbred and forget that businesses go through cycles. We took our eye off the ball."[3]

Type 1—Excessive Major: Closed Community. As Levi's focused on internal issues such as values, culture, and process reengineering, its attention was diverted from the market. Its work-and-family advisory task force, for example, sent a colossal twenty-five-page questionnaire to 17,000 employees—a costly waste of time just when everyone's attention most needed to be directed outside the firm rather than in. Said Robert Siegel, who left Levi's after twenty-nine years to become CEO of Stride Rite, "Almost all of my time was spent in meetings that were absolutely senseless." So much effort went into issues like participation and empowerment that people forgot

Beware of brand insularity.

The greatest danger facing successful brand builders may be insularity. Firms become so concerned with preserving a brand, its image, and the cultural rituals that support it, that they lose track of the needs of the marketplace. Another very different threat is that the brand will be spread too thinly and thereby devalued.

what they were being empowered for. Yet despite the firm's enlightened work practices, managers were not getting things done; they ceased to renew the brand. The consensus approach, it seems, led to paralysis. Said former CFO George James, "Unless you could get everyone to agree with your idea, you didn't have authority to make a decision. That made it very difficult to be responsive."[4]

Levi's also dragged its feet in a mammoth reengineering effort. Over 200 of its best managers were pulled out of their regular jobs to help in revamping the supply chain. Along with 100 management consultants from Andersen Consulting, the team kept broadening its mandate, ultimately to include redesigning virtually every job and forcing incumbents to reapply for their positions. Employees rebelled, and clients got confused by the new system, which after two years was still hobbling along. The inclusive culture, once an asset, had become a quagmire.[5]

Type 3—Eroding Complements: Insipid Command and Severed Connection. Bob Haas had always sought the opinions of others. But his management style moved from consultative to indecisive. Instead of telling managers what they were doing wrong, he would sit down and ask them what they thought about the situation. And he insisted on consensus before moving forward. Peter Thigpen, former president of Levi Strauss USA, said, "I love Bob to death, but he has a tendency to involve everybody in decision making." Even minor issues got decided, or shelved, after endless meetings, e-mails, and task forces. Said Robert Siegel, "Everything had to go into a corporate process so nothing ever got resolved."[6]

Inevitably, another complementary priority to fall at Levi's was connection—contact with the market. As internal matters distracted managers and slowed response time, the company strayed farther and farther from its market. The company was late in recognizing trends—too arrogant to acknowledge their relevance and too sluggish to respond once Levi's did. So it continued to sell yesterday's products to yesterday's customers, and at a declining rate.

Misguided Craftsmen

Coors and Nordstrom reveal opposite problem scenarios for craftsmen: becoming too wed to quality at the expense of relevance, or losing a quality edge. Coors, believing quality alone would save the day, refused to market or update its product lines, even though it was being besieged by its rivals. In contrast, Nordstrom, under a nonfamily leader, began to lose its sense of identity and its service quality.

Coors: Stubbornly Ignoring the Market

Today, Coors continues as a thriving brewery with a rising market share. It is America's third-largest brewer, second largest in the United Kingdom, and it employs more than 8,700 people. Its earnings per share have quintupled since 1995 to a record $4.68 in 2002. But in the late 1970s, the company began to run into trouble. Competitors arrived on the scene with very intensive marketing, trying to lure Coors customers away. Miller (owned by tobacco giant Altria) and Anheuser-Busch were the most aggressive. Miller, still a small hungry company in the 1980s, had its eye on Coors's market position and began spending $3 a barrel on ads: twice the industry average. But when Bill Coors tasted his rival's product, he just laughed, saying the beer was entirely inferior, and he refused to think anymore about it. Anyone who suggested that Coors should respond by raising its minuscule ad budget would hear Bill recite his mantra: "Nobody

Beware of craftsmanship that ignores the market or fades.

Coors let continuity become stagnation, and converted strong values into rigidifying dogma. Its connection with markets disappeared. Nordstrom departed from its craftsmanship and traditions, and lost its distinctiveness, confusing customers and employees alike.

is going to decide what beer to drink on the strength of a thirty-second commercial . . . I'm not going to turn my back on the way my father and grandfather did business just because a bunch of cigarette people decided to make beer."[7]

After rivals introduced the popular light beers, marketing and distribution director (and CEO-to-be) Peter Coors approached his Uncle Bill for the umpteenth time about responding. "We are 'America's Fine Light Beer,'" he was told. "Let's advertise ourselves as a light and be done with it." Asked Peter, "Then where would that leave heavy-beer drinkers? The whole point is to have two beers on the market." Still, Bill insisted, "But our beer is the best. Make a good product, sell it at a reasonable cost, and the people will buy."[8] Unfortunately for Coors, that had become less true. Market share shrank and the competition grew ever stronger.

Type 1—Excessive Major: Hidebound Continuity. Coors's strong sense of identity and commitment to quality were rare and laudable. But over time, they ossified the organization and crowded out all other considerations. Change just didn't happen. Coors wouldn't broaden the line, wouldn't decentralize operations to reduce costs, wouldn't allow beer to be sold off the shelves, and wouldn't advertise. Those tactics went against the Coors genes. So continuity turned into stagnation. The elders, moreover, prevented new blood from having a say. Traditions by now had driven out all thought about the long-term health of the business and the product line.

Type 2—Eroding Major: Defensive Community. Coors's internal community, always engineer- and engineering-dominated, now became intolerant, defensive, and rife with conflict. It went from being pro-quality to being anti-marketing, branding all marketers "Visigoths." Although keenly aware of the need for change, Peter Coors was no match for his powerful father, Joe, and his Uncle Bill. He pushed for better marketing and new products, but was constantly rebuffed. And because he lacked the "sacred" credentials of an engineering diploma, he was immediately suspect as being the emissary from the promotion and distribution side of the business. When Peter brought in former ad executive John Nichols to help with the marketing, they fought an uphill battle. According to reporter Dan Baum, "No matter how many marketing brains Peter recruited, they couldn't make significant progress in a company that treated them like invaders . . . Marketing couldn't be grafted onto a corporation that was institutionally hostile to it."[9]

Type 3—Eroding Complements: Theocratic Command and Broken Connection. The Coors values were so strong that the firm was run almost as a theocracy: The family "priests" made the decisions and brooked no dissent. At board meetings, dominated by Coors cronies, there were no formal votes; senior family members Bill and Joe decided matters and expected everyone to follow. But this was control, not command. Missing now was TMT diversity and frank discussion—and consequently the courage to act. The result was paralysis. When at one meeting, Bill called for "those opposed," and Peter raised his hand, Joe growled, "Never before."[10] Dissent just was no longer an option on the board. Lower down, however, Coors began to spawn levels of hierarchy to insulate the family from day-to-day affairs. The Coorses became more and more remote from operations, while their administrative staff dragged their feet. The pace was glacial, and against the new competition, this began to hurt.

An important complementary priority for craftsmen is connection with the market: relationships with major customers, distributors, or partners that keep quality relevant. Coors, however, broke that connection by angering its distributors and alienating its customers. When Peter wanted to hire a director of marketing research, Bill waved him off: "What's to research? People drink beer because they like it. The better the beer, the more they'll drink." So Coors dismissed shifting market tastes. It also termed its distributors ungrateful parasites and ignored their clamoring for lighter beers, premium beers, and more advertising support.[11] When the distributors complained about a can press tab that was almost impossible to open, Marketing Director Nichols protested: "The distributors are ready to wring our necks." Peter replied, "[D]on't talk about the distributors, that's the last thing Dad and Uncle Bill want to hear."[12] The family also began to attract adverse publicity from its right-wing political pronouncements and the company's lack of programs for minorities. Coors, in effect, had closed itself off from the outside world.

Eventually, with market share shrinking and profits sinking, the family realized they had one core priority: *save the business,* even if it meant listening more to the customer and doing some advertising. Finally, power began to shift to Peter, who after years of wavering, and with the help of a marketing whiz from Frito Lay, began to act. Today, with Peter as Chairman, Coors sells a full range of successful brands, distributes broadly, and markets as aggressively and creatively as any of its rivals. Coors is, after a period of painful layoffs and a modernization of administrative and control systems, a far more competitive company. In 2002, it acquired Interbrew's Carling brand for $1.7 billion—the first acquisition in Coors's history. And it still has that quality edge to fall back on.

Nordstrom: Losing Its Craft

Whereas the Coors example reveals a craftsman taking its tried-and-true strategy to extremes, Nordstrom shows one losing its way with the arrival of its first non-family CEO. In the late 1990s, under CEO John Whitacre, Nordstrom began to depart from its quality tradition. To lure a younger crowd, the exclusive retailer began to carry more daring lines, changing its luxurious, upscale, classic stores into more trendy venues with hip, piped-in music, and younger staff. Service remained good, but no longer superb, and the surroundings and much of the merchandise became unfamiliar to the store's fans.[13] Exacerbating the problem was Nordstrom's expansion all over the country at a faster and faster pace. Its information and logistics systems, never state of the art, just couldn't keep up. The company, which still depended partly on handwritten notes from sales clerks to keep track of inventory, was too slow to alert buyers about what was moving and what wasn't. Markdowns mushroomed, selling, general, and administrative expenses rose to $100 per square foot, compared with $60 for the industry. For the first time, customers found their sizes out of stock—a forgivable error elsewhere, but not among Nordstrom's expectant shoppers. In 2001, Neiman Marcus rose to number one, surpassing Nordstrom in customer service, and it sold $490 per square foot versus Nordstrom's $342.[14]

Type 2—Eroding Majors: Interrupted Continuity and Divided Community. Continuity deteriorated as the firm departed from its winning ways. The ambience had changed to such a degree that loyal customers no longer felt at home in the stores. They came to Nordstrom's to find conservative, tasteful clothing of the finest quality—in all shapes and sizes—proffered in relaxing surroundings by unfailingly attentive associates. Instead they were confronted with bright lights; loud, upbeat décor; disagreeable music; and fashions that were uncomfortably avant garde and incompletely stocked.

The Nordstrom community, too, began to change. Rapid expansion made for a climate of strangers working with strangers, as people were relocated to staff the new stores. A schism opened between the old guard and the new: those struggling to preserve the class and glorious traditions against those willing to embrace a more modern outlook. Values also became fuzzier as norms of efficiency began to encroach on those of quality and service, and associates became less clear about core priorities.

Continuity and community, in other words, shriveled as a non-family CEO abandoned too many retailing traditions, at the same time overtaxing the resources of the system. Soon there was less to distinguish the company from its rivals. Today, a new generation of Nordstroms is back running the business and has returned to the core strategy of superb service and excellent merchandise, albeit with more efficient processes and systems.

Insensitive Operators

Tyson Foods and Wal-Mart still make a lot of money and continue to grow, but they seem to be exhibiting more and more "antisocial" behavior. Never ones to coddle their employees, they are now using hardball tactics to keep costs—and unions—down. They also have managed to raise the ire of the general public; they have been accused both of insensitivity to community interests and of ignoring the law.

Tyson: Disconnected

Tyson Foods continues to be the market leader in the "center-of-the plate" meat industry, and Don Tyson still controls 80 percent of the voting shares, while his son runs the company. But since 1996, the firm has been struggling to improve its profitability. In part, this is because commodity

---

Beware of dehumanized operations.

At Tyson, continuity deteriorated as a result of incautious diversification, and connection became cronyism. At Wal-Mart, a cost-cutting fixation alienated key stakeholders. Significantly, both firms experienced erosion of community: They became so obsessed with efficiency that they stopped worrying about their staff. Because most workers at these companies perform routine tasks, companies get away with this attitude for a long time. In the end, many firms must pay the costs of labor strife, productivity declines, and poor service.

---

prices have been unfavorable. But Tyson also got cocky, entering businesses it paid too much for and knew too little about, skirting lobbying rules, and creating friction with its workers.[15]

Type 1—Excessive Major: Crony Connection. Connection, as noted, can devolve into cronyism as a firm competes less through service or efficiency and more through political muscle. Over the years, Tyson seems to have become prone to tarnishing alliances. Don Tyson was grilled by Mike Wallace of *60 Minutes* regarding his alleged influence peddling during the Clinton administration, and prosecuted for giving inside information on prospective acquisitions to his friends. He also signed a plea bargain in 1998, admitting that his firm gave former Secretary of Agriculture Mike Espy freebies such as football tickets and $12,000 in "gratuities" for official acts Espy was to perform. Don Tyson, in fact, was so *in* with the political regime in Arkansas that he often benefited from liberal treatment by "friendly" authorities. For ages the Tyson plant of Green Forest, Arkansas, got away with polluting local wells; the government turned a blind eye. It took years for a local citizen's group to win a suit ordering Tyson to pay damages.[16] Cronyism plagued even the company's board of directors, which was stacked with Tyson yes-men. So bad was it that the California Public Employees Retirement System (CalPers) tried to oust Tyson's board in 2000, claiming it was not responsive to current shareholders.[17]

Type 2—Eroding Major: Lapsed Continuity. Tyson had expanded in part by acquiring businesses in meat processing that it absolutely knew how to run, and it thrived. But its executives began to stray from areas of competency, believing they could manage any business: "If we can buy it, we can run it," was their slogan. When Don bought Arctic Alaska, owner of the biggest fishing fleet in the Pacific Northwest, the executives were proven wrong. Tyson was buying into a business it did not understand, and ended up with a fleet of boats in a terrible state of disrepair.[18] Moreover, it had bought at the peak of the market, contrary to its usual bargain-driven practice, and had to take a $214 million write-off for the fish fiasco. It also went into the pork business in an unusually tentative way. As a result, it could not generate enough interest in its products to get up to scale, and dropped its usual practice of hyper-efficient, integrated, multiple-shift processing. Ultimately, it had to downsize its money-losing live-swine operations.

Type 3—Eroding Complement: Shaky Community. Tyson was never a nir-vana for its employees, most of whom performed routine jobs. But it began to use rough (and illegal) tactics in dealing with some of its unions. After it bought Holly Farms in 1989, Tyson fired its unionized drivers, who refused to take pay cuts. The U.S. Supreme Court ordered Tyson to rehire the drivers and give them the wages they had lost.[19]

Wal-Mart: Losing Its Culture

Since Sam Walton's death in 1992, Wal-Mart has continued to grow and move into international and grocery markets. Looking only at the top and bottom lines, it would seem the company has done well. But there are unmistakable signs of erosion, both in the internal corporate community and the relationship with outside communities.

Types 1, 3, and 2—Excessive Continuity, Eroding Community, and Connection. Wal-Mart without Sam seems to have become more and more a moneymaking machine with less of a soul. The continuity elements of stewardship and parsimony got out of hand as control over expenses turned into a hazardous obsession with costs. Many top managers, it appears, left because of the overwhelming workload and the pressure for constant performance enhancement and budget slashing. Indeed, the company has focused so narrowly on cost cutting that its workers, many of whom are part-timers, earn less than $20,000 per year. Without the soar-ing stock price, or the charismatic Sam to talk with employees and put a folksy human face to the company, there have been more attempts to gain entry by labor unions. Wal-Mart reacted by firing would-be organizers and threatening to close down any union-organized store.[20] The Wal-Mart community, it seems, isn't what it used to be.

Connection also has been a problem. The Wal-Mart image was hurt by Bangladeshi and other suppliers shown to be using prisoner or child labor toiling under inhumane conditions.[21] The company was also charged with arranging "sweetheart" deals with landlords related to the Walton family, to whom Wal-Mart paid excessive rents. And it embar-rassed itself in failing to penetrate the German market by making little attempt to understand the consumer, culture, or language. Perhaps most damaging of all to its reputation was the retailer's insensitivity to commu-nity interests and demands in locating its mega-stores, and putting small retailers out of business. Print and television exposés on more than one occasion portrayed the company as an irresponsible corporate citizen, using powerful public relations firms to bully a community into accepting a sprawling store.[22]

Inept Innovation

Motorola and Corning today are facing serious problems, problems that have depleted financial and human resources and forced both firms to reconsider the most fundamental aspects of their strategies. Motorola lost its way in a maze of too many products and technologies, and a weighty bureaucracy. Corning, on the other hand, focused too narrowly, risking everything on optic fiber for the telecom industry.

Motorola: A Strategy of Muddling

By 2003, with the Galvins owning less than 3 percent of the shares, and with the resignation of CEO Chris Galvin, Motorola had ceased to be a true family business. The company had grown into a diverse empire that encompassed personal communications such as pagers and mobile phones, semiconductors, large networks (from broadband infrastructure to police radios), integrated electronic systems (e.g., for automotive navigation), and customer solutions.

Most of these businesses were suffering. In wireless infrastructure, market share fell from 22 percent in 1995 to 13 percent in 2001, and profits were decimated because Motorola lacked an integrated all-in-one switch that the phone companies wanted. In cell phones, Motorola presented clients with a confusing array of models, many of them antiquated and overly expensive. And the division was losing hundreds of millions of

---

Beware of too much focus in innovation— or too little.

The command dimension is challenging. When it is too unrestrained, risks become excessive and continuity is lost, as at Corning. Too weak, and direction vanishes in inertia and a raft of minor innovations, as at Motorola. Innovation also places heavy demands on the organizational community. It is easy, for example, to over-empower tech-loving engineers who disconnect from the market.

dollars. It also lost dominance in the market to Nokia and saw its share fall from 33 percent to 14 percent in five years (Nokia's went from 22 percent to 35 percent). Motorola even allowed its semiconductor unit to flag as receding economies of scale doomed it to ever-shrinking margins.[23] Although all in the industry were hit by the telecom bust, Motorola has underperformed its peers since 1997, and has had to cut more than 50,000 jobs from its precious workforce. What went wrong?

Type 1—Excessive Major: Closed Community. Motorola's high-tech engineering culture over the years produced numerous innovations and ever-increasing quality. But as that culture grew insular and intolerant, it got the company into trouble. Motorola became more and more of a technology farm, paying scant attention to the marketing end of the business. Its products were slow to hit the market, too costly to make, and not stylish enough for consumers. Said one commentator, "The engineers are still running the asylum."[24]

It didn't help that many Motorola devices were overly complex, reflecting engineering passion more than customer demands. The company sold 120 models of cellular phones when 10 would have covered the bases. Worse, it produced very similar products with little hardware or software complementarity. Two StarTAC phones, for example, might have only 5 to 15 percent of their software and hardware in common, and each device would have as many as 600 parts! (The aim now is to cut that to 150.)[25] It is fine for a technology company to rally around its engineers and R&D people; it is not fine to sequester them from the rest of the world and let them call all the shots.

Type 2—Eroding Major: Indecisive Command. One reason for the culture run amok was a lack of strong leadership. The last decisive family executive was Bob Galvin. When son Chris became CEO of Motorola in 1997, he inherited a company that had become too diverse and unwieldy under former CEOs George Fischer and Gary Tooker. Product lines proliferated while hopeless money-losers like the Iridium global satellite were allowed to linger and bleed the company. Divisions hid such weak results from Chris, who acted more like a visionary than a turnaround executive. In fact, Chris delayed making tough decisions and left a vacuum at the top. Analyst Mark Veverka wrote in 2001, "The insular paternal culture seemingly continues to deprive Motorola of a leader who is free to make dramatic strokes such as selling the semiconductor division."[26]

To promote an entrepreneurial spirit over the years, dozens of small units developed, each with its own product or technology, marketing, and profit center. In 1998, to improve integration and unify technologies and standards, Galvin put many of the units together under an umbrella department, Communications Enterprise, employing 500 executives in charge of cell phones, infrastructure, and broadband. A dozen or so managers reported to Merle Gilmore, an engineer, who insisted that all decisions be passed up to the top of the unit. Despite the resulting paralysis, Chris Galvin still kept mostly out of the picture.[27]

Eventually, Motorola became so diversified that the old legacy businesses were now distracting executives from the core focus of making and selling personal wireless devices and infrastructure. So the company was late in shifting from analog to the more efficient, better-quality digital technologies demanded by wireless service providers. Said one industry observer, "They still see themselves as a radio company. And if they don't begin realizing they are a communications company, they will marginalize themselves to second tier."[28] Crucial for innovators, as we argued, is strong command. In its absence, rivals soon come to take the innovative initiative—and that is exactly what happened.

Type 3—Eroding Complement: Weak Connection to Market. The insular engineering culture at Motorola distanced the firm from its markets—even from its giant telecom clients. Verizon Wireless's Chief Marketing Officer John Stratton actually called the company arrogant. For example, Motorola dictated to carriers exactly how to sell its products, refused to take suggestions into account, and missed key deadlines for product delivery; sometimes, it never bothered to send the product at all. Motorola, as a result, was deemed a "bossy, know-it-all supplier . . . Listening, for Motorola, was waiting for you to stop speaking so they could tell you what to buy . . . It was endemic to their culture."[29]

Corning: Too Many Eggs in One Basket

Like Motorola, Corning today is less of a family business. The Houghtons own less than 1 percent of the shares—which is fortunate for them, as the stock price had fallen from a high of $113 in 2000 to under $3 in 2002. Although in the process of a turnaround under a recalled Jamie Houghton, Corning faces a crisis because of its narrow high-tech focus and woeful overexpansion.

Error Types 1 and 3—Excessive Major and Eroding Complement: Unbridled Command; Faltering Continuity. Under the first non-family CEOs, Roger Ackerman, and his successor, John Loose, Corning took too many risks. It let continuity flag, and allowed the business to change too quickly. It also cast off old lines—lighting in 1989, medical testing in 1996, and housewares in 1998—solid businesses that could help support higher-tech ventures such as new types of optical fiber for the telecommunications industry. So, Corning was left with most of its eggs in one basket.

True, the company rode the communications boom; its telecom sales surged 38 percent to $3 billion in 1999, and to $5.1 billion in 2000—70 percent of total revenues. But to take that ride it had to spend a staggering $10 billion on high-priced acquisitions to serve the telecom market. And breaking with 149 years of tradition, Corning began to *buy* innovations instead of develop them. Then, to lock in business, it signed take-or-pay contracts with suppliers, which required that Corning purchase components whether it needed them or not. The company ultimately had to write off inventory it didn't even own. At the time of this writing, the outcome of Corning's story is still uncertain, but Jamie Houghton has returned as chairman and CEO to steer the company back onto the path to more controlled development.[30]

Dangerous Deal Making

Olympia & York and Bechtel illustrate the problems that can come from an overly cocky and independent CEO. Paul Reichmann and Steve Bechtel Jr. both became too confident about their ability to predict and

Beware of hubris and chance taking.

At some deal makers, excessive command manifests as hubris and grandiosity—a winner's curse. The executive team deteriorates with a leader's growing sense of infallibility. So firms bet too heavily on a single project or type of project. Bechtel, ultimately, realized that this approach had to change. O&Y did not, and compounded its risks with high-flying financing strategies and major investments in industries it knew nothing about.

control the future. So they threw away their safety nets, ignored their advisers, and jeopardized corporate survival. Eventually, Bechtel recovered; O&Y did not.

Olympia & York: Unbridled Expansion

We summarized O&Y's problems at the start of this chapter, problems that manifest all three types of errors.

Type 1—Excessive Major: Command Hubris. The late 1980s and early 1990s saw telling excesses of command at the real estate giant. Paul's growing hubris, in particular, had a profound influence on the risks his company was willing to assume. In one of his pronouncements on Canary Wharf, Paul told a reporter for the Toronto *Globe and Mail*, "This is not a risky project . . . on a scale of one to ten—if the Battery Park was nine— here it would be one." His estimate of the time it would take to complete Canary was seven years, half that of the projections of other highly experienced developers. Paul, moreover, now wanted total control, and hence would accept no minority partners in the massive project. Nor would he take out any construction loans, thus engaging in a scale of self-financing that was unheard of.[31] And although Paul's brothers and advisers warned him of the great difficulty of attracting lessees from City of London to the Docklands area, he never listened. One adviser said of Paul, "Dreamers don't like to be awakened." It was only after the collapse of O&Y that Paul admitted, "The fact that I had never been wrong created character flaws that caused me to make mistakes."[32]

Type 2—Eroding Major: Command, Again. While some elements of command were taken to excess, others were neglected. At O&Y, a cohesive and vigorous team at the top became a Greek chorus and then a one-man show. The business, in effect, went from being a family enterprise to, for all intents, an entrepreneurial venture completely dominated by a single Reichmann. As Paul became more dominant, Albert went his own way, occupying himself with charities and his own real estate partnerships. According to Anthony Bianco, O&Y's risk taking became " . . . exacerbated as Paul, the most driven and prodigiously gifted of the brothers, gained dominance over the family and the family company, transforming the highest councils of each into echo chambers for his own increasingly daring propositions."[33] One of the key safeguards of a family business—the frank intervention of family members—had been lost.

Type 3—Eroding Complement: Fractured Continuity. Overconfidence led to deterioration in continuity—stewardship and focus in particular. Strategic coherence and concern for the long-term health of the business were neglected. Risks were no longer being controlled, and O&Y embroiled itself in an increasingly precarious balancing act. With Canary Wharf, for example, the Reichmanns broke with their long-standing policy and took the project on "spec," building first and leasing later—a very significant risk. They also abandoned their contrarian ways by jumping into a supercharged rental market. Perhaps most hazardous, O&Y limited itself to short-term financing to get the lowest interest rates. This was a dangerous tactic given the constant need to refinance—and the difficulty of doing so during periods of negative cash flow. At the same time, O&Y was pursuing other major development deals across the globe, straining its human and financial resources to the maximum.

The Reichmanns also diversified beyond O&Y's area of expertise, investing billions of dollars to purchase major chunks of Gulf Canada, Abitibi Price, Allied-Lyons, Santa Fe Southern Pacific, and the dangerously leveraged Campeau Corporation, an aggressive acquirer of troubled department stores run by the eccentric Robert Campeau. O&Y took huge stakes in these companies, even though it did not understand their business fundamentals and exercised virtually no governance influence. The investments performed very badly. Because O&Y's stock price was a key source of collateral, this left the Reichmanns vulnerable, as they kept being pushed back to the market to borrow short-term funds for Canary Wharf. It was just a matter of time before the bubble burst.

Bechtel: Focus Frenzy

Bechtel hit its trouble patch during the 1980s, when Chairman Steve Bechtel Jr. began to focus ever more narrowly on petroleum engineering and nuclear power plants. After the Three Mile Island nuclear accident in 1979, his firm ignored the writing on the wall. Instead of diversifying, it used its formidable lobbying muscle to push the Nuclear Regulatory Commission to license more plants and lift restrictions on exporting nuclear technology. Although Bechtel succeeded in winning many contracts for nuclear plants, these became ever less the technology of choice, and many projects were canceled after the company had spent vast sums tooling up for them. Bechtel's other focus was oil: petroleum refineries, depots, and pipelines. But by 1984, oil prices had plunged, third-world debt was mounting, and the U.S. dollar was strong. So Bechtel's oil projects too were terminated. Its unprecedented concentration had proved devastating. Between 1982 and 1987, the firm had to cut 22,000 people from the payroll, almost half the workforce.[34]

Type 1—Excessive Major: Cocksure Command. Part of the problem was that unlike his dad, Steve Bechtel Jr. behaved like an exclusive potentate at his firm, especially after the departure of President George Shultz. By the 1980s, Steve Sr. had ceased to be a strong voice in the company, and the younger generation had not yet taken authoritative positions. So although command was "strong," in that there was a leader with courage and entrepreneurial initiative, there was also deterioration in the top team. Steve Jr. had a nasty habit of dressing down anyone who would bring him bad news. Said one Bechtel manager, "Most of the corporate vice presidents were afraid of upsetting the chairman. The upshot was, if there was a problem, you simply swept it under the rug."[35]

Type 3—Eroding Complements: Capsized Continuity and Demoralized Community. It is no surprise then that no one spoke up when Bechtel ignored stewardship and bet too heavily on the nuclear and oil businesses. To make things worse, the builder would take on only mega-projects, shunning smaller opportunities. When energy prices fell and a few large nuclear projects were canceled, the business was decimated. In another lapse in stewardship, Bechtel began investing in businesses it knew nothing about. Incongruously, the firm bought control of the white-shoe investment bank Dillon, Read & Co., which it was forced to unload in 1986.

Bechtel also let its internal community deteriorate. Certainly the need for the massive layoffs in 1984 and 1985 did not help. People said the firm had lost the family feel. Claimed one manager, "I don't think that Bechtel will ever be thought of as 'family' again." Said another, "They tend to act like God, but without the compassion."[36] Bechtel had become sluggish and bureaucratic as well, with too many layers of managers who were afraid to question the chief's absolute authority.

The turnaround began in earnest in 1986, with Steve Jr.'s admission that he needed some help. He assembled a high-powered group of business advisers to put on the board, flattened the structure, and did away with many of the stifling rules. On Saint Patrick's Day 1987, Steve Jr., looking drawn and tired, discussed his new intentions: "We've got to put more emphasis on marketing, on strategic planning, on business management.

We need to get back to the attitudes and work practices of twenty years ago. That means less formality, more flexibility, more speed and responsiveness, more teamwork." Bechtel was on the road to recovery.[37]

Two Unhealthy Syndromes

What have we learned from all these examples? Certainly, that even great FCBs are not immune to problems. Deterioration can, in fact, be especially quick when the leader of an innovator or deal maker, in unchecked command mode, makes dangerous moves. Decline is slower but potentially as devastating when eroding connection to the market brings irrelevance to the products of a brand builder or craftsman, or bad will to an operator; or when a faltering organizational community knocks the edge off a craftsman. But there are more general lessons here about the dangers of going too far with the major C priorities, neglecting any one of them, or letting the complementary Cs, so necessary for resilience, to deteriorate. These lessons come in the form of more general, "higher-level" patterns in our findings, syndromes that occur again and again, and against which companies must be especially vigilant, regardless of the strategy they are pursuing.

In table 8-2, the column totals summarize the prevalence of the different errors among the nine companies discussed here. The most striking fact is that type 3 errors, eroding complements, are more common than types 1 and 2. As we probed further to discern patterns among the findings, it seemed that most of the problem cases could be classified into two syndromes: the first we call the *Icarus Paradox*, and the second, *blunting*.

The Icarus Paradox

Type 1 and 3 errors often combine in a common syndrome we have called the *Icarus Paradox*. The paradox is that, as with Icarus's power of flight, the very practices and capabilities that create success can often pull organizations toward dangerous extremes. They also may drive out vital complementary practices and ultimately bring failure. Here's how it happens: Excesses in a major C are accompanied by erosion in a complementary one as a firm becomes too obsessively focused, too extreme, and too simple, thereby losing its resilience. The tendency is to become overly preoccupied with whatever function or capability the company believes is responsible for success, whether marketing, innovation, operations, etc.

Table 8-2

Risks of Error by Strategy

	Type 1: Excessive Major Priority	Type 2: Eroding Major Priority	Type 3: Eroding Complementary Priority
Brand Building			
• Command			x
• Continuity			
• Community	x		
• Connection			x
Craftsmanship			
• Command			x
• Continuity	x	x	
• Community		xx	
• Connection			x
Operations			
• Command			
• Continuity	x	x	
• Community			xx
• Connection	x	x	
Innovation			
• Command	x	x	
• Continuity			x
• Community	x		
• Connection			x
Deal Making			
• Command	xx	x	
• Continuity			xx
• Community			x
• Connection			
Total Count	8	7	11

Thus, excesses are reached in the Cs supporting those capabilities—command elements, in the case of innovation, say, or continuity elements for operations excellence. The preoccupation drives out consideration of complementary elements. The innovator, for example, may neglect continuity and connection, allowing risk management and market relevance to fall. The craftsman may become too mired in quality traditions and perfect processes to listen to the client. All the attention, resources, and power, in other words, go to the dominant priority, creating excesses there and gaps within the complementary priorities.[38]

Recall that it is imperative to have constructive tension among the C priorities. Organizations, in order to function properly, need to accomplish a variety of things that pull in opposite directions. As discussed in chapter 2, that is certainly the case with the Cs, not only across them, but even among the elements within. The clearest example of a tension—in fact, of a natural counterpoint—is between connection with outsiders and community among insiders. Cohesive, homogeneous community cultures may be slow to recognize the need to adapt to a changing market. Conversely, a constant attempt to adapt to every fad will cause confusion and pull apart the internal community. Therefore, too much market connection can compromise community, and vice versa. The same tension or counterpoint exists between continuity and command. Command favors action, change, and reorientation. Continuity favors momentum, focus, and tradition. Too much change erodes tradition; too much tradition constrains change. Going back to our error types, then, it is no surprise that excesses in a major are often accompanied by erosion in a complement. One occurrence facilitates the other.

Make no mistake: We are not arguing for moderation or bland balance, either among the priorities or the elements of strategy. These businesses were great *because* they embraced a powerful theme that configured their elements. Firms were skewed to back *core* capabilities, as opposed to peripheral ones, and major Cs, not complements. How could a craftsman reach unparalleled excellence without profound continuity—deep investment, dedicated traditions, and disciplined focus? How could a great brand builder do well without a tight, cohesive community that indoctrinates everyone with the values to support the brand?

Firms, in other words, were *required* to focus their resource allocations and efforts. But they offset the dangers of that concentration with multifacetedness, both within and across Cs. Brand builders worked hard at internal community building, but also at reading and adapting to the market (connection). There was multifacetedness *within* the Cs, too. Craftsmen were fortified by tradition, but also invested in extending capabilities for the future—traditions and investment *both* being aspects of continuity. Both these types of multifacetedness, and the constructive tension and debate they engender, determine the *long-term* viability of an organization.

Back to our syndrome. The Icarus Paradox shows a loss of multifacetedness, resilience, and complexity. The organization therefore becomes too simple, too specialized, obsessive, narrowly focused, intolerant, oblivious, and excessive.[39] The prevalence of that mistake shows up in the high totals at the bottom of columns 1 and 3 of table 8-2.

Why the Icarus Paradox Happens. Although most of these firms avoided this paradox, it was the most common problem for those that did run into trouble. Some of its causes were specific to family business, others were more general. Change in governance was a common driver. At O&Y and Bechtel, a family leader became unusually dominant after other strong managers departed. Without an influential sounding board, the leader began to behave rashly. Similarly in 1997 at Levi's, Bob Haas executed a leveraged buyout (LBO) to buy out most of his relatives so he could do whatever he wanted. That marked the beginning of the firm's community excesses. Such changes at the top can restrict CEOs' worldviews, reduce their accountability, and lead to dangerous extremes.

Another driver of Icarus is success itself. Success can lead to overconfidence, giving top managers a false sense of security. It also rigidifies the favored practices, policies, departments, and managers to which success is attributed. Craftsmen, like the Coorses, ignored marketing and marketing people because they "knew" the real source of their success was quality. Indeed, sometimes firms attribute success to pet parties and practices, whether those are vital to performance or not. They ignore crucial elements that they never respected to begin with, even though those elements represent important ingredients in a firm's competitiveness. The problem is that frequently it is hard to tell exactly what the drivers of success are. And as focus narrows and the environment changes, risks increase.

What happens can be compared to a natural selection process occurring within successful companies, such that favored practices and parties get more attention, resources, and power, while others are left to atrophy. At the same time, managers pull too hard on their favorite strategic levers. The firm, in essence, becomes a caricature of its former self.[40] The thriving FCBs were able to resist this trap because they paid attention to *all* of the Cs.

Blunting the Family Edge

The second major syndrome, less common than the first, we call blunting. It is, simply, the erosion of a major priority—a type 2 error. Here we have the *loss* of an edge, versus the overly sharp edge wrought by Icarus. This occurred at firms like Nordstrom, where continuity suffered with the ascent of a non-family CEO, and at Motorola, where eroding command and misdirected community evolved under Chris Galvin's wavering leadership. Such blunting can erode competitive advantage. It may torpedo a company with indecision, as happened at Motorola; or, as at Tyson and Wal-Mart, it may reveal a growing sloppiness in managing relationships with stakeholders. In some cases, there appears to be a decrease in what may be called the "familiness" of the business. Leaders begin to act in a more shortsighted way. They have less passion for the company as an institution, for its social contribution, and for the excellence of its products. Time horizons contract in the pursuit of a short-term profit opportunity or quick-fix efficiency. And companies fail to build on thematic strength and to think about the future.

In most blunting examples, changes in leadership again seemed to play a role. The family or non-family successors were not as committed to, did not understand, or were not able to lead their organizations. Or they embraced a more distanced style of management. The company, as a result, lost a part of its soul.[41]

All that said, this seems like a good place to caution against pessimism. The vast majority of these firms continue to shine, in many cases after more than a hundred years. And others that were experiencing problems are well on the way to recovery.

Conclusion

Clearly, looking at the C priorities one at a time provides an incomplete picture of what an organization must do to succeed. These Cs, and the practices they engender, represent not just important pillars of advantage, but key checks and balances that must complement one another to support a successful configuration. This constant balancing and tension is needed to sustain any strategy, and to counter the natural tendency for majors to mushroom and complements to atrophy. Reverting to the musical analogy with which we began this book, chapters 3 to 7 show how the C notes need to be orchestrated to play different melodies; and this chapter shows what happens when notes are dropped or played too stridently.

Appendix B builds on this chapter to help managers launch a conversation about their own organizations, to discover gaps within and imbalances among their priorities, and to initiate a tune-up process. In chapter 9, managers will begin to learn immediately how to manage for the long run.

Managing for the Long Run

T HE ACTIONS OF the great FCBs should reveal more to managers than any set of prescriptions. Indeed, it is not so much
our invocations as the details of the earlier chapters that will provide the
greatest inspiration. However, the long-run approach has many facets, and
victory will come only by fighting on many fronts. So it is useful to summarize the concrete actions that board members and managers at all levels
can consider for their own firms. But first some words of caution.

Our firms succeed because they are harmoniously configured totali-
ties; their priorities and practices are tailored to a particular strategy, and
are blended and balanced for complementarity and to offset extremes.
Consequently, the very gesture of listing individual and general recommendations runs counter to our approach of configuration. Readers, therefore,
should go through the exercise in appendix B to discover the most crucial
recommendations for their firms, and then review the concrete examples
of these recommendations in the relevant chapters.

We admit that some of our recommendations will be politically challenging—especially at non-FCBs. Family ownership often gives top managers
the latitude to be farsighted, inclusive, and generous; this produces a real
edge in managing for the long run. Executives at companies without this
edge may be forced to please short-term shareholders, and that is a limita-
tion. So if you are a manager of a private or family business, rejoice! You
may have at your disposal levers of competitive advantage that most of
your rivals will find hard to access. Treasure your differences and make
the most of them.[1] If you are not at an FCB, however, do not despair:
There is still a lot you can do.

This chapter will reveal how everyone from the upper echelon to line
operatives can embrace the long-term approach, in big ways and small.
Although some of the governance recommendations are ambitious, many

of those at the functional and individual levels are attainable at almost any company. And where that is not the case people may consider moving to where they have more scope to act.

We begin the chapter with a set of enabling preconditions for a long-run approach. These, of necessity, reside in the incentives and evaluation criteria at the very top of the firm: for boards, CEOs, and top teams. Next we recap the overall management philosophy and organization design levers needed to implement the long-run approach. From there, we address the actions that can be taken by each of the major functional areas: human resources, marketing, operations, R&D, finance, and information technology. Finally, we talk about the attitudes and initiatives everyone in the company can embrace to further the long-term agenda.

Levers of Governance

Executives at long-term winners act as stewards, not careerists. Their concerns are the long-run interests of the company and *all* its stakeholders, not just shareholders but employees, clients, partners, and the society at large. It is truly a blessed paradox that shareholders, ultimately, will gain the most only when these other interests are taken care of. Here is a happy situation in which traveling the high road benefits everyone—in time.

Shareholder Attitudes: Longer Time Horizons

As we said in chapter 1, many shareholders today are traders at heart who prefer to hold a stock for a short time, make a fast profit, and sell. They favor CEOs who boost earnings quickly and reward those executives accordingly—even if the quick gains are at the expense of the long-term health of the company. Where ownership is concentrated in the hands of a group with this attitude, it becomes especially challenging for a CEO to act in a farsighted manner.[2]

So we begin by reminding shareholders that the long-term approach, in the end, may be the most rewarding of all. Recall the tables in chapter 1, which showed how FCBs outperformed other firms not only in survival but also in total returns to shareholders and profitability. And keep in mind that the quintessential long-term investor is superstar Warren Buffet, who buys and holds large parts of companies that really do manage for the future: companies that sell quality products in an honest way, generously maintain their infrastructure, and are truly decent places to work. Through his

Berkshire Hathaway Ltd., Buffet has been one of the most successful investors of the century. He is not alone. Benjamin Graham, Peter Lynch, and other market experts also have argued the merits of holding good investments for the long term, while continuing to monitor the evolution of their broad performance fundamentals—financial *and* nonfinancial.[3]

Shareholders should also care about the *risks* of short-termism. How many savvy traders were caught in the collapse of companies like Enron and WorldCom, and the dot-coms and high-techs? If stock picking is difficult, stock timing is even more so. Maybe in today's soberer economic environment, investors will be more willing to look for firms with enough substance and discipline to go the distance.

Finally, but most important, there are the social and economic costs of shortsightedness. Shoddy products, labor strife, dehumanized jobs, and devastated communities have shaken people's faith in today's executives and corporations. Short-termism has been costly not only for the individual investor and company but for the community at large.

Board Responsibilities: Diligent Oversight

The directors are the critical nexus between shareholders and top managers. It is they who must establish and oversee the executive incentives and monitoring mechanisms. It is they who must be motivated to assess and reward the CEO, not according to rapid, lock-step revenue and profit growth, but for a host of substantive, long-term contributions that cannot be measured simply in dollars and cents. But to do so, board members themselves have to have the right incentives and capabilities.[4]

Board Incentives: Ownership and Compensation. If our accounts tell us anything, it is that proprietorship can induce a sense of responsibility and pride. So for board members to act more like long-term stewards, they need to feel like proprietors—they need to own a meaningful quantity of stock. Professor Don Hambrick of Penn State University suggests that board members' investments in a company should amount to at least 10 percent of their capital.[5] Members' farsightedness can also be encouraged by granting them rights that are exercisable only after several years of good performance. As long as the performance lasts, awards may compound into the future, even beyond a member's tenure.

Board Composition. Boards benefit from a blend of insiders and independent outsiders—a broad mix of talent that combines those with profound insight into the business, its markets, and its technologies.[6] Ideally, each key dimension of performance should have its champion. In fact, the board could benefit by including representatives with special insights into the interests of all of the critical stakeholders of the firm—clients, employees, suppliers, even community leaders.

Some firms employ an ex-CEO as chairman. Indeed, intelligent oversight is a good reason for separating the CEO and chairman roles. An ex-CEO is often someone who deeply understands the business and symbolizes corporate values. Such members provide rare expertise. At the same time, their commitment to the firm and concern about its future make them more willing to consider long-term investments.

One of the most important factors in selecting board members is character. And the best testimony to character is prior achievement. Firms would do well to find executives who have a track record of developing organizational capabilities, selling great products, building a committed workforce, and satisfying a diverse set of stakeholders. "Shooting stars" and quick turnaround artists are in most cases to be avoided, as are overly busy members serving on many other boards, or members too beholden to a CEO.

In the case of family businesses, there is sometimes a tendency for family board members to push their personal agendas—dividends and nepotism being high on the list. Clearly, an FCB can thrive only when those with the power hold the soundness of the business above the aims of individual relatives. It is useful, therefore, to confer significant control or governance influence only on those who take the interests of business most seriously and have the greatest competency to oversee those interests in recruitment, financial policy, and executive action. The appointment of expert board members from outside the family should also help. The family, ultimately, will do best when the business does best, even if that means disappointing Uncle Bill and Cousin Sam.

Evaluation Criteria and Monitoring. Managing for the long run requires that board members resist the urge to push impatiently for bottom- or top-line results. Instead, they must monitor progress along various substantive "interim" indicators and probe for the facts behind the numbers—behind the relevant elements of all four Cs. What is quality like (from production reports)? What do the customers and employees think of the company and its products? What are the trends in market share, new product acceptance, employee turnover? The board or its committees should also examine subtle indicators of how the firm is managing for the future. How much is being invested at two-, five-, and ten-plus-year time horizons? How much of this money goes to training, infrastructure, product and process research, pure research, alliance building, and so on? How does this compare to the firm's objectives and the behavior of its rivals? Boards should have the right to call in independent assessors from time to time to help conduct these inquiries, especially when they sense that all is not well. When problems arise, board committees may become more fine-grained in their inquiries, examining, for example: Which key executives have left the company and why? Who is being promoted? Which are the best and worst business units and departments, and why?

CEO Incentives, Grooming, and Selection: Leading for the Long Run

Like the board, the CEO will pursue the long-run interests of the firm and its stakeholders only if rewarded for doing so and possessed of the right values and abilities.

Compensation and Incentives. As a board's performance time horizons lengthen, so will those of the CEO. Again, the interim performance indicators suggested above can be useful, as can compensation that increases as long-term performance grows over the years.[7] Compensation and incentives may be based on a combination of near- and long-term outcomes. The former might include successful product introductions, enhanced client satisfaction, increasing quality, growing market share in new niches, retention of key employees, and effective new partnerships or alliances.[8] These criteria avoid penalizing executives for weaker bottom-line performance during a build-up or investment phase. Compensation based on a moving average may also insulate CEOs from penalties during heavy investment periods, while it rewards them for average performance over a longer interval. Indeed, longer-term compensation might be based on both the level *and* duration or timing of performance. Therefore, a CEO might even be rewarded for good performance that extends years after he or she retires. Requiring executives to hold onto their stock options longer before they can exercise them may also lengthen time horizons.

Apprenticeship and Succession Planning. Some of our FCBs use intensive, career-long apprenticeships to instill within potential CEOs the right capabilities and attitudes. In addition to structured career ladders, broad job rotations, and extensive training, these programs involve regular contact with and feedback from upper-echelon mentors. The more promising candidates are assigned the most talented tutors—and are exposed to a variety of them. Recall that at Gore, close interaction with "sponsors" ensured that not only skills but values were imparted, as well as critical contacts. In this way, the teacher has ample chance to evaluate the student up close and in all kinds of situations. At its highest levels, in firms like Michelin and Motorola, the apprenticeship took the form of co-CEO positions, with the more senior executive not only training and monitoring, but also learning from his younger colleague. Such apprenticeships can be used to build a pool of promising succession candidates for a whole roster of top management positions.[9]

CEO Selection. CEOs need to be chosen not only for their technical competencies but for their character and commitment to the mission. Crucial assets are integrity, the courage to take tough stands, and a willingness to do the right thing for the company and all its stakeholders. Close apprenticeships make it possible to scrutinize candidates to assess their skills *and* personalities. This opportunity and the training benefits of long apprenticeships favor going to internal successors wherever possible. Of course, a candidate's track record is also important. Did he or she make substantive improvements and build capability, or just go for quick results and move on?

In the case of FCBs, there is often a preference for CEOs who are family members. This is fine, as long as the person chosen has the attitudes and competencies we've been discussing. (We have written elsewhere of the succession processes that will make it more likely that a family can develop such a candidate from within.)[10] Sometimes, however, there is no fully competent family member willing to take over, and firms must overcome parochialism to find the best non-family candidate, preferably from a roster of talented, well-trained, thoroughly committed insiders.

CEO Retention. Recent research has shown that CEOs keep getting better with years served. The profitability and growth of their companies peak very late in their tenures, with some studies suggesting a peak of eight years, and others fourteen to sixteen years (the lower figure pertaining to the more turbulent industries).[11] The FCBs in our study encouraged very long CEO tenures, which no doubt contributed to their success. Clearly, there are a number of governance implications here. First, boards should understand that the first few years of a CEO's tenure might be difficult as the person learns the ropes and develops a network. They must also realize that learning and performance improvement keeps occurring, even after many years. So keeping a good CEO in the company should be a high priority. Methods of doing that include incentives and benefits that grow with performance *and* with time. These may include funding an executive's pet projects or charities, and providing opportunities for brief sabbaticals. Useful, too, are assistance with different roles as a CEO ages (even the use of co-CEOs) and a gradual phaseout from the job, allowing for a thorough tutoring of successors.[12]

Top Management Team Characteristics: Family Frankness

Unfortunately, insider selection and long apprenticeships and tenures risk that CEOs will become insular—too imbued with tradition to adapt and update the firm and its strategies. This threat makes it crucial that there be enough variety of perspective on the top management team for alternative points of view to be debated. Chapter 8 described how a narrow, obsessive top team hurt Coors's marketing capability. The Cargill-MacMillans, Michelins, Rausings, Galvins, and Nordstroms, on the other hand, benefited from having empowered executives on the team with different points of view. The rule of thumb in all these instances was that the overall mission and core values and ethics of the firm were inviolate. But the required strategies, methods, products, and processes were fair game for heated "family-like" discussion.[13]

One of the greatest assets of the FCBs we studied was that managers, even across the generations and cohorts, could speak frankly with one another. They could be critical and convey bad news, knowing that their jobs would remain secure. Clearly dissenting executives can speak truth to those in power only within a climate of openness and an insistence on fact-based decision making that welcomes questioning and dialogue. That means the top team needs to be constantly surfacing data from all over the firm and from the outside on all kinds of potentially contradictory indicators, in an attempt to identify promising and threatening trends and facts. For *useful* discourse, there must be an understanding that those with dissenting opinions will not be punished.

Long-Run Philosophy of Executives

These governance enablers should stimulate the essential attitudes and policies among executives that underlie top performance: courageous stewardship to do what is best for the firm and its stakeholders; commitment to a substantive mission; and an unusual focus on capability building. Much of this book has been devoted to these qualities and how leaders and outstanding firms manifest them, so we will only reiterate the headlines here. In the discussion of the functions, we will highlight the more practical hands-on levers.

Courage and Stewardship

Farsighted boards that select leaders for character and focus on substantive accomplishment must provide a platform for courageous leadership—for doing the right thing for the future, even if it means being unorthodox, demands bold action, and entails slow payoffs. Ultimately, such courage must manifest in novel business models, decisive investments, and exceptional resource commitments.

Yet for all this courage, stewardship over the enterprise must come first, specifically, risks must be carefully managed. Investments, for example, might be steep, but covered by large war chests and minimal debt. Business models might be unorthodox, but endlessly fine-tuned and incrementally implemented to fit market needs.

One of the most important aspects of stewardship is the ability to listen. In the very best companies—those that thrived the longest—perhaps the most salutary courage came in the form of admitting fallibility. Although this is often easier in the atmosphere of a supportive family, it is a personal strength that all executives must develop. Arrogance or smugness were rare among these leaders. And success, for the most part, did not go to their heads.

A Meaningful Mission

The best leaders rally their firms around a mission that has real social and economic importance and market appeal, and enough scope to be relevant for decades. They feel these missions in their gut, often as a consequence of their social philosophies and their ethical or religious beliefs. Such passionate convictions, coupled with a sense of the firm's special competencies and market opportunities, tend to breed the most evocative missions.[14] These go beyond logic and analysis, beyond brainstorming about competencies and competitive forces; they appeal to emotions and fundamental values.

Substantive missions inspire commitment. They might be as grand as Hallmark's contribution to social harmony, the Family Timken's "overcoming friction," or the *New York Times'* serving as the vehicle for an informed electorate. Or they might be as basic as Estée Lauder's drive to teach women how to be more beautiful, or S.C. Johnson's commitment to add substantial value to basic consumer products. Either way, missions require the specificity to give employees a sense of purpose, the relevance to attract markets, and the breadth to remain fresh. Profit and sales targets take a back seat or are not mentioned at all.

Leaders, of course, must clarify not only the mission but the concrete policies, capabilities, and action plans needed to pursue it. Interim objectives and performance indicators are essential. Timken's quality mission, for example, is institutionalized in its perfectionist product, process, and materials standards. It is backed by policies of generous investment in equipment and training, and assessed by rates of improvement in bearing durability, customer loyalty, and the ability to capture demanding new clients.

Relentless Capability Building

Stretch missions become attainable only through focused capability building. By focus, we mean concentrating on what the organization needs to do best to satisfy both its mission and its markets. This typically involves an allocation of resources that is more skewed, intensive, and long-term than that of one's rivals, and more of an attempt to bootstrap capabilities and leverage them. We recounted dozens of examples of this: Recall Michelin, which spent more than its competitors on process and product R&D; and Estée Lauder, which out-invested every competitor in building its brand.[15]

An important outcome of focus is that firms will deliver value that their competitors cannot imitate—at least not economically. They will have developed "asymmetric" or inimitable competencies that enable them to sustain competitive advantage.[16] In short, their concentration has given them a distinctive set of resources and capabilities, devotedly augmented over the years, that defy duplication. Perhaps that is one reason many of these companies are so long-lived. Who would relish competing with

Bechtel at mega-projects, with Tetra Pak in packaging, or with Corning in glass-related technologies?

Organizational Design

We have shown throughout how long-term winners developed cohesive, high-commitment cultures to get everyone on board. Their methods of doing this included shared values, socialization, and mentorship programs, along with a deep consideration of people. It is worthwhile drawing attention here to other organizational design practices that contribute to rich internal communities, but that we have emphasized less in our discussion.

Flat, Informal Organizations

Many great FCBs we studied liberated their staffs to stimulate creativity and exploit grassroots wisdom. Organizational designs were kept as simple as possible, with few levels of hierarchy and lots of authority residing at lower levels. As values and priorities were clear, and staff loyalty had been earned with generous treatment, people could be trusted with ample discretion. At numerous plants, the operators themselves decided how to get the job done and how to improve things. In companies like Timken, Gore, Corning, and Michelin, many job descriptions were open-ended.

Implicit in the notion of a flat organization is a relative absence of bureaucracy. Initiative arises when people can contact one another without going through the hierarchy, and when common objectives rather than confining rules guide actions. So even firms that are very large can have a small-company feel to them. Shoppers at Nordstrom, for example, felt as though they were being served by the proprietor of a store, rather than a sales representative. The only rule was to "please the customer."[17]

Company Subunits: United, Not Siloed

Too many organizations today become fiefdoms in which people focus primarily on their own department or profit center. Although cost and profit centers are useful administrative devices, they must not be allowed to become divisive silos, obsessed with local interests. Ways of avoiding that tendency include firmwide values, socialization, hiring for collaborative skills, and compensation and rewards based on firm—not unit—objectives.[18]

Collaboration across units can also be enhanced by universal training programs (as at Motorola), and sponsorship programs that provide recruits with readymade networks outside their unit (as at Gore). Job rotations that expand contacts and broaden perspectives help as well. Common formal mechanisms for cross-unit collaboration include task forces, committees, project groups, and integrative personnel who serve as liaisons and coordinators among departments.

Table 9-1 contrasts our recommendations with the approaches prevailing at so many of today's companies.

Table 9-1

Governance, Philosophy and Organization: Winning FCBs Versus Common Practices

Our Winning FCBs	Common Practices
Governance	
Shareholders: act as long-term proprietors.	*Shareholders:* act as traders after quick profits.
Board: deeply invested; free, informed, and motivated to do disciplined monitoring of financial and nonfinancial results.	*Board:* token ownership; dominated by those beholden to CEO; CEO may also be chairman; monitoring mostly of financial results.
CEO: compensated mostly via long-term incentives; an insider with lots of experience and substantive accomplishment; value- and mission-driven; stays in job for decades.	*CEO:* given short-term stock options; recruited from outside; record of financial achievement; stays in job for 3–4 years and retires rich.
Top team: strong voice, diverse functional backgrounds, multigenerational, long tenures.	*Top team:* perhaps politicized, one function dominates, often of the same cohort, with short tenures.
Philosophy of Leaders	
Careful stewardship over mission as well as assets and resources; willingness to listen and invest in capabilities to enhance prospects of long-term success.	Willing to trade long-term for the short; mission and capability building take a back seat to top- and bottom-line results.
Organizational Designs	
Flat, informal, and collaborative to unite the team and make the best use of people's skills and initiative.	Siloed functions and business units; hierarchy to enforce financial accountability.

The Business Functions

To make the balance of our recommendations more actionable, we organize them by function. In all cases, the primary objective is to help managers to take a long-term, broader view in every aspect of operations, one that is more expansive in time horizons, constituencies, and substantive objectives. Again, readers must select those recommendations most relevant to their particular strategies. Table 9-2 compares the functional practices of our stellar FCBs with today's more common practices.

Human Resources: To Nurture the Tribe

Long-term objective: To attract and keep, for their entire careers, talented employees who believe in the mission, fit with the culture, keep learning, and collaborate without much guidance.

The only way to encourage people to act for the long-run good of the organization is to get them on board. To that end, managers must attract employees whose values jibe with the mission. Then they need to socialize them in the importance and means of the organization's craft and motivate them with unusual consideration. This approach contrasts starkly with today's temporary hiring practices, job hopping, tight job descriptions, and incentives based largely on pay and promotion.

Be Choosy on Many People Dimensions. Long-run players have to be fussy recruiters, hiring not for jobs but careers. They must find people who will contribute to the organization for the long haul, those with talent and character who buy into the mission. A good fit with company values is absolutely essential. So some of our best firms put the family in charge of recruitment and hired only a very small percentage of applicants—people with just the right aptitudes (well-tested), ethics, achievements, and personal interests. In some cases, proof of initiative and an ability to work well with others were primary hiring criteria; and firms contacted ten or more references to establish these qualities. Frequently, hobbies and activities that fit a firm's mission and culture (e.g., nature buffs at L.L. Bean) were used as key suitability indicators. Because employment is seen as a big investment, extreme caution in hiring is the rule. The policy is always: If in doubt, say no.

Table 9-2

Contrasts in Functional Approaches

	FCBs in Our Study	Common Practices
Human Resources	Fussy hiring for careers and fit with values; understaff; avoid layoffs; lots of training and development allows jobs with scope; satisfaction from job accomplishment, sense of belonging, career opportunities.	Hire as needed, but lean and mean practices with layoffs; less training requires narrower, more boring jobs; pecuniary incentives dominate.
Marketing	Base on superior value-added for client, build around special competency; invest in enduring relationships with favored clients; patiently build reputation and share.	React to emerging market opportunities; chase hot areas of the market that yield quick results; make a splash.
Operations	Original business models; invest deeply in a superior infrastructure to enhance competency, efficiency, or quality; go for constant improvement; pay for it with creative leveraging, focus, and partnering; avoid frills and fads.	Tried-and-true business models; invest in infra-structure with rapid payback, augmented by fashionable new techniques, tech-nologies, and processes.
R&D/Engineering	Time-staggered portfolio of research projects; idea- and market-driven research; inspired impracticality and forgiveness; a balance of research and commercialization.	Shorter-term, market-driven research projects; strict bottom-line accounta-bility; bias in favor of commercialization.
Finance and Information Systems	Conservative—low debt, lots of cash, steep reinvestment in the business; attention always on substance, not costs or revenues; wide variety of indicators tracked.	Financial leverage to increase returns and grow faster; financial numbers drive decision making.

Understaff. Complements are kept small, and there is a tendency toward understaffing. This reduces the chances of demoralizing layoffs and obliges people to assume larger roles and to show initiative at work. The resulting demands quickly weed out less capable employees and make jobs more interesting for the rest. Having fewer positions to fill also means the firm can be more selective in choosing candidates.

Invest Deeply in Training and Development. Firms do not simply want to *keep* good people, they want them to fully develop their potential so that their value increases every year—to the benefit of both company capabilities and personal fulfillment. Companies like S.C. Johnson, Timken, Motorola, Estée Lauder, Gore, Hallmark, and Levi Strauss invested far more in education than their rivals. This could take the form of on-the-job training, courses, sabbaticals, and job rotation programs. Some of the best training vehicles, in fact, were mentorship programs, placing newcomers with veterans who were expected to teach the subtleties of the job and the values and social system of the company. The idea always is to increase employee versatility and skill, not just in technical aspects, but in social and managerial skills as well. That way firms can get most of their managers from among their own ranks—people who know intimately the culture and craft of the enterprise and thrived within it.

Design Jobs with Scope. Broader job definitions, too, help personal development. Workers at Corning's Blacksburg, Virginia, CELCOR ceramics plant rarely saw any supervisors and could do virtually every job in the plant; and they were in charge of final decisions about warehousing, quality, and other critical functions. To guide them, they were given access to all the financial and technical information needed to make intelligent decisions. Workers also were encouraged to create special projects for themselves—for example, to enhance plant efficiency. They even dealt directly with customers, and they worked in cohesive teams in which every member was expected to pitch in wherever needed. Such scope gave staff ample latitude to explore their talents and interests and to keep learning.[19]

The People Are the Place—Care for Them. Our own prior research has shown that the more firms invest in their people, the more they are able to benefit from sound strategies and processes. Without unusual loyalty and commitment to employees, even the most inspired strategies and approaches do not result in superior profitability.[20] The human resources philosophies of many of our firms seemed to reflect that finding, and were starkly simple: If you want exceptional loyalty and devotion, first you have to demonstrate it. Given the effort they spend in finding and training excellent people, these companies want to keep them. Good compensation and benefits go a long way in achieving that, and certainly many FCBs pay better than average.

As important as compensation, however, are corporate culture, career opportunities, and loyalty to staff. Strong corporate values give employees pride in their work and workplace. And promising paths for advancement allow people to rise and stay in the company. Nordstrom, recall, expanded for the express purpose of giving upward mobility to its talented staff. Corning allowed great scientists to advance to high positions and salaries without having to become managers and leave their beloved labs. In order to keep such good people and reward them for their lengthy service, there was often a seniority component to compensation and status; "lifetime achievements" were celebrated. People were not valued simply for their latest contribution but for what they had done over their entire careers.

Finally, staff often felt gratitude because firms had been loyal to them in times of trouble. Companies minimized layoffs during recessions and downturns, and involved those affected directly in any essential restructuring processes (as at Levi's and Corning). People remember that kind of care and become harder to lure away. In the best of circumstances, employees act in the interests of the company because they believe in what it does and stands for, and feel loyalty to it as an institution. While that seems to be a lot to strive for in today's corporations, it is a realized goal in many of the companies we studied.

Minimize Vertical Distinctions. Our winners try to make their employees feel that they are all on the same team. Where possible, they avoid symbols of rank, power, and wealth, preferring instead to foster a sense of comradeship. Executives' offices, salaries, and expense accounts are modest, and limos are rare. The motto is: "Curb luxury at the top. People are watching." Lines of communication are always open, to give employees down the hierarchy the freedom to talk with their bosses and perhaps their bosses' bosses. Even high-level executives spend a lot of time on the shop floor and out in the field.

Be Cheerleaders. The HR department in many of our firms was charged with celebrating organizational values and the people who best exemplified them. House news organs glorified company milestones and community contributions. HR units also orchestrated the celebratory hoopla and rewards for personal accomplishments and service anniversaries. Many even set up "Walls of Fame" to showcase the veterans and recount their contributions, as well as museums that poignantly related the history of the company and its people. Other firms commissioned biographies. All of these initiatives make people aware of what a company stands for and of the myriad actions that prove its worth and commitment.

Marketing: To Build Firm Reputation and Client Relationships

Long-term objective: To create and sell superior offerings that engender reputation, and to form long-term relationships with the client. Marketing is about demonstrating value, not glitz, and aims for client loyalty, not one-shot sales.

Develop Superior Offerings. Marketing here starts with a great product. In fact, product differentiation underlies most of these successful strategies— quality, great brands, innovation, even superior operations—that deliver customer "solutions." Superiority is always gauged vis-à-vis the competition, and is measured not in abstract standards but in what a specific target market will value.

Because reputation and customer loyalty are fundamental to the long-term view, companies absolutely avoid shoddiness in products and services. Even small mistakes can destroy reputation, especially when customers are currently paying more or going out of their way to obtain these firms' offerings. So new offerings must never hurt the image of the firm or risk bringing disrepute. In fact, many of our firms were especially selective in their product introductions, bringing out far fewer new products and selling far narrower lines than their rivals. In developing a new offering, they took the time to get it absolutely right. And, most emphatically, they avoided copycat products in favor of original ones whose attractiveness would last.

Form Enduring Relationships with the Client. Long-run players build and grow enduring relationships with their clients. They exploit their product and service superiority to create loyalty, and it is this closeness to customers that helps them understand the market and improve offerings. Relationships with the client can be forged by doing something as simple as making a follow-up sales call based on a well-maintained "client book." We saw how Estée Lauder and Nordstrom associates call up customers to let them know about new products especially suitable to their tastes. They may also offer gifts and special discounts to reward loyal customers. In other words, these firms look for every excuse to stay in touch with clients and their needs and to signal that they care.

Sometimes, however, enduring client relationships can issue only out of major, customer-specific investments. Tyson and Simplot made heroic efforts to create those relationships, building special plants and logistics systems for a particular client, and tailoring "customer solutions" to deliver the right goods to the right locations just in time. Again, clients appreciate the investment these companies are willing to make to accommodate them. What keeps these relationships growing are the extras, like the new products the firm develops expressly for a large client, or added services. Bechtel, recall, gave former clients critical information about international political and economic trends, even when they were no longer doing business with them. This kept the relationship alive.

Develop Good Relationships with the Community. An important part of marketing for many companies is building a positive image in the community. Most of these FCBs were philanthropic or did pro bono community work because they believed it was the right thing to do. They wanted to "give something back." But their contributions also created an image of responsible citizenship, and that in turn drew good clients, public support, and superior job applicants.

Promote Patiently. Promotional efforts can be unusually farsighted. Recall Hallmark's pioneering broadcasts, which took years to build the brand. For deal makers and operators, a decade of personal networking might occur before a major client was landed. But these companies were willing to put lots of money up front in a deal that might pay off only years later. Bombardier and Morgan made themselves useful to, and hired people from, government and potential customers in the hope of eventually landing business. Promotion here was not cheerleading. It was a concerted attempt to communicate the character of the company, the superiority of the product, or the willingness to do more than others to accommodate.

Operations: To Create an Evolving, Inclusive System

Long-term objective: To build a superior infrastructure that adds more value at less cost and evolves with the needs of the products and markets. The system incorporates not just insiders, but outside partners, and is geared to tomorrow as well as today.

Devise a Better Business Model—Mind the Configuration. To deliver superior offerings, some firms adopt a different way of doing things—an original, cohesive business model. At IKEA, Wal-Mart, and Fidelity, the value proposition is shaped by a whole constellation of complementary parts: the breadth and depth of the product line, choice of value-chain stages, capabilities at which to excel, and the activities for which to partner. The business is treated as an integral system. So, for example, IKEA's product line, locations, store layouts, marketing methods, and outsourcing policies are all complementary aspects of a unique business model. Similarly, Fidelity's fund families, service centers, sales approach, automated client interface, and fee structure are all indispensable parts of *its* system. Such integrated systems are both effective and hard for rivals to imitate, and so they help sustain advantage. We are not arguing for automation or knee-jerk integration here, but for the need to periodically take a fresh, bird's-eye look at the business model to search for additional complementarities. One might ask, for example: Does the infrastructure suggest new outsourcing opportunities? Does the distribution configuration favor broadening the product line?

Use "Miserly Extravagance" to Build a Better Infrastructure. Our winners invested generously in their operations. Wal-Mart had the most modern stores and warehouses and the most sophisticated computer and logistics systems; Fidelity deployed the most automated and user-friendly client interfaces. Whenever it was a question of investing to patch things up or to build a lasting, more effective system, firms opted for the latter. Their calculations were always based on making long-term returns, not shaving current expenses. Michelin and Cargill kept building the most efficient plants in the business and bought only the best equipment. But they abhorred spending on frills: Offices were rudimentary; furnishings, Spartan. The money went only toward enhancing critical capabilities.

Leverage Capability. Firms support these generous investments by leveraging them for maximal use. Fidelity, for example, employs its back-office capabilities to outsource for institutional clients. Tyson runs three shifts in its highly automated plants. Michelin and Timken leverage their operations across all kinds of tires and bearings. Where possible, facilities are fashioned to increase such flexibility. Product designs, too, can be leveraged. Bechtel has scalable power plant designs, and it can mix and match modular components to efficiently create a customized installation.

O&Y codified its knowledge of building so it could use standard design components and techniques across different projects.

Partner to Focus on Your Strengths. Focus and partnering combine to make for highly efficient operations. Companies concentrate on those processes and products they are best at, and partner for less critical activities.[21] Bechtel, for example, concentrates on the high-margin businesses of design and financing. It can afford to do this because it has excellent partners to help with construction. So beneficial are such alliances, in fact, that sometimes companies invest deeply in their partners to make them better, as did Wal-Mart and IKEA. In the long run, everyone gained.

Keep Improving the Business System. The best firms never rest. They are constantly adapting their systems to improve effectiveness, meet new opportunities, and stay ahead of the competition. This system improvement, however, is anything but haphazard. The focus is always on the most critical parts, and building a pivotal competency.

Firms do especially well when combining product and process improvement. As designs evolve, so must operations, and vice versa, such that a virtuous circle is initiated between product and process enhancement. Corning, Michelin, and Motorola made sure this happened by getting the various engineering departments together. Timken exploited the growing quality of its steel-making process to vastly improve the designs and durability of its bearings—which in turn pushed its steel-making limits.

Quality Always Counts. Obviously, firms ride herd over quality. Here's the trick: By careful infrastructure design they often enhance quality while reducing cost. For Timken and Motorola alike, economy and quality improvement were never considered independently.

R&D and Engineering: To Provide Generously for Tomorrow

Long-term objective: To keep offerings at the cutting edge and renew product lines.

Stagger Project Time Horizons. To endure, companies have to invest in the products and processes of the future, *and* for the shorter term. We've recounted many examples, but it is worth stressing the importance of staggering project time horizons. Firms like Corning and Motorola, for most of their histories, embraced research and development projects with very different time horizons. Some projects had payoff and commercialization prospects decades away, others less than two years away. The theoretical research was for the very long term, while the applied work was expected to have a much quicker payoff.

Broaden the Philosophy of Research. The best firms research and try to improve *many* different things. R&D can be seen as a state of mind, a philosophy of preparing for the future that can show up everywhere and in better and more original ways of doing business. Novel products are worked on, of course, and processes as well. But sometimes the biggest gains come from new approaches to selling, distributing, organizing, or partnering.

Be Impractical Sometimes, and Celebrate Glorious Mistakes. One of Corning's top scientists said that the best research is not product-driven but idea- and technology-driven. CEO Jamie Houghton confirmed this, saying that it is impossible to know the market implications of many technologies or discoveries when they are still at an early stage. He praised Corning for its long-term orientation that allows "unpredictable exploration."

The biggest gains typically come from surprising corners, and the best firms probed those corners. Of course, the price came in the form of failures—some, like Michelin's sagging locomotive, with comical outcomes. But leaders have to muster the courage to praise the positive qualities of such brave and sensible efforts, no matter what the results. Otherwise, no one ventures forth, and tomorrow will look too much like today. That's why Gore celebrates each and every project completion—failures as well as successes—with equal enthusiasm.

Open the Doors to the Lab. High-minded research and tolerance for errors only take companies to the edge of innovation. To cross the threshold of commercial viability, there has to be a match with the market. These firms, with their flat, networked structures, made it easy for departments and business units to share knowledge. Thus, Corning's marketing people, very early on in a project, went scouting for applications, and brought back ideas to people in R&D and product development. At Gore, teams were small and multifunctional right from the start, thereby uniting research, production, and marketing staff, whose dual function was to give researchers new ideas *and* figure out ways of commercializing inventions. As jobs were broadly defined, everyone was responsible for success, all could contribute, and no one worried about "speaking out of turn." Further stimulation of the research types at Corning came from alliances with other firms—clients, universities, and other partners—which, again, could provide ideas for exploration and signal avenues for exploitation. Frequently, these associations involved co-location to bring people into the closest possible connection.

Finance: To Safeguard the Future

Long-term objective: To fund competency development and keep the firm sound and financially healthy for years to come. Financial levers assure longevity instead of celebrating the bottom line.

Be Financially Conservative—But Invest Generously. Although financial policy will have to vary with a firm's strategy and competitive environment, most of the great FCBs were unusually conservative. They avoided excessive financial leverage and built up significant cash reserves. Borrowing was seen as either a necessary evil or an unnecessary one. Best-practice fads, offices, fancy cars, luxuries, even computer systems were viewed with great suspicion. And dividends were modest, as was pay to the top executives. Good-time Charlies, these were not. That said, firms *were* unfailingly generous investors. Depending on their strategy, they put more money into competencies, infrastructure, R&D, marketing, and training than most of their peers, and they were willing to wait longer to receive a return. This generosity, of course, was made possible in large part by the parsimony just noted—and by families' constant reinvestment of almost all their profits in the business.

"Contain" the Finance Guys. This stark recommendation gets at an underlying truth. Too many firms are dominated by accounting and finance types who draw attention to costs and profits without considering the substance behind the numbers. So the focus and rewards become too tightly centered on dollars and cents, and people start gaming the system and starving capabilities. That is what happened to General Motors and Ford during the decades when the cost accountant whiz kids took over.[22] The firms lost their manufacturing edge—and market share—to Japanese rivals that cared more about their craft. The lesson: Bottom-line and

top-line growth must be seen as natural outcomes of a superior mission and capability, not as ends in themselves.

Information Systems: To Open Up the Discussion

Long-term objective: To make managers aware of how the firm is doing now and for the future in all aspects of its operations (not just financial) and for all of its stakeholders (not just owners or managers).

Go Beyond the Numbers and Cast a Wide Net. The philosophy of most great FCBs is that if you deliver on your mission, the financial rewards will follow. Putting financial concerns into perspective does not mean that these firms don't have good information systems. They do. But they are less formal, less structured, and they employ many nonfinancial indicators. Managers, from the highest levels on down, spend a great deal of time physically present "on the ground": in the plants, with customers, with line employees, and with suppliers. They collect qualitative as well as quantitative data in order to focus on substantial matters like quality, customer satisfaction, and emerging opportunities. These are key leading indicators of the financial results and are more useful in guiding intelligent action. Great FCBs like Coors and Hallmark, for example, are not afraid to make ample use of informed judgment in evaluating truly subjective quality indicators like taste. This inevitable need to treat professional judgment and intuition as real information is celebrated, not concealed.

Data gathered should fall into the domains of all key stakeholders. For *customers,* it might be market share, as well as satisfaction with service, quality, and price. Information may also be collected on the preferences of individual clients so they can be better served and retained. For *employees,* one might track satisfaction, turnover, and skills; for *suppliers and partners,* opinions, repeat business, and expansion and duration of the relationship.

It is useful to regularize the collection of soft, episodic information: Solicit employee suggestions, collect data on customer complaints, and get "stories from the outside." Some firms reward for good suggestions and leads.

Aggregate Information in Space and Time. Information broken down too finely into units and brief intervals can cause people to focus on those slices at the expense of the whole. Wherever possible, the emphasis should be on true and ultimate contributions to overall firm performance. Again, this suggests using abundant nonfinancial information and looking at a unit's long-term contributions. Some of the products and divisions most promising in the long run may be costly losses in the short. Don't let the information systems fool you into aborting these.

Share Information Broadly. Great FCBs let everyone know how the firm is doing and what improvements are needed. They circulate celebratory information: on victories, heroic decisions, employee successes. The company newspaper can be an important part of the information system. Indeed, the best information is useless unless it is talked about by the right people at the right times.

What Everyone in the Company Can Do

The long-term view is not just for CEOs and managers; it must enlist everyone. It relies on attitudes of commitment, integrity, generosity, and consideration throughout the organization. Here are some starting tips for those wishing to play a part.

- *Follow your passion.* Adopt goals that are personally meaningful. Don't squeeze yourself into the job; instead, find the job that fits you and the part of the job that resonates.
- *Use your initiative, not your job description.* Think beyond the boundaries—not about what *is* your job but what *should be* your job—to take best advantage of your skills and help you contribute more to the firm.
- *Do "sweat the small stuff."* There are *some* aspects of your job where doing a little extra contributes a lot and says a good deal about you. Usually, it is those aspects that tie in most closely with the company mission: taking more time with a key client or job, perfecting a design or project, searching for that extra bit of data on a deal.
- *Time stagger your objectives.* Even in the face of short-term demands, keep an eye on long-term goals. Don't just put out fires, work on finding better people, tuning your systems, building the business with new clients, identifying strong partners, and thinking up new ventures.
- *Get people on your side.* Help them before they ask you to. Build networks through your generosity; give before demanding.

- *Communicate face to face.* Keep it simple and informal. Take the shortest distance between two points; go lateral rather than vertical.
- *Resist the urge to be petty about perks and salaries.* Worry more about having enough room to grow and to show your talents.
- *Make decisions that tell people who you really are.* Your decisions should reveal your character and principles. If these don't fit the firm, you may be better off elsewhere anyway.

To close the circle, table 9-3 relates the major recommendations of this chapter to the four C priorities and practices.

Conclusion

The theme behind all these recommendations echoes our message throughout the book: that the only way to sustain good performance is to *act in the long-run interests of the company and all its stakeholders.* First, boards and top managers must be motivated to be courageous and farsighted stewards. Second, they need to concentrate on and invest deeply in a substantive, enduring mission. Third, they must assemble a unified, value-driven staff that uses its initiative for the interests of the whole firm. Finally, they must form enduring, win-win relationships with external partners.

People may object that in all these respects our great FCBs will be hard for non-FCBs to emulate. Patient shareholders are rare, as is family-like trust among top managers and the board. Our governance recommendations, therefore, may sometimes fall on deaf ears. That does not, however, make them any less valid. We know that the path is steep and the difficulties many. But if we look at what these great family businesses have accomplished, the trip seems to be worth it, for owners, employees, clients, and partners, and for society as a whole. Maybe the current economic difficulties Americans are facing, as well as the crisis in corporate confidence, will awaken us all to the weaknesses of the short-term approach and to the promise of a different way.

Table 9-3

The Basis for Recommendations in the C Priorities

	Realm	C Priorities
Governance, Philosophy, Organization	Boards • Incentives and evaluation • Composition and diversity	← Continuity ← Command
	CEO • Selection; apprenticeship; retention	← Continuity
	Top management team • Voice; diversity; tenure	← Command ← Continuity
	Long-run philosophy • Stewardship; substance; capability	← Continuity
	Organization design • Flat organizations; unsiloed	← Community
Functions	Human resources • Choosy; understaffing; training and development; job scope; consideration; minimized distinctions; cheerleading	← Community
	Marketing • Superior offerings; enduring relationships with client and community • Patient promotion	← Connection ← Continuity
	Operations • Infrastructure investments; core capability leveraging; constantly improving the system • Partnering for value chain focus • Better business model	← Continuity ← Connection ← Command
	R&D/Engineering • Broad research philosophy; impracticality and glorious mistakes • Stagger time horizons • Open doors to the lab	← Command ← Continuity ← Community and Connection
	Finance • Generous conservatism	← Continuity
	MIS • Beyond the numbers • Information aggregated and shared	← Continuity ← Community

Description of the Research

O UR RESEARCH BEGAN as a quest for companies that had been able to "survive their success" and keep succeeding for decades. In examining Collins and Porras's classic book, *Built to Last,* we were struck that eleven of their eighteen firms were FCBs at the time of the book's publication or for most of their histories.[1] Things were very different for the fallen stars Danny wrote about in *The Icarus Paradox* (HarperBusiness, 1990)—firms that had thrived, then crashed. Only five of these twenty-four were FCBs. So here FCBs constituted 61 percent (11/18) of the long-term winners versus 21 percent (5/24) of the fallen stars. Was this pure chance? Or could it be that these FCBs were the Paradox beaters: the deliberate ants who could survive the grasshoppers? We decided to dig deeper. We identified over a dozen rigorous empirical studies comparing FCBs and NFBs and found the contrasts reported in the tables of chapter 1. FCBs, it seemed, outlived NFBs, performed better along virtually all indexes of financial performance, and invested more deeply in their people and their capabilities. Given these results, we decided to focus our search for long-term winners on that breed. Just as appealing to us was the neglect of "FCBs *as* FCBs" by organizational researchers and management gurus, and the possibility that these peculiar companies might be marching to a different drum—a new approach that we all could learn from.

The Research

Ours was in every respect an exploratory journey, with many false starts. We will begin by describing our early *pilot study* that identified the common FCB strategies and many of the driving priorities and practices. Then we will describe the sample and methods of the *current study*.

Phase 1: The Pilot Study

Our pilot study had three aims: (1) to find a sample of successful FCBs that had lots written on them; (2) to distinguish among the most common strategies these firms used to build capability and achieve competitive advantage; and (3) to understand and characterize the sources of those capabilities and advantages.

The Sample. We sought the advice of six experts in generating a list of major FCBs that had thrived for a long time and risen to prominence in their markets. From a roster of over 100 firms, we got down to 50 by deleting those for which there was too little information. Files were compiled for each company. These consisted of books, articles, annual reports, Web site information, and financial and market share information. The object was to gather enough qualitative information, usually spanning at least two decades, to gain some insight into what had made these firms succeed.

Different Strategies—Different Animals. From the beginning, it was clear that this was a heterogeneous group whose members pursued very different strategies and competitive advantages. Some companies succeeded primarily through unsurpassed product quality, others via innovation, and still others through brand creation, hyperefficiency, or an ability to seize new opportunities. Clearly, we needed some way of partitioning the sample to reflect these differences. Fortunately, previous research over the years had converged on a number of common strategies believed to sustain competitive advantage.[2] From a master list of ten such strategies we sorted our FCB sample into the different types and found five that were by far the most common. We called them *brand building* (brand differentiation), *craftsmanship* (quality differentiation), *superior operations*, *innovation*, and *deal making*. Over 80 percent of our firms strongly favored one of these. We could now group the companies by strategy and probe the data in a more targeted way.

The Categories for the Analysis. The next challenge was to richly describe the companies to get at the driving priorities, policies, and practices that seemed to support the strategies. Based on our own earlier research on non-FCBs, we started with the broad descriptive categories of organizational culture and structure, decision-making process, and leadership. We employed a checklist of elements for each (e.g., values and indoctrination for culture; decisiveness for leadership; and information technologies for process)—over 100 elements in all.[3] After reading case material on dozens of firms and discussing our findings by category, we found ourselves in a quandary. First, according to many of these categories and elements, the firms were bland—we found few novel organizational designs, little charismatic leadership, and seemingly primitive approaches to decision making. Second, and more important, we were not capturing what *was* clearly exceptional about these firms.

So we returned to the case data, now looking inductively for patterns (trends and gaps) among the original elements and seeking out new ones that might provide clues about the distinctiveness of our firms. Four underlying themes began to emerge, each reflecting a driving priority within the companies. We called these priorities the *four Cs*, and they are described in detail in chapter 2. A new checklist was then created to incorporate their elements.

Performance. Although most of these firms had done well for a long time, some occasionally ran into trouble. Using indicators such as returns (where available), changes in market share, layoff announcements, and other indicators that a firm was struggling, we bifurcated the sample into good and poor performance groups based on double-blind rater assessments.

Extracting and Analyzing Data. Using the new checklist, the team (both authors and an experienced researcher with a master of science in business) reread the materials on each company. We then ticked off the elements that were clearly present within the firm, and provided supportive anecdotal and factual evidence. Checklists were completed double-blind, and resulted in 88 percent agreement about the elements present in each firm.

Findings. The first outputs from our analyses were a set of five typical profiles, one for each strategy for the successful group of firms. We were excited that the firms within each strategy group were remarkably similar both in strategy components and priority elements: If one firm had an element, chances were good that many other successful firms pursuing the same strategy would as well.

When we examined the unsuccessful group, also by strategy, we found similar patterns, except that elements were spottier in their occurrence. Moreover, some priorities manifested especially strongly and consistently, and others hardly at all.

What Was Missing. Although suggestive, the pilot study suffered a number of shortcomings. First, its sample was not systematic: The firms fulfilled no clear selection criteria other than fame, perceived achievement, and availability of information. We wished to have a sample in which *all* firms had achieved true market leadership over a longer period. Second, the strategies, C priorities, and configurations of elements, although evocative, were not sufficiently fine-gained. We needed to peel away additional layers of the onion to characterize strategy more richly, understand the priorities and their elements more deeply, and begin to appreciate their interactions. We also wanted to understand what happens when things go wrong by following the transitions of some outstanding companies from success to failure. Only then would we begin to see how good performance intervals differ from poor ones in the same organization.

Phase 2: The Current Research

The Sample. The first step in the current research was to assemble a sample of truly accomplished FCBs, those that had reached and sustained the number-one or number-two market share in their domains and survived for more than one generation. To identify our long-term winners we applied a set of filters.

1. As a rough surrogate for "accomplishment," we first looked for size, sifting through *Family Business Magazine*'s lists of America's 150 Largest Family Businesses and the World's 200 Largest Family Businesses.
2. We deleted all firms founded within the last forty-five years, as these may not have survived more than one generation of family leadership. (The median age of our *final* sample of winners was 104 years.)
3. We eliminated highly diversified businesses and firms our raters could not reliably classify by strategy. We also eliminated businesses outside America and Europe to avoid steep cultural differences.
4. We selected only businesses that had risen by 1982 or earlier to the number-one or number-two market share positions in their domains, and maintained that position in 2001. Share information was obtained from "The Market Share Reporter," Hoover's, "Off-the-Shelf" Industry Reports, Value Line, 10Ks, and company Web sites.

5. Firms had to be FCBs by our definition for most of the period of study: specifically, the family had to play a key role in setting strategy and fill the office of chairman, CEO, or president. Family members also had to control the largest block of equity or votes.
6. Finally, it was essential that the firms selected be documented sufficiently for us to study them over at least thirty years of history.

These screens resulted in a sample of forty companies, to which we added a single one—J.P. Morgan, a quintessential deal maker, which was our rarest type. Morgan, since the 1940s, is no longer a family business, although Morgan family members have been involved as partners until recently, and many of the bank's policies, practices, and best clients today date back to the family years. The company ruled investment banking under three generations of Morgans, and its history is well documented, evocative, and full of lessons. We couldn't resist.

Any study of success is incomplete without an analysis of failure. Otherwise, it risks celebrating qualities of winners that are just as prevalent among losers. So we gathered a sample of FCBs that had lost their way. These too had done well, but had run into difficulties. We hoped to learn more about success by examining what happens when a thriving organization begins to decline. That is the topic of chapter 8. For that purpose, we identified a troubled sample with the aid of four consultants and academic experts. Seventeen of the candidates identified either had a good deal written about them or were firms we had worked with personally. Another eight were taken from especially challenging intervals in the lives of our winners.

The presentation of findings would be terribly scattered had we written about all forty-one winners and seventeen losers. Although we structure our presentation based on the overall pattern of the findings, chapters 3 to 8 refer directly only to those twenty-four businesses with the richest data, most telling lessons, and for which we have *not* served as consultants. We deliberately salted chapters 3 to 7 with the one or two companies that would run into trouble down the road (e.g., Motorola, O&Y, Nordstrom) in order to revisit them in chapter 8. Table A-1 recaps the sample we feature in the book.

Data Gathering. We assembled extensive files for each company in the sample. Secondary data were collected in the form of series of articles and books that recounted key facts and decisions regarding a company's mission, goals, policies, strategy, leadership, culture, administrative practices, competencies, challenges, and performance.

Secondary sources were identified through Pro-Quest, library, and Internet searches, and searches of business indexes such as the *New York Times* and *Wall Street Journal* indexes. Sources included lengthy book histories, fact-based articles in trade and business magazines, and lengthy investigative newspaper profiles. We also collected information on the public firms in the sample from 10K, Hoover's, and Value Line reports. Hundreds and sometimes thousands of pages of material were collected on each firm, much of it overlapping to ensure the reliability of the data.

We also attempted to interview a firm's executives, consultants, customers, and partners, and succeeded in doing so for ten of our firms. Given the secretive nature of many family firms and our sensitive questions on strategic decisions and mess ups, we assured most of our respondents confidentiality. Consequently, the interviews provided mainly context, as well as a sense of a firm's mission, values, strengths, and weaknesses. Our ultimate quest here was for hard facts that would show the *actual* strategies and practices of the firms, and most of that information came from secondary sources. We should say also that our notions about FCB conduct, advantage, and challenge were significantly influenced by our consulting engagements with thriving and faltering FCBs that we could not mention in the book.

Data Analysis. The analysis was structured based on the preliminary results from the pilot: specifically, the five most common FCB strategies and four C driving priorities. The successful sample was split into five strategy groups by raters working double-blind. There was 95 percent agreement on the classifications; the "disagrees" were deleted. The text and interview materials were then closely read for all firms within a strategy, with each firm being discussed individually.

In extracting information, we were guided by a lengthy checklist of elements: specifically, the strategy components, driving priorities, policies, and practices taken from the pilot study. The list grew, however, as the analysis progressed. For each firm, facts and quotations were gathered to exemplify the operative elements. We then met to ask the following kinds of questions: What were the components of strategy the company used to compete? What were the related core capabilities? How were these supported or impeded by the priorities, policies, and practices? How did the interplay or configuration among all these elements complement or compromise each other?

Having analyzed each firm within a strategy, we then met to go over the data to discuss the key commonalities among *all the successful firms within a given strategy*. We asked which components, elements, and connections seemed common to most firms following the strategy, and which patterns in the data kept appearing again and again. We then performed separate analyses of the troubled firms or periods, again by strategy, following the method described.

At the end of the analysis of a type, we had a skeletal model and a linked array of qualitative data, quotes, and evidence for a strategy chapter. Each chapter went through numerous versions, with the authors meeting to question each draft and target additional data gathering.

Limitations and Future Directions. This book is an exploration, not a proof. It will be useful for subsequent research to employ more rigorous means of operationalizing the priorities and practices we identified, and to determine more systematically their impact on performance in different strategic and industry contexts—for FCBs and non-FCBs alike.

Table A-1

Characteristics of Featured Companies

Notes to this table are found under "Table A-1" in Notes.

	Industry	Strategy	Public/ Private	Founding date	Family name	Sales (millions) 2002	Market position 2002	Number of family in TMT 2002/2003	Number of family directors 2002/2003	Family ownership/ control 2002/2003	Forbes/ Fortune ranking 2002*
1. Adolph Coors Company	Beer	Craftsman	Public	1873	Coors	$3,776	U.K. #2 and U.S. #3 brewer[a, b]	2	2/8	100% Class A (voting power)/33.2 % Class B	†† = 603
2. Bechtel Group, Inc.	Construction services	Deal maker	Private	1898	Bechtel	$11,600	World #2 construction U.S. #1 contractor[b, c]	1	2/16	Majority ownership	† = 6
3. Bombardier Inc. (Canada)	Aircraft and railway equipment	Deal maker	Public	1937	Beaudoin (in-law)/ Bombardier	$13,778	World #1 regional jet and #3 civil aircraft[b]	3	3/13	82% Class A or 63% voting power	††† = 360
4. Cargill, Incorporated	Process/ market agricultural/ food products	Operator	Private	1865	MacMillan (in-law)/ Cargill	$50,826	World #1 grain trader and grower of genetically modified foods[d]	1	6/17	83%	† = 1
5. Compagnie Générale des Établissements Michelin (France)	Tire maker	Innovator	Public	1832	Michelin	$15,645	World #1 or 2 tire maker[b, e]	≥1	1/5	Ownership and voting control	††† = 342

Table A-1

Characteristics of Featured Companies (continued)

	Industry	Strategy	Public/Private	Founding date	Family name	Sales (millions) 2002	Market position 2002	Number of family in TMT 2002/2003	Number of family directors 2002/2003	Family ownership/ control 2002/2003	Forbes/ Fortune ranking 2002*
6. Corning Incorporated	Communications technology	Innovator	Public	1851	Houghton	$2,631	World #1 fiber-optic maker[b]	1	1/13	0.8%	†† = 289
7. The Estée Lauder Companies Inc.	Personal care products	Brand builder	Public	1946	Lauder	$4,744	World #2 prestige cosmetics/ U.S. #1 prestige cosmetics[a, b, c]	4	3/9	91% Class A (voting power)	†† = 360
8. Fidelity Investments (part of FMR Corp.)	Investment services	Innovator	Private	1946	Johnson	$8,900	World #1 mutual fund company[b]	3	4/n.d.	49% (voting power)	† = 10
9. Hallmark Cards, Inc.	Printing and publishing	Brand builder	Private	1910	Hall	$4,200	World #1 greeting cards[b]	≥2	3/≥7	67%	† = 32
10. IKEA International A/S (Sweden)	Furniture retailer	Operator	Private	1943	Kamprad	$10,980	World #1 furniture retailer[f]	≥4	≥4/n.d.	100% (Kamprad foundation)	n.a.

Table A-1

Characteristics of Featured Companies (continued)

	Industry	Strategy	Public/ Private	Founding date	Family name	Sales (millions) 2002	Market position 2002	Number of family in TMT 2002/2003	Number of family directors 2002/2003	Family ownership/ control 2002/2003	Forbes/ Fortune ranking 2002*
11. J.P. Morgan & Co., Inc.	Financial services	Deal maker	Public	1838; family-led until 1943	Morgan	$43,372	1910-30: U.S. #1 security underwriter; 2002: U.S.#1 private bank/ #2 financial services [b, g]	n.a.	n.a.	n.a.	†† = 21 ††† = 54 ** = 38
12. J.R Simplot Company	Processs/ market food/ agricultural products	Operator	Private	1929	Simplot	>$3,000	World #1 processor of frozen potatoes/ World #2 processor of frozen vegetables [b, h]	2	4/9	100%	† = 51
13. L.L. Bean, Inc.	Outdoor sporting goods and apparel	Brand builder	Private	1912	Gorman (Bean descen-dants)	$1,070	World #1 outdoor speciality products and sports retailer catalog [c]	≥1	n.d.	majority ownership (>95%)	† = 221

Table A-1

Characteristics of Featured Companies (*continued*)

	Industry	Strategy	Public/ Private	Founding date	Family name	Sales (millions) 2002	Market position 2002	Number of family in TMT 2002/2003	Number of family directors 2002/2003	Family ownership/ control 2002/2003	Forbes/ Fortune ranking 2002*
14. Levi Strauss and Co.	Apparel	Brand builder	Private	1853	Haas, Stern (Strauss descendants)	$4,137	World #1 brand-name apparel manufacturer[b]	1	4/14	100%	† =23 ** = 23
15. Motorola, Inc.	Communication technology	Innovator	Public	1928	Galvin	$26,679	World #2 mobile handsets[b]	1	1/13	2.6%	†† = 56 ††† = 138
16. Nordstrom, Inc.	Apparel retailer	Craftsman	Public	1901	Nordstrom	$5,975	US #2 upscale department store[c]	4	3/11	27.9%	†† = 314 * = 92 ** = 36
17. Olympia & York Developments Ltd. (Canada)	Real estate	Deal maker	Public	1955–1992	Reichmann	n.a.	n.a.	n.a.	n.a.	n.a.	n.a.

Table A-1

Characteristics of Featured Companies (continued)

	Industry	Strategy	Public/ Private	Founding date	Family name	Sales (millions) 2002	Market position 2002	Number of family in TMT 2002/2003	Number of family directors 2002/2003	Family ownership/ control 2002/2003	Forbes/ Fortune ranking 2002*
18. S.C. Johnson & Son, Inc.	Personal and household products	Brand builder	Private	1886	Johnson/ Lewis (cousins)	$5,000	World #1/2 consumer household brands in 15 product categories/ U.S. #1 or #2 in nearly every major category[i]	2	3/10	100%	† = 20 * = 29 ** = 37
19. Tetra Pak AB (part of Tetra Laval S.A.) (Sweden)	Packaging	Innovator	Private	1943	Rausing	€7,500	World #1 liquid food processing and packaging company[j]	n.d.	3/n.d.	100%	n.a.
20. The New York Times Company	Diversified media	Craftsman	Public	1851	Sulzberger (Ochs descen- dants)	$3,079	N.Y. #1 and U.S. #3 circulation/ #1 news- paper site on the Web[c, k]	2	4/13	35.4% Class A and 87.6% Class B (voting power)	†† = 500 * = 93
21. The Timken Company	Bearings and alloy/ specialty steel	Craftsman	Public	1899	Timken	$2,550	America #1 and World #3 bearing co.[b, l]	3	4/12	18.9%	†† = 598

Table A-1

Characteristics of Featured Companies (*continued*)

	Industry	Strategy	Public/Private	Founding date	Family name	Sales (millions) 2002	Market position 2002	Number of family in TMT 2002/2003	Number of family directors 2002/2003	Family ownership/control 2002/2003	Forbes/Fortune ranking 2002*
22. Tyson Foods, Inc.	Processor and marketer of beef/chicken/pork	Operator	Public	1935	Tyson	$23,367	World #1 meat processor and marketer (beef/chicken/pork)[b]	2	3/15	99.9% Class B and 80.2% voting power	†† = 177 ††† = 468
23. W.L. Gore and Associates, Inc.	Textiles–non-apparel	Innovator	Private	1958	Gore	$1,230	Gore-Tex world #1 waterproof, windproof, breathable fabric[m, n]	≥2	"Several family members on its board"[o]	75%	† = 199 * = 27
24. Wal-Mart Stores, Inc.	Retail	Operator	Public	1945	Walton	$244,524	World #1 retailer[b]	1	2/13	38.9%	†† = 1 ††† = 1

†† U.S. 500 Private Companies ("America's Private Giants," *Forbes* November 25, 2002, 174+); †† U.S. 500 Public Companies ("Fortune 500: Largest U.S. Corporations," *Fortune*, April 15, 2002, F1+); ††† Global 500 Public Companies (Paola Hjelt, "Fortune Global 500: The World's Largest Corporations," *Fortune*, July 22 2002, 144+); * U.S. 100 Best Companies to Work for (Robert Levering and Milton Moskowitz, "100 Best Companies to Work for," *Fortune*, January 20, 2003, 127+); ** U.S. 50 Best Companies for Minorities (Jonathan Hickman, "50 Best Companies for Minorities," *Fortune*, July 8, 2002, 110+).

Assessment Grid and Checklist

THIS APPENDIX PRESENTS a grid and checklist for you to use to start a conversation about your firm's priorities and capabilities and how they stack up against our winners and losers. The first part consists of a simple assessment grid. The second part presents a checklist of potentially helpful policies and practices by strategy, all derived from chapters 3 to 7. After scoring the instrument and discussing the results, it will be useful to examine the relevant parts of the checklist to get a more fine-grained idea of what may be missing in your firm and some possible steps for improvement.

It is important to bear in mind that it is not the individual items on the list that are so critical; it is their *configuration,* their fit with the selected strategy, and their comprehensiveness and complementarity in supporting that strategy.

Assessing Your Own Company

Classifying Your Company

The grid is quick to complete. First, to determine which grids to fill out, you need to identify the primary strategy or strategies of your company—classified here according to the major sources of competitive advantage being pursued. Chose a maximum of two *primary* sources of intended or actual competitive advantage from among the following:

- A superior brand (Grid A)
- Exceptional quality capabilities (Grid B)
- Business model superiority and excellence in operations (Grid C)
- New products and technologies (Grid D)
- Spotting and executing on diverse opportunities or one-off deals (Grid E)

Respond *only* to the one or two grids you just selected. To verify that the strategy chosen is indeed the one most central to your firm's mission, you should confirm that more than half the items of the Strategy section are company objectives, realized or not. Now you are ready to complete the grid.

Scoring the Grid

In responding to the grid, insert a checkmark opposite the question in the "Your firm" column *only* if the statement holds true for your firm, or at least seems more true than false. This indicates that the statement describes the *current reality* at your firm. Where possible, use your major competitors as the comparison. For now, ignore the last two prerated columns. Instructions for interpretation follow the grids. It would be useful for several members from different managerial levels and functions of the firm to fill out the grid independently.

Grid A

Brand Building

Mark a "√" in the "Your firm" column if the statement describes the current reality at your company. Otherwise leave the space blank.

	Your firm	Levi's A	Levi's B
Strategy			
Products stand out as being distinctive and have special appeal to the targeted client		√	
Promotion is exceptionally original, and effective			
Brand quality and consistency keep products attractive		√	√
Brands are well leveraged and grown via careful variations		√	
Proportion of √ (__/4):	__ %	0.8	0.3
Continuity—Major priority			
The firm invests more generously than its rivals in brand creation and development		√	
A focused mission or competency prevents polluting or over-extending brands		√	√

Brand Building *(continued)*

	Your firm	Levi's	
		A	B
The company is very patient in getting its brands just right		√	
There is great reluctance to depart from traditional market segments*			√
Most sales come from products over 5 years old*			√
Proportion of √ (__/3):	__ %	1.0	0.3
Community—Major priority			
Strong traditions and shared values make for a clear brand identity		√	√
Training and indoctrination communicate well the essence of the brand		√	√
Generous treatment of staff builds a corps of brand boosters		√	
Tight parameters guide hiring			
Questioning any aspect of the brand is frowned upon*			
Core time is spend ensuring the integrity of the brand than determining its appeal*			√
Proportion of √ (__/4):	__ %	0.8	0.5
Connection—Complementary priority			
Executives serve as good brand ambassadors			
Relations with the outside community improve and complement the brand image		√	√
Market reactions are monitored carefully to adapt and renew brands		√	
Proportion of √ (__/3):	__ %	0.7	0.3
Command—Complementary priority			
Leaders are free to act courageously to build or reshape the brand		√	
Leaders can be original in their branding and promotion strategies		√	√
Proportion of √ (__/2):	__ %	1.0	0.5

Craftsmanship

Mark a "√" in the "Your firm" column if the statement describes the current reality at your company. Otherwise leave the space blank.

	Your firm	Coors	
		A	**B**
Strategy			
The firm creates the best products and processes in its domain		√	√
Quality keeps improving year after year		√	
Core competencies are focussed and keep growing		√	√
Those competencies are effectively leveraged across different product or market opportunities			
Proportion of √ (__/4):	__ %	0.8	0.5
Continuity—Major priority			
There is a proud quality tradition		√	√
An inspiring mission elicits a deep sense of purpose		√	
Sacrifice and unusually deep investments underwrite quality		√	√
Lengthy apprenticeships foster craftsmanship		√	
Core competencies and tacit knowledge are key competitive advantages here		√	√
The company is often inflexible and blinded by tradition*			√
Changes to adapt or cater to the market opportunities are slow*		√	√
Proportion of √ (__/5):	__ %	1.0	0.6
Community—Major priority			
People at all levels use their initiative to improve quality			
Compelling values get everyone on the quality bandwagon		√	
Reward, punishment and hiring practices support these values; misfits are ejected		√	
Training and indoctrination are superior		√	
The firm is generous to its people, and elicits their loyalty		√	√
The engineering or operations functions are far too influential*			√
There are major conflicts between the functions*			√
Proportion of √ (__/5):	__ %	0.8	0.2

Craftsmanship *(continued)*

	Your firm	Coors	
		A	B
Connection—Complementary Priority			
The company works well with suppliers to improve inputs and quality		√	
Managers work closely with clients to renew and adapt offerings			
Good relations with the community attract excellent employees		√	
Proportion of √ (__/3):	__ %	0.7	0.0
Command—Complementary Priority			
Leaders are free to impose, and are effective in attaining, the highest standards		√	√
A robust TMT helps ensure relevant and evolving quality		√	
Proportion of √ (__/2):	__ %	1.0	0.5

Superior Operations

Mark a "√" in the "Your firm" column if the statement describes the current reality at your company. Otherwise leave the space blank.

	Your firm	Tyson A	Tyson B
Strategy			
An unusually potent, often original business model is embraced		√	√
Effectiveness is enhanced via state-of-the art infrastructures		√	√
The firm focuses on parts of the value chain it excels at, partnering well with others for the rest		√	
Price and cost-driven clients are the primary market targets		√	√
Proportion of √ (__/4):	__ %	1.0	0.8
Continuity—Major priority			
Executives think constantly about improving the infrastructure			
All resources are husbanded with painstaking care		√	
Leaders happily sacrifice returns until the system is just right		√	√
Top management tenures are especially lengthy		√	
The company exhausts resources by rapidly expanding its infrastructure and scope*			√
There is great reluctance to modify systems and procedures*			
Proportion of √ (__/4):	__ %	0.8	0.3
Connection—Major priority			
Generous investments are made to form good relationships with value chain partners		√	√
The company works to be responsive to and expand relationships with major clients		√	√
The firm acts with honesty and openness towards all its partners (and the public)		√	
Extensive lobbying and political connections help skirt competition or regulations*			√
Partnerships are stressed by a lack of cooperation or complementarity*			
Proportion of √ (__/3):	__ %	1.0	0.7

Superior Operations *(continued)*

	Your firm	Tyson	
		A	**B**
Command—Complementary Priority			
Leaders can quickly commit major resources to improve and expand infrastructure		√	√
Leaders are free to evolve a bold, original business model		√	√
Proportion of √ (__/2):	__ %	1.0	1.0
Community—Complementary Priority			
Good ideas surface from throughout the firm for system improvement			
Client-facing employees are well trained, reliable, and responsive		√	√
The system is dehumanizing to many employees*			√
Proportion of √ (__/2):	__ %	0.5	0.5

Innovation

Mark a "√" in the "Your firm" column if the statement describes the current reality at your company. Otherwise leave the space blank.

	Your firm	Corning	
		A	**B**
Strategy			
The firm makes path breaking innovations		√	√
These are separated by long periods of persistent incremental innovation		√	
Commercialization is avidly enhanced by cost reduction and product improvement		√	√
The firm itself is often the one to obsolete its products		√	√
Proportion of √ (__/4):	__ %	1.0	0.8
Command—Major priority			
Executives are free to be creative and original		√	√
The top management team has broad skills, and members work well together		√	√
Executives invest boldly and wisely to encourage innovation		√	
Focus has been on more and more ambitious projects*			√
Tolerance for risk keeps growing*			√
Proportion of √ (__/3):	__ %	1.0	0.7
Community—Major priority			
Units from across the firm collaborate well on innovation projects		√	
People are treated exceptionally well—in compensation, benefits and challenge		√	√
People deeply believe in the values and mission of the organization		√	
Staff have lots of leeway and motivation to start new initiatives		√	√
Rich, informal communication networks span the organization		√	
Many departments have little voice in the organization*			
This is a company dominated by engineers and technology geeks*			√
Proportion of √ (__/5):	__ %	1.0	0.4

Innovation *(continued)*

	Your firm	Corning	
		A	B
Continuity—Complementary Priority			
The company invests more resources than its rivals in long term innovations		√	√
Innovations build on a thematic core competency		√	
Risks are managed well and the firm is a careful steward of resources		√	
Proportion of √ (__/3):	__ %	1.0	0.3
Connection—Complementary Priority			
Productive innovation partnerships are formed with leading edge clients		√	√
The firm is close enough to its markets to tailor innovations to opportunities		√	
Productive alliances exist between your firm and other organizations to enhance innovation		√	√
Proportion of √ (__/3):	__ %	1.0	0.7

Deal Making

Mark a "√" in the "Your firm" column if the statement describes the current reality at your company. Otherwise leave the space blank.

	Your firm	O&Y A	O&Y B
Strategy			
The firm excels at being first to spot opportunities		√	√
It has a high hit rate to capture those opportunities		√	√
Superior execution comes from deep knowledge		√	√
Superior execution comes from partnering abilities		√	
Learning is transferred effectively across projects and opportunities		√	
Proportion of √ (__/5):	__ %	1.0	0.6
Command—Major priority			
Leaders are free to act quickly to commit resources		√	√
Trust and complementarity characterize the top team		√	
Leaders are free to pursue brave, contrarian deals		√	√
The CEO is becoming more and more powerful versus others on the top team*			√
Risks have been growing with every project*			√
Proportion of √ (__/3):	__ %	1.0	0.7
Connection—Major priority			
Long term relationships are favored over transactions		√	
Contacts are cultivated easily with partners, potential clients, governments		√	√
Reputation and trustworthiness elevate contacts into relationships		√	√
The company works well with external partners to carry out projects and deals		√	√
Partnerships are driven by cronyism more than functionality*			
Lobbying and political connections are seen to be as important as skills and merit*			
Proportion of √ (__/4):	__ %	1.0	0.8

Deal Making *(continued)*

	Your firm	O&Y	
		A	**B**
Continuity—Complementary Priority			
Deals and projects build on core competencies		√	
Ample stewardship prevents excessive risk taking or squandering of resources		√	
Apprenticeships pass along contacts and deal making skills to new leaders		√	
Proportion of √ (__/3):	__ %	1.0	0.0
Community—Complementary Priority			
The culture is lean and entrepreneurial (informal, flat, decentralized)		√	√
People work together well in temporary project teams		√	√
Proportion of √ (__/2):	__ %	1.0	1.0

Scoring and Interpretation

The first step in scoring is to count the number of checkmarks you have indicated in each category (strategy, continuity, etc.) next to the *unstarred* items (i.e. items not marked with an asterisk), and express this as a fraction of the total number of unstarred items in the category.

If half or fewer of the unstarred items are marked, this may point to significant weakness in a category. For the Strategy category, this outcome suggests that essential capabilities are missing. This same result will be of particular concern in a category that is a *major* C priority for the strategy in question. Here category weakness indicates that a central pillar of long-run success is not in place—recalling the blunting syndrome of chapter 8. To show strength on a major C, at least 75 percent of the items should be marked. Specific items left blank give clues about what is missing—about gaps in the configuration.

For the *complementary* C priorities of a strategy, potential weakness again is suggested by having half or more of the items blank. Although these weaknesses are less serious than those in a major category, they indicate that the firm is "not covering all the bases," that it lacks the full complement of tools, and therefore the resilience to support the strategy over the long haul. This danger is compounded where a checkmark is filled in for the *starred* items in a major C. Here the Icarus Paradox described in chapter 8 threatens. Indeed, checking off any of the starred items suggests that excesses may be occurring in a major priority category, and these will be especially dangerous when accompanied by a weakness in any complementary priority. A firm may do well in the short run with only a few strengths. But as illustrated in chapter 8, a few gaps or excesses can torpedo even a company with very profound capabilities and resources.

Scores for Some of Our FCBs

To give raters a basis for comparison, we scored some of the firms of chapters 3 to 8. The scores are presented in the last two columns of the grid. Column A shows the firm's ratings when it was doing well; column B scores the troubled situations reported in chapter 8. The brief descriptions that follow describe what went wrong as the firm ran into trouble.

Grid A: Levi Strauss's strategy scores in column B indicate that the brand is not being renewed or leveraged. Some aspects of continuity (sticking to traditional market niches) have become excessive, while others (investment in the brand) have declined. Community has become too insular, resulting in weaker connection with the market. In the terminology of chapter 8, column B gives evidence of "excessive majors" (continuity and community) and "eroding complements."

Grid B: Coors too showed excesses of the continuity major (the starred items) as it became mired in stifling traditions. Community exhibited both excesses and weaknesses: excesses in a clannishness that empowered only brewmasters while alienating marketers, and weaknesses in an intolerant organization rife with labor conflict. The connection complement atrophied as well as the firm failed to adapt to its market.

Grid C: Tyson Foods got into legal trouble with excesses of cronyism (connection) and problems with the unions (community). It also expanded into areas it knew too little about—a lapse in stewardship (continuity).

Grid D: Corning displayed excesses of command as it undertook too much risk in the fiber-optics business and got out of more stable lines. Continuity also declined as the company abandoned incremental innovation in favor of pathbreaking discovery—with risks poorly managed and traditions weakening. Ultimately, community and connection suffered from the required downsizing.

Grid E: The O&Y profiles show hubris affecting command as the CEO seized too much power and took excessive risks. Continuity faltered as O&Y departed from its areas of competency and failed to exercise appropriate stewardship over resources.

Discussion of Grid Results

As noted, it will be especially useful if several managers from different levels and functions in the firm complete the grid independently, and then meet to discuss the scores. Discrepancies may be due to people having different experiences or to genuine disagreements about the situation in the company. Where there are many respondents, it will be helpful to sort results by function, division, or level of hierarchy to surface areas of difference within the company. Those differences can be used as a backdrop in discussing the firm's current and intended sources of advantage, capabilities, and gaps along the Cs.

Self-Assessment Checklist

Having attained some sense of your firm's gaps and excesses, it may be useful to revisit the salutary elements we have extracted from the histories of our great FCBs. The balance of this appendix lays these out on a checklist, organized by strategy and by Cs.

Of course, each firm and the challenges it faces are different. So managers must use the list not as dogma but as a basis for conversation. Focus will ultimately have to be on the melody not the notes; the configuration, not its elements. We also caution that our recommendations typically need to be viewed *relative to one's rivals*. So if we say "pay, promote, or invest generously," it should be read as "versus one's better competitors," not "versus some minimal standard."

The checklist concentrates *only* on the C practices and policies, which are more actionable than the complex capabilities that make up a strategy. Managers should therefore review chapters 3 to 7 for the more subtle capability and market positioning components of their chosen strategy, as well as for the rich examples of how the Cs play out in configuration.

A. Brand Building

A.1—*Pursuing the Dream: Continuity*

1. *Patience* is not just a virtue in brand creation, it is a top priority. Brands that stand out and attain popularity are usually of high quality, original, or capable of forming a unique emotional relationship with a customer. All these things take time to achieve, and their absence can be fatal, so the best brand builders wait until they get things absolutely right before fully launching their brands.
2. If there is one thing that stands out among successful brand builders, it is the depth, consistency, and duration of *investment,* vis-à-vis rivals, in promotion, product improvement, and all other aspects of marketing.
3. A brand is a treasure, never to be cheapened or threatened by inadequate *stewardship* or *focus*. Banned absolutely are elements that might contaminate the brand, along with extensions that erode it.
4. Brands are subtle, as much in the mind of the customer as in the product. Through lengthy *executive apprenticeships*, often extending to several decades, top managers learned what their brands were all about: image, psychology, scope, and limits; how to relate to the customer; and how to sell, distribute, and leverage. It was only by watching the previous generation make decisions in these realms that such subtleties could be understood.

A.2—Uniting the Tribe Behind the Brand: Community

1. More fundamental than the image of a brand are the *values* and *traditions* that support it. These compel delivery of a fine product in an ethical way, help employees understand the brand, motivate them to nurture it, and ultimately, enhance the image of the company. Recall the many ways in which L.L. Bean celebrated its value of enhancing life experiences through nature: training programs, outings, summer camps, dress code, employee benefits, charitable work—even idyllic location of facilities.

2. As important as values are *indoctrination* and *socialization*, which extend from the top to the bottom of the organization, and are relentless. Indoctrination via courses, meetings, policies, and personal feedback makes the brand something to believe in. It explains *very specifically* a brand's mystique, and defines its elements, so people will know how to sell, make, and develop it (recall Estée Lauder's choreographic sales manuals).

3. *Selectivity* determines whom to hire and promote. Firms evolve criteria on who fits exactly the image of the brand and the values of the firm. And they follow through on this in all their human resources decisions. Even at some of the largest companies, the families personally were in charge of all key hires.

4. Because brands rely so much on feelings, emotions, and gently connecting with the client's psyche, highly motivated people may be needed to create or deliver superior offerings. To accomplish that, firms get everyone on board through *genuine consideration*, generous treatment, and putting people into jobs that best use their talents.

A.3—Being Good Neighbors: Connection

1. Brand builders connect robustly with the market. Occasionally, leaders help that process by acting as *ambassadors* and *figureheads*. But firms also connect in another way: by *taking the pulse of the market*, listening to salespeople, distributors, and clients, and making sure the brand is still in tune with what people want.

2. Brand builders stand to benefit from a positive connection to the broader community, via good *corporate citizenship*, charitable works, exemplary trade and employment decisions, and so on. These are not token gestures, but ethical practices so outstanding as to attract attention.

A.4—Freedom to Act Courageously: Command

1. Unless an offering is original, it is not a brand. In creating a brand, leaders do best when they are *empowered to go against the grain,* to experiment with new products, client relationships, and modes of promotion. Thus, the best brands are fashioned not by copycat committees that shave the edges off a good idea, but by courageous leaders marching to their own drum.
2. All brand leaders risk stagnation and insularity, in part because of their emphasis on continuity and community. Therefore, executives require the *courage* to phase out their fading brands early, and to create new ones before the old ones go bad.

B. Craftsmanship

B.1—Pursuing the Dream: Continuity

1. Craftsmen are imbued with their *quality mission*, and this is evident everywhere. We are not talking about credos on a bulletin board, but substantive matters such as where the money goes, who is hired and promoted, what they are rewarded for, the scope of the product line, vertical integration decisions, and so on. Otherwise, the firm only delivers quality, it doesn't lead in quality; still less does it sustain that leadership. *Traditions* are also very rich here. These, however, do not mire firms in yesterday or make them victims of tomorrow but serve as quality sentinels that eternally bar mediocrity.
2. Craftsmanship is not about making an excellent product. It's about doing something better than anyone else. Managers must discover exactly what that something is: what tacit knowledge and collective skills the firm has that gives it its quality advantage. They need, in short, to identify the *core competencies* that distinguish the firm, the ones that create advantage and must serve as the focal points for development and leveraging. Great FCBs were extremely centered in this regard. They knew where and why they were good, and played these strengths for all they were worth.
3. Quality is not about dollops of investment but *continuous investment*. Our companies invested in products and processes, in short- and in long-term projects, in supplies, and in distribution. They also outstripped their rivals in the focus and intensity of this

investment. Consequently, payouts to shareholders were modest to keep capability-building resources within the company.

4. Quality takes time to institutionalize and time to teach. It is complex, and a product of lore, values, and tradition as much as technique. Therefore, executive *tenures* and *apprenticeships* are helpful.

B.2—*Uniting the Tribe: Community*

1. Craftsmen must articulate values as *priorities* everyone understands, so people know what and what not to do, understand that X is more important than Y, and grasp how to make the inevitable trade-offs. The values must be reflected not only in what managers say, but in who runs the company and how they behave and decide. Actions speak, as credos sleep.

2. Our firms hire, train, promote, and fire on the basis of *quality*. They stack the company with quality-conscious people, and indoctrinate them until they are quality addicts. Everyone at the company subscribes to the motto: "The people make the place."

3. Craftsmen are *generous to employees,* according them loyalty, good compensation, and the opportunity for glory. That is why people put their heart and soul into the pursuit of excellence. But those who perform poorly are rejected. These are intolerant cultures.

4. Craftsmen *liberate initiative* and harness ingenuity as well as effort. They are not big on bureaucracy. Instead, clear priorities, reward systems, and symbolic actions get people thinking the right way. Rules and operating procedures are pared down to essentials, while people are encouraged to think about how to improve quality. Firms have few layers of management, broad job definitions, and an atmosphere of informality.

B.3—*Being Responsive to Customers: Connection*

Firms avoid too narrow a definition of quality by *connecting closely* with clients and prospective clients to understand their reactions to the firm and its offerings. Joint ventures with suppliers and customers also keep the firm relevant, as can a close watch on the competition. It is not that craftsmen follow their rivals; rather, they know why they are doing things differently and why that makes sense in the light of their capabilities and opportunities.

B.4—*Spry Top Teams: Command*

1. Without diversity and *frank interchange* on the top management team, quality can become the road to irrelevance. Family marketing executives at some winners could confront their relatives in engineering. Of course, they would never let quality take a back seat; but they could adapt it to be more pertinent.
2. Quality leaders in it for the long haul ultimately have to make *courageous trade-offs*. They sacrifice family time for commitment to work, marketing for quality, easy improvements for truly ambitious ones, and quick profits and growth for ultimate excellence.

C. Superior Operations

C.1—*Pursuing the Dream of the Perfect System: Continuity*

1. Inimitable efficiency comes only from *superior long-term investment* in capabilities and infrastructure. Operators invest more deeply than their rivals in facilities and equipment. And they never stop improving the system via standardization, integration, and expansion.
2. Managers patiently *sacrifice* to keep building and improving the system until they get it just right. They give up profits today for rewards well down the road. They also *stay at the job* for many years to amass the resources and influence needed to build an integrated system with enough critical mass to survive.
3. Operators must be *good resource stewards* because of the steep investment requirements. They need to conserve capital for building the system, get costs down to preserve their tight margins, and stick to essentials. They also need to concentrate only on what they do best. Which brings us to connection.

C.2—*Being Good Partners: Connection*

1. To thrive with their business model, operators find good partners. This usually requires them to be the first to ante up to build a relationship. To gain access to the best candidates up and down the value chain, firms are especially *generous with partners*. Recall IKEA's major investments to build its *suppliers'* infrastructures.

2. Operators work hard to *protract and expand their better relationships*. They do this not only with investment but by being especially *open and responsive*: for example, tailoring outputs to specific clients, tuning their logistics systems to outsiders, sharing information, and so on—and always doing more than their rivals in these respects.

C.3—*Freedom to Act Boldly and Differently: Command*

1. The greatest economies come not from brute effort but *creative, unorthodox business models*: original ways of doing things that offer a unique value proposition by devising a novel system of production and delivery. Original models like those of IKEA, Wal-Mart, and Cargill can only be pursued by independent leaders who are not threatened by shortsighted investors.
2. There is a real danger of stagnation among Operators, as they focus so intently on efficiency and integrated operations that they may neglect to change to capture new opportunities and adapt. But leaders here had the *power to make big changes*, even to dismantle and radically adapt the infrastructure.

C.4—*Community—Sometimes*

There is a temptation among many operators to treat their workers as cogs. But the best ideas for improving the system often come from the lower echelons. At IKEA and the old Wal-Mart, *legions were enlisted* in the battle to improve operations and offerings and reduce costs. Community matters, especially for those operators whose systems require a great deal of adaptation and where there is much contact between employees and clients.

D. Innovation

D.1—*Freedom to Innovate Boldly: Command*

1. Conformity and convention are the sworn enemies of innovation. So these leaders and executives have the courage and the freedom to be *unorthodox* and to chart new paths. They embrace projects with uncertain payoffs and unfamiliar parameters. They also act with *speed* to get the jump on rivals and stay ahead of them in what often proves to be a long and exhausting race.

2. A *diverse, collaborative top management team* brings a multiplicity of viewpoints to complex innovation projects. Diversity of perspective mitigates risks, while easy collaboration allows for speedy action. Leaders benefit from being part of a tight-knit team that spans both technical and commercial spheres. Another wrinkle is having *older and younger* managers serve as coleaders to preserve tradition while heeding the winds of change.

D.2—Uniting the Tribe in Creative Collaboration: Community

1. *Strong values* concerning discovery and its purpose guide and motivate innovation. They channel people's daily decisions and provide a sense of the job's importance. Hence, they must be clearly prioritized and communicated.
2. Innovators never forget that employees are the sole sources of innovation, via their knowledge, talents, and ideas. So firms *invest deeply in human resources*, finding and hiring the right people, training and socializing them (recall Gore's mentors), and putting them in a harmonious work environment in which their skills and creativity will blossom.
3. Especially key is the provision of *latitude:* (1) to grow in a job and use one's initiative, (2) to move into positions that make the best use of one's talents, and (3) to fail without fear of punishment in the pursuit of innovation. That is the only way to get people to use the full power of their minds to contribute.
4. Innovation happens only when there is ample *collaboration* among those with different skills and from different units and functions. As at Gore, networks and networking is promoted via sponsorship, co-location, and cross-functional team formation, so that innovation is not simply creative, but market-relevant. Bureaucracy, vertical silos, and labyrinthine hierarchies are avoided, as are incentives focusing only on the individual and the bottom line.

D.3—Managing Innovation's Risks: Continuity

1. The risks of innovation must be moderated by careful stewardship. To do that, firms stayed within their realms of *core competency*. Tetra Pak stuck to packaging, Michelin mostly to tires. That way they could focus investment and build cumulatively on past discoveries

to stay ahead. That said, they avoided overdependence on any one product or market.

2. Firms carefully *husband resources*. Michelin did indeed spend a good deal more on R&D than its rivals, and it invested relentlessly in developing the best process technology. But it skimped on all the extras. Offices were Spartan and costs were policed without mercy.

3. Leaders of innovative companies are often meddlers, closely monitoring the company and *assessing the risk* of major projects. They involve themselves in the details because innovation *is* such a risky strategy.

D.4—*Being Good Partners to Assure Relevance: Connection*

1. *Connection with outsiders*—customers, suppliers, and research partners—can help counter insularity in a tight culture and ensure that innovations will be relevant. Corning's myriad partnerships with clients like RCA and GE allowed it to combine its own expertise with its partners', while ensuring the desirability and market of its product.

E. Deal Making

E.1—*Freedom to Pursue Opportunities: Command*

1. A conventional deal is of little advantage. Leaders therefore are *free* to take *calculated risks,* to make unconventional arrangements and boldly commit resources when the occasion demands. Paradoxically, it was the ingenuity and contrary nature of many of our companies' deals that actually *reduced* their risks. Bombardier, Bechtel, and O&Y, for example, would buy when the market was depressed, and pioneered unorthodox construction and financing techniques that greatly cut costs.

2. The best *top teams* bring to bear multiple perspectives to a complex deal, and communicate with frankness and speed. Member differences in risk tolerance and perspective ensure that the bolder members will not overextend the company.

3. Leaders must have the *"magic"* to sniff out and consummate good deals. This is as much an art as a science, which means that getting the right executives is critical.

E.2—Being Good Partners: Connection

1. Contacts are the lifeblood of most of these firms, and what distinguish them from their rivals. Successful executives *cultivate* these contacts, and get to know those who might help flag opportunities and execute projects. They build these contacts by striving to be useful to clients and potential partners well before the prospect of business is at hand.
2. Relationships are *prolonged* by investing in them, even when there is no imminent chance of new business. Partners stay in touch because the firms serve them with useful advice, connections, and resources—whether they are currently working together or not.
3. Because of their honesty, expertise, and the useful network they bring to projects, firms *work well with partners* to execute jobs.

E.3—Learning and Managing Risks: Continuity

1. Deal makers try to offset their significant risks by *sticking to areas of expertise* and continually deepening their knowledge to safeguard the company. They focus on projects they understand better than anyone else. In fact, they do so much homework before any deal that there is little chance for surprise. To reduce uncertainty and enhance economies of *learning*, companies modularize the work, using the same elements or templates in numerous projects. Recall Bechtel's scalable power plants and O&Y's standardized building modules.
2. Firms *spread their risks*. Although there is focus, it is not too narrow, too dependent, say, on one sector of the economy or type of project, client, or region. These firms also reduce risks by getting partners to invest in major projects.
3. To avoid the risks of a "one-man show," gifted deal-making executives pass on their skills through tutoring, coaching, and close *apprenticeships*.

E.4—Uniting the Tribe: Community

1. The culture is *entrepreneurial*, with few levels of hierarchy and lots of discretion at the project and business unit level.

2. Given the project nature of much of the work, firms are *flexibly organized*: able to recombine staff from various functions, business units, and geographies, and to marshal them around different projects. Staff work together for a while and then disband, only to reorganize with a different set of partners. Thus people are good communicators and able to work well in teams and across units—they are, in fact, hired for those skills.

Chapter 9 goes into greater detail on specific actions everyone can take to manage for the long run, and in the interests of *all* of their stakeholders—not just managers, but employees, owners, customers, partners, and the larger community.

Notes

Introduction

1. Thomas J. Peters and Robert H. Waterman Jr., *In Search of Excellence: Lessons From America's Best-Run Companies* (New York: Harper & Row, 1982); James C. Collins and Jerry I. Porras, *Built to Last: Successful Habits of Visionary Companies* (New York: HarperBusiness, 1994); Michael Treacy and Fred Wiersema, *The Discipline of Market Leaders: Choose Your Customers, Narrow Your Focus, Dominate Your Market* (Reading, MA: Addison-Wesley, 1995); Danny Miller, *The Icarus Paradox: How Exceptional Companies Bring About Their Own Downfall* (New York: HarperBusiness, 1990).

2. Alfred D. Chandler, *Scale and Scope: The Dynamics of Industrial Capitalism* (Cambridge, MA: Belknap Press, 1990).

3. 2001 Academic Conference. "Theories of the Family Enterprise: Establishing Paradigms for the Field" (Edmonton, Alberta: University of Alberta, September 27–28, 2001).

4. Ronald C. Anderson and David M. Reeb, "Founding-Family Ownership and Firm Performance: Evidence from the S&P 500," *Journal of Finance* 58, no. 3 (June 2003): 1301–1328; Kelin E. Gersick et al., *Generation to Generation: Life Cycles of the Family Business* (Boston: Harvard Business School Press, 1997).

5. Melissa Carey Shanker and Joseph H. Astrachan, "Myths and Realities: Family Businesses' Contribution to the U.S. Economy—A Framework for Assessing Family Business Statistics," *Family Business Review* 9, no. 2 (Summer 1996): 107–119; Family Firm Institute Web site <www.ffi.org>, 2002.

6. Although many of these firms were highly profitable, we did not use profits as a performance measure for this study, for two reasons: first, half of our FCBs were private and did not report profits; second, high returns without growth are not what most long-established FCBs shoot for. These firms have substantive objectives—in most cases, nothing less than significant technological, human, or social progress. What counts for them is the ability to have that progress reflected in overall impact, best measured by market share in a national or international market. Their success is confirmed by their number-one or -two market share positions and a median age of 104 years.

7. Gersick et al., *Generation to Generation*; Ivan Lansberg, *Succeeding Generations: Realizing the Dream of Families in Business* (Boston: Harvard Business School Press, 1999); John L. Ward, *Keeping the Family Business Healthy: How to Plan for Continuing Growth, Profitability, and Family Leadership* (San Francisco: Jossey-Bass, 1987).

Table I-1

a. Joseph Weber et al., "Family, Inc.," *BusinessWeek*, November 10, 2003, 100+.

b. Ronald C. Anderson and David M. Reeb, "Founding-Family Ownership and Firm Performance: Evidence from the S&P 500," *Journal of Finance* 58, no. 3 (June 2003): 1301–1328; Kelin E. Gersick et al., *Generation to Generation: Life Cycles of the Family Business* (Boston: Harvard Business School Press, 1997).

c. Hasnehn Jetha, "The Industrial Fortune 500 Study," working paper, Loyola University, Chicago, 1993.

d. John L. Ward, *Keeping the Family Business Healthy: How to Plan for Continuing Growth, Profitability, and Family Leadership* (San Francisco: Jossey-Bass, 1987).

e. Philip H. Burch Jr., *The Managerial Revolution Reassessed: Family Control in America's Large Corporations* (Lexington, MA: Lexington Books, 1972).

f. Daniel L. McConaughy, "Founding-family Controlled Corporations" (Ph.D. diss., University of Cincinnati, 1994).

g. Melissa Carey Shanker and Joseph H. Astrachan, "Myths and Realities: Family Businesses' Contribution to the U.S. Economy—A Framework for Assessing Family Business Statistics," *Family Business Review* 9, no. 2 (Summer 1996): 107–119; Family Firm Institute Web site <www.ffi.org>, 2002.

h. Raphael La Porta, Florencio Lopez-de-Silanes, and Andrei Shleifer, "Corporate Ownership Around the World," *The Journal of Finance* 54, no. 2 (April 1999): 471–517.

i. Maria Faccio and Larry H. P. Lang, "The Ultimate Ownership of Western European Corporations," *Journal of Financial Economics* 65, no. 3 (September 2002): 365–395.

j. Christine Blondel, Nicolas Rowell, and Ludo Van der Heyden, "Prevalence of Patrimonial Firms on Paris Stock Exchange: Analysis of the Top 250 Companies in 1993 and 1998," working paper 2002/83/TM, INSEAD, Fontainebleau, France, July 2002.

Chapter 1

1. Lisa Munoz, "Next-Generation Leaders: Money Grows on Family Trees," *Fortune*, April 2, 2001, 128.

2. William S. Schulze, Michael H. Lubatkin, Richard N. Dino, and Ann K. Buchholtz, "Agency Relationships in Family Firms," *Organization Science* 12, no. 2 (March–April 2001): 99–116; Harold Demsetz, "The Structure of Ownership and the Theory of the Firm," *Journal of Law and Economics* 26, no. 2 (June 1983): 375–390; Andrei Shleifer and Lawrence H. Summers, "Breach of Trust in Hostile Takeovers," in *Corporate Takeovers: Causes and Consequences*, ed. Alan J. Auerbach (Chicago: University of Chicago Press, 1988).

3. Ivan Lansberg, *Succeeding Generations: Realizing the Dream of Families in Business* (Boston: Harvard Business School Press, 1999).

4. Danny Miller, Lloyd Steier, and Isabelle Le Breton-Miller, "Lost in Time: Patterns of Intergenerational Succession in Family Business," *Journal of Business Venturing* 18, no. 4 (July 2003): 513–531.

5. Larry D. Singell Jr. and James Thornton, "Nepotism, Discrimination, and the Persistence of Utility-Maximizing, Owner-Operated Firms," *Southern Economic Journal* 63, no. 4 (April 1997): 904–919; Peter Leach, Bruce Ball, and Garry Duncan, *Guide to the Family Business* (Scarborough, Ontario: Carswell Thomson Professional Publishing, 2000).

6. Alfred D. Chandler, *Scale and Scope: The Dynamics of Industrial Capitalism* (Cambridge, MA: Belknap Press, 1990).

7. Excellent books about how family businesses can address these problems have been written by Kelin Gersick and associates: Kelin E. Gersick et al., *Generation to Generation: Life Cycles of the Family Business* (Boston: Harvard Business School Press, 1997); Ivan Lansberg (*Succeeding Generations*), and John L. Ward; *Keeping the Family Business Healthy* (San Francisco: Jossey-Bass, 1987).

8. Thomas J. Peters and Robert H. Waterman Jr, *In Search of Excellence* (New York: Harper & Row, 1982); James C. Collins and Jerry I. Porras, *Built to Last* (New York: HarperBusiness, 1994).

9. Hermann Simon, *Hidden Champions: Lessons from 500 of the World's Best Unknown Companies* (Boston: Harvard Business School Press, 1996); Daniel L. McConaughy, Charles H. Matthews, and Anne S. Fialko, "Founding Family Controlled Firms: Performance, Risk, and Value," *Journal of Small Business Management* 39, no. 1 (January 2001): 31–49; Jose Allouche and Bruno Amann, "Le retour triomphant du capitalisme familial?" (The Triumphant Return of

Family Capitalism?), *L'Expansion Management Review* 85, (Juin 1997): 92–99. The last authors studied a sample of French companies and found that FCBs also grew faster than other firms and, when matched for size and industry, had higher returns on assets (7.6 versus 6.1 percent) and equity (18.5 versus 12.6 percent); Ronald C. Anderson and David M. Reeb, "Founding-Family Ownership and Firm Performance: Evidence from the S&P 500," *Journal of Finance* 58, no. 3 (June 2003): 1301–1328. These authors found the superiority of return on assets for FCBs to hold also for the S&P 500 (6.2 versus 4.7 percent), and a 10 percent premium in market valuation as measured by Tobin's Q (company market value to replacement cost of assets); confirmatory evidence appears in Belén Villalonga and Raphael Amit, "How do Family Ownership, Management, and Control Affect Firm Value?" working paper (Boston: Harvard Business School, March 2004). David L. Kang, "The Impact of Ownership Type on Performance in Public Corporations," working paper 98–109, (Boston: Harvard Business School, 1998: Kang showed that textile firms in which families owned a large block of shares had higher returns on sales and more investment in modernization; Paul Bornstein, "All in the Family," *Forbes*, August 29, 1983, 152–153; Robin Mackie, "Family Ownership and Business Survival: Kirkcaldy, 1870–1970," *Business History* 43, no. 3 (July 2001): 1–32; Dirk Junge, "The Pitcairns," in *The factors determining the success of the family/enterprise relationship*, by Family Business Network, Joachim Schwass, and Rik Donckels, eds., *Proceedings of the Fifth Annual Family Business Network Conference*, Lausanne, Switzerland, September 15–18, 1994, Lausanne, Switzerland: Family Business Network, 1995: 171–172.

10. Paul Solman, "Executive Excess," *Newshour with Jim Lehrer*, PBS, December 3, 2002. See also Steve Werner, "The Structure and Effects of Compensation Strategy in Owner-Controlled, Owner-Managed and Manager-Controlled Firms" (Ph.D. diss., University of Florida, 1994).

11. Business Section, *Globe and Mail* (Toronto), December 20, 2002:1–4. The agency problems of public, managerially controlled firms have been extensively discussed. See, for example, Andrei Shleifer and Robert W. Vishny, "A Survey of Corporate Governance," *Journal of Finance* 52, no. 2 (June 1997): 737–783.

12. George A. Ackerlof, "The Market for 'Lemons': Qualitative Uncertainty and the Market Mechanism," *Quarterly Journal of Economics* 84, no. 3 (August 1970): 488–500; Solman, "Executive Excess."

13. Some economists have argued that "agency costs" are reduced under family owner-management. Agency costs occur when an agent, due to superior information and differing interests, is able to exploit a principal, in this case an owner. In public companies, managerial agents often have an incentive to grow the firm in a way that jeopardizes the investments or profit streams of the owners (see, for example, Yakov Amihud and Baruch Lev, "Does Corporate Ownership Structure Affect Its Corporate Diversification?" *Strategic Management Journal* 20, no. 11 (November 1999): 1063–1069; and Michael H. Lubatkin, Yan Ling, and William S. Schulz, "Fairness in Family Firms," working paper (University of Connecticut, Storrs, 2002). In family-owned and -managed businesses, however, these costs are reduced where the interests of the managers and owners are better aligned (see the classic analyses of Michael C. Jensen and William H. Meckling, "Theory of the Firm: Managerial Behavior, Agency Costs, and Ownership Structure," *Journal of Financial Economics* 3, no. 4 (October 1976): 305–360; Eugene F. Fama and Michael C. Jensen, "Separation of Ownership and Control," *Journal of Law and Economics* 26, no. 2 (June 1983): 301–325; Eugene F. Fama and Michael C. Jensen, "Agency Problems and Residual Claims," *Journal of Law and Economics* 26, no. 2 (June 1983): 325–344; and Harold Demsetz and Kenneth Lehn, "The Structure of Corporate Ownership," *Journal of Political Economy* 93, no. 6 (December 1985): 1155–1177). There are a number of reasons for this. First, the principal family shareholder running the business has an incentive to be vigilant to protect the family assets—both in caring for personal wealth and for the good of the family (James H. Davis, David F. Schoorman, and Lex Donaldson, "Towards a Stewardship Theory of Management," *Academy of Management Review* 22, no. 1 (January 1997): 20–47). Second, there are often close ties of loyalty among family members, wrought by kinship, joint socialization, and common values. Typically, family

members try to be more helpful to one another than to outsiders. This reduces the propensity for self-interested opportunism (Gary S. Becker, "A Theory of Social Interaction," *Journal of Political Economy* 82, no. 6 (November–December 1974): 1063–1093). Third, self-interest is further tempered by altruism, whereby the giver's perceived enjoyment or "utility" is enhanced by giving to others in the family—children, relatives, even veteran managers (Lubatkin, Ling, and Schulz, "Fairness in Family Firms"). Moreover, as the business is a central vehicle for such giving, it is cherished and managed for long-term survival. Indeed, when the intent is to keep the business within the family, managers are inclined to invest for the future (Harvey S. James Jr., "Owner as Manager, Extended Horizons and the Family Firm," *International Journal of the Economics of Business* 6, no. 1 (February 1999): 41–55; Jeremy C. Stein, "Efficient Capital Markets, Inefficient Firms: A Model of Myopic Corporate Behavior," *Quarterly Journal of Economics* 104, no. 4 (November 1989): 655–669). Stability of management and ownership so typical in family businesses also gives top executives deep expertise in making decisions, as well as close associations with other employees—whom the family comes to understand, support, and evoke loyalty from (Anderson and Reeb, "Founding-Family Ownership and Firm Performance").

Of course, these benefits do not accrue in all family businesses. First, the great power of family executives and their relative freedom from "professional" controls and outside directors can allow them to behave in a self-serving way for long periods (Harold Demsetz, "The Structure of Ownership and the Theory of the Firm." Moreover, family conflicts may come to the fore, whereby generations fight, cousins vie against cousins for control, or parents spoil their children and grant them short-term rewards at the expense of the business (Miller, Steier, and Le Breton-Miller, "Lost in Time"; Lubatkin, Ling, and Schulze, "Fairness in Family Firms").

14. Daniel Altman, "Downsizing Could Have a Downside," *New York Times*, December 26 2002, C1.

15. See Amihud and Lev, "Does Corporate Ownership Structure Affect Its Corporate Diversification?"; and David J. Denis, Diane K. Denis, and Atulya Sarin, "Agency Theory and the Influence of Equity Ownership on Corporate Diversification Strategies," *Strategic Management Journal* 20, no. 11 (November 1999): 1071–1076.

16. The tactical view of strategy is explained by authors such as Michael E. Porter, in *Competitive Strategy* (New York: Free Press, 1980), who are concerned with positioning companies to achieve competitive advantage. This approach is to be contrasted with the more recent resource-based and dynamic capability views, which argue that competitive advantage comes mainly from the distinctive capabilities within an organization (David J. Teece, Gary Pisano, and Amy Shuen, "Dynamic Capabilities and Strategic Management," *Strategic Management Journal* 18, no. 7 (August 1997): 509–533; Danny Miller. "An Asymmetry-Based View of Advantage: Towards an Attainable Sustainability," *Strategic Management Journal* 24, no. 10 (October 2003): 961–976).

17. See Davis, Schoorman, and Donaldson, "Towards a Stewardship Theory of Management." When the going got tough at the *New York Times* because of a controversial position the paper was about to take, some editors reminded Punch Sulzberger, the family publisher, that the public shareholders might be unhappy. Punch replied, "They can always sell their shares."

18. Kang, "The Impact of Ownership Type on Performance in Public Corporations"; Allouche and Amann, "Le retour triomphant du capitalisme familial?"; Joseph Weber et al., "Family, Inc.," *BusinessWeek*, November 10, 2003, 100+.

19. Bettye H. Pruitt, *Timken: From Missouri to Mars—A Century of Leadership in Manufacturing* (Boston: Harvard Business School Press, 1998), 6–8.

20. Danny Miller and Jangwoo Lee, "The People Make the Process: Commitment to Employees, Decision Making, and Performance," *Journal of Management* 27, no. 2 (2001): 163–189.

21. Allouche and Amann, "Le retour triomphant du capitalisme familial?"; Werner, "The Structure and Effects of Compensation Strategy in Owner-Controlled, Owner-Managed and Manager-Controlled Firms."

22. William G. Ouchi, *Theory Z: How American Business Can Meet the Japanese Challenge* (Reading, MA: Addison-Wesley, 1981); Gary S. Becker, *A Treatise on the Family* (Cambridge, MA: Harvard University Press, 1991); Theodore C. Bergstrom, "On the Evolution of Altruistic Rules for Siblings," *American Economic Review* 85, no.1 (March 1995): 58–81.

23. Robert Levering, Milton Moskowitz, and Michael Katz, *The 100 Best Companies to Work for in America*, (Reading, MA: Addison-Wesley, 1984).

24. Michael Winerip, "Canton's Biggest Employer Is Out of Step, and That's Fine with Him," *New York Times*, B8, December 2, 1996, quoted in Pruitt, *Timken: From Missouri to Mars*, 407.

Table 1-1

a. Jeffrey A. Tannenbaum, "Family Business Index," *Wall Street Journal*, June 6, 1996, B2.

b. ODDO Generation, June 1996, 2.

c. Paul Bornstein, "All in the Family," *Forbes*, August 29, 1983, 152–153.

d. Denis Leech and John Leahy, "Ownership Structure, Control Type Classifications and the Performance of Large British Companies," *Economic Journal* 101, no. 409 (November 1991): 1418–1437.

e. *Forbes*, May 22, 1995.

f. David L. Kang, "Family Ownership and Performance in Public Corporations: A Study of the U.S. Fortune 500, 1982–1994," working paper 00–0051, Harvard Business School, Cambridge, MA, 2000.

g. Robert Kleiman et al., "An Index of Family Controlled Publicly Traded Companies: Comparison of Performance Relative to Traditional Indices," in *Frontiers of Entrepreneurial Research 1996* (Babson Park, MA: Babson College, 1996).

h. David L. Kang, "The Impact of Ownership Type on Organization Performance," (Ph.D. diss., Harvard University, 1996).

i. Daniel L. McConaughy, Charles H. Matthews, and Anne S. Fialko, "Founding Family Controlled Firms: Performance, Risk, and Value," *Journal of Small Business Management* 39, no. 1 (January 2001): 31–49.

j. Miguel A. Gallo and Alvaro Vilaseca, "Finance in Family Business," *Family Business Review* 9, no. 4 (winter 1996): 387–401.

k. Ronald C. Anderson and David M. Reeb, "Founding-Family Ownership and Firm Performance: Evidence from the S&P 500," *Journal of Finance* 58, no. 3 (June 2003): 1301–1328.

l. MassMutual Financial Group/Raymond Institute, *American Family Business Survey*, MassMutual Financial Group and Raymond Institute, 2003.

m. Jose Allouche and Bruno Amann, "Le retour triomphant du capitalisme familial?" (The Triumphant Return of Family Capitalism?), *L'Expansion Management Review* 85 (Juin 1997): 92–99

n. Joseph Weber et al., "Family, Inc.," *BusinessWeek*, November 10, 2003, 100+.

Table 1-3

a. Jose Allouche and Bruno Amann, "Le retour triomphant du capitalisme familial?" (The Triumphant Return of Family Capitalism?), *L'Expansion Management Review* 85 (Juin 1997): 92–99.

b. Daniel L. McConaughy, Charles H. Matthews, and Anne S. Fialko, "Founding Family Controlled Firms: Performance, Risk, and Value," *Journal of Small Business Management* 39, no. 1 (January 2001): 31–49; Daniel L. McConaughy et al., "Founding Family Controlled Firms: Efficiency and Value," *Review of Financial Economics* 7, no. 1 (1998): 1–19.

c. Robert Kleiman et al., "An Index of Family Controlled Publicly Traded Companies: Comparison of Performance Relative to Traditional Indices," in *Frontiers of Entrepreneurial Research 1996* (Babson Park, MA: Babson College, 1996).

d. MassMutual Financial Group/Raymond Institute, *American Family Business Survey*, MassMutual Financial Group and Raymond Institute, 2003.

e. Ronald C. Anderson and David M. Reeb, "Founding-Family Ownership and Firm Performance: Evidence from the S&P 500," *Journal of Finance* 58, no. 3 (June 2003): 1301–1328.

f. Allouche and Amann, "Le retour triomphant du capitalisme familial?".

g. McConaughy, Matthews and Fialko, "Founding Family Controlled Firms: Performance, Risk, and Value"; McConaughy et al., "Founding Family Controlled Firms: Efficiency and Value."

h. Robin Mackie, "Family Ownership and Business Survival: Kirkcaldy, 1870–1970," *Business History* 43, no. 3 (July 2001): 1–32.

i. Arie de Geus, *The Living Company* (Boston: Harvard Business School Press, 1997), 2–3. See also the Family Firm Institute Web site <www.ffi.org>, and the study by Ellen De Rooij, *A brief desk research study into the average life expectancy of companies in a number of countries* (Amsterdam: Stratix Consulting Group, August 1996).

j. de Geus, *The Living Company*.

k. MassMutual Financial Group/Raymond Institute, *American Family Business Survey*.

l. Christine Blondel, Nicolas Rowell, and Ludo Van der Heyden, "Prevalence of Patrimonial firms on Paris Stock Exchange: Analysis of the Top 250 Companies in 1993 and 1998," working paper 2002/83/TM, INSEAD, Fontainebleau, France, 5 July 2002

Table 1-4

a. MassMutual Financial Group/Raymond Institute, *American Family Business Survey*, MassMutual Financial Group and Raymond Institute, 2003.

b. David L. Kang, "The Impact of Ownership Type on Organization Performance," (Ph.D. diss., Harvard University, 1996).

c. Joseph Weber et al., "Family, Inc.," *BusinessWeek*, November 10, 2003, 100+.

d. Jose Allouche and Bruno Amann, "Le retour triomphant du capitalisme familial?" (The Triumphant Return of Family Capitalism?), *L'Expansion Management Review* 85 (Juin 1997): 92–99.

e. MassMutual Financial Group/Raymond Institute, *American Family Business Survey*.

f. Allouche and Amann, "Le retour triomphant du capitalisme familial?"

g. MassMutual Financial Group/Raymond Institute, *American Family Business Survey*.

h. Ronald C. Anderson and David M. Reeb, "Founding-Family Ownership and Firm Performance: Evidence from the S&P 500," *Journal of Finance* 58 no. 3 (June 2003): 1301–1328.

i. Allouche and Amann, "Le retour triomphant du capitalisme familial?"

Chapter 2

1. We are referring here to the "configuration school" of strategy as discussed in Danny Miller, "The Architecture of Simplicity," *Academy of Management Review* 18, no. 1 (January 1993): 116–138; Danny Miller, "Configurations Revisited," *Strategic Management Journal* 17, no. 7 (July 1996): 505–512; and Danny Miller and Peter H. Friesen, *Organizations: A Quantum View* (Englewood Cliffs, NJ: Prentice-Hall, 1984).

2. For more about the four Cs, see Danny Miller and Isabelle Le Breton-Miller, "Challenge Versus Advantage in Family Business," *Strategic Organization* 1, no. 1 (January 2003): 127–134. We will be describing the practices of FCBs that have succeeded, indeed thrived, for decades. As we detail in chapter 8, many of these qualities do not apply to poorer performing FCBs—certainly not with anywhere near the same degree or consistency. As a result of mismanaging the Cs, some former "winners" like Corning, Motorola, and Olympia & York are no longer performing well, while others like Bechtel, Nordstrom, Coors, and Timken have hit an occasional rough patch.

3. Susan E. Tifft and Alex S. Jones, *The Trust: The Private and Powerful Family Behind the New York Times* (Boston: Little, Brown, 1999), xix.

4. There is a growing evidence and broader discussion of the tendency for family businesses to adopt a longer-term time horizon in caring for their business. See, for example, Jeremy C. Stein, "Efficient Capital Markets, Inefficient Firms: A Model of Myopic Corporate Behavior," *Quarterly Journal of Economics* 104, no. 4 (November 1989): 655–669; Harvey S. James Jr., "Owner as Managers, Extended Horizons, and the Family Firm," *International Journal of the Economics of Business* 6, no. 1 (February 1999): 41–55; James H. Davis, David F. Schoorman, and Lex Donaldson, "Toward a Stewardship Theory of Management," *Academy of Management Review* 22, no. 1 (January 1997): 20–47; Mark Casson, "The Economics of the Family Firm," *Scandinavian Economic History Review* 47, no. 1 (1999): 10–23. Such extended horizons are critical in developing inimitable core competencies or capabilities. The latter are said to be economic resources that are "valuable, inimitable, rare and nonsubstitutable," and so will yield abnormal profits or "economic rents." See Jay B. Barney, "Firm Resources and Sustained Competitive Advantage," *Journal of Management* 17, no. 1 (March 1991): 99–120; Ingemar Dierickx, Karel Cool, and Jay B. Barney, "Asset Stock Accumulation and the Sustainability of Competitive Advantage," *Management Science* 35, no. 12 (December 1989): 1504–1513; and David J. Teece, Gary Pisano, and Amy Shuen, "Dynamic Capabilities and Strategic Management," *Strategic Management Journal* 18, no. 7 (August 1997): 509–533.

5. Bettye H. Pruitt, *Timken: From Missouri to Mars* (Boston: Harvard Business School Press, 1998), 138–140, 340.

6. Joseph C. Goulden, *Fit to Print* (Secaucus, NJ: Lyle Stuart, 1988), 226–229; Tifft and Jones, *The Trust*, 518.

7. Tifft and Jones, *The Trust*, 588.

8. Continuity can be a real drawback if taken to excess (more on this in chapter 8). See Miller and Le Breton-Miller, "Challenge Versus Advantage in Family Business."

9. Tifft and Jones, *The Trust*, 779. See also Richard Grassby, *Kinship & Capitalism* (Cambridge, MA: Cambridge University Press, 2000), 405–435.

10. Tifft and Jones, *The Trust*, 588.

11. *Hallmark's Beliefs and Values Statement*, formally codified in 1989. Jeff Mauzy and Richard A. Harriman, "Three Climates for Creativity," *Research Technology Management* 46, no. 3 (May–June 2003): 27–30.

12. Thomas Goldwasser, *Family Pride* (New York: Dodd, Mead, 1986), 7–44; Scott Robinette and Claire Brand, *Emotion Marketing: The Hallmark Way of Winning Customers for Life* (New York: McGraw-Hill Trade, 2001).

13. Robert Levering and Milton Moskowitz, *The 100 Best Companies to Work for in America* (New York: Doubleday, 1993). Jennifer Mann, "New Profit-Sharing Plan Lets Hallmark Employees Diversify Portfolios," *Knight-Ridder Tribune Business News*, November 1, 2002, 12.

14. The notion of community is mirrored in the classic sociological literature that makes a fundamental distinction, first posited by Ferdinand Tonnies, between *gemeinschaft* and *gesellschaft* (*Community and Society* (New York: Harper, 1963; German original edition, 1887)). The former refers to primary, family-like, face-to-face social groups with relative permanence and intimacy and encompassing interactions (Charles Horton Cooley, *The Social Group* (New York: Harper, 1909)). It also evokes the more traditional, affectual, value-based groups that Max Weber contrasts with purely rational forms of organization in *The Theory of Social and Economic Organization* (New York: Macmillan, 1947). Dimensions that define *gemeinschaft* in its purer forms are, according to Talcott Parsons, in *The Structure of Social Action* (Glencoe, IL : Free Press, 1949), affectivity (versus neutrality), collectivity (versus self-orientation), diffuseness (versus specificity), and quality or "ascription" (versus achievement). Although our FCBs are never pure types, the majority do incorporate many more elements of *gemeinschaft* than the typical bureaucracy, among them strong values, socialization, loyalty, caring and informality. See, for example, Davis et al., "Toward a Stewardship Theory of Management," and Grassby, *Kinship and Capitalism*. The dark side to community in FCBs is that they can become cultlike, insular, and

slavish to family interests, and thereby often lose touch with the outside world and its needs (see chapter 8; and Andrei Shleifer and Robert W. Vishny, "Large Shareholders and Corporate Control," *Journal of Political Economy* 94, no. 3 (1986): 461–489; William S. Schulze et al., "Agency Relationships in Family Firms: Theory and Evidence," *Organization Science* 12, no. 2 (March–April 2001): 99–116; Miller and Le Breton-Miller, "Challenge Versus Advantage in Family Business."

15. Tifft and Jones, *The Trust*, 471.

16. Dan Baum, *Citizen Coors: A Grand Family Saga of Business, Politics, and Beer* (New York: William Morrow, 2000), 31.

17. Tifft and Jones, *The Trust*, 591.

18. François Michelin with Ivan Levaï and Yves Messarovitch, *Et pourquoi pas?* (And Why Not?), (Paris: Bernard Grasset, 1998), 81.

19. William S. Schulze, Michael H. Lubatkin, and Richard N. Dino, "Toward a Theory of Agency and Altruism in Family Firms," *Journal of Business Venturing* 18, no. 4 (July 2003): 473–490.

20. Laton McCartney, *Friends in High Places: The Bechtel Story* (New York: Ballantine Books, 1989), 27. There is a growing literature on the advantage that family businesses have in building enduring relationships. Stability and continuity of the family is said to preserve reputation and perpetuate and extend connections. See Donald Palmer and Brad M. Barber, "Challenges, Elites, and Owning Families," *Administrative Science Quarterly* 46, no. 1 (March 2001): 87–120; Grassby, *Kinship and Capitalism*.

21. The dark side of such relationships is that FCBs have been accused of competing via cronyism and long-standing social contacts rather than effectiveness or merit (see Randall K. Morck, David A. Stangeland, and Bernard Yeung, "Inherited Wealth, Corporate Control, and Economic Growth," in *Concentrated Corporate Ownership*, ed. Randall K. Morck (Chicago: University of Chicago Press, 2000)). Some powerful families form cabals of the rich and famous and circumvent the forces of the market. Consider J.P. Morgan's voting trusts, which locked up most of the U.S. railroads at the turn of the twentieth century and held them hostage to Morgan bondholders. Likewise, consider the widely reported incidents of executives bribing government officials and making illegal campaign contributions.

22. The increasing importance of interfirm relationships has been documented by Adam M. Brandenburger and Barry J. Nalebuff, *Co-opetition* (New York: Currency Doubleday, 1996); Nitin Nohria and Robert G. Eccles, eds., *Networks and Organizations* (Boston: Harvard Business School Press, 1992); Robert G. Eccles and Dwight B. Crane, *Doing Deals: Investment Banks at Work* (Boston: Harvard Business School Press, 1988); Christopher A. Bartlett and Sumantra Ghoshal, *Managing Across Borders: The Transnational Solution* (Boston: Harvard Business School Press, 1989). This importance has grown with the increasing necessity of strategic alliances, outsourcing, global partnerships, and joint ventures.

23. Robin Mackie, "Family Ownership and Business Survival," *Business History* 43, no. 3 (July 2001): 1–32; Danny Miller, Lloyd Steier, and Isabelle Le Breton-Miller, "Lost in Time: Patterns of Intergenerational Succession in Family Business," *Journal of Business Venturing* 18, no. 4 (July 2003): 513–531.

24. The issue of top management discretion is key, as it determines the scope of action top managers have to direct the company as they see fit. Where the top managers are well intentioned and talented, discretion can be a profound asset for the firm (see Donald C. Hambrick and Sydney Finkelstein, "Managerial Discretion," in *Research in Organizational Behavior,* vol. 9, Barry M. Staw and Larry L. Cummings, eds. (Greenwich, CT: JAI Press, 1987), 369–406). Where executives are self-serving, incompetent, or irresponsible, such discretion can hurt. The winners we studied overwhelmingly had talented managers devoted to their companies, and thus their discretion was a profound advantage in combating stakeholders with short-term and purely pecuniary objectives. In low-discretion situations, researchers have found that no matter how good a top manager is, he or she will have a very limited impact on organizational performance

(Donald C. Hambrick, Marta A. Geletkanycz, and James W. Fredrickson. "Top Executive Commitment to the Status Quo," *Strategic Management Journal* 14, no. 6 (September 1993): 401–418).

25. The downside of freedom is abuse. Some FCB leaders behave irresponsibly in the absence of governance mechanisms to stop them (see chapter 8; Shleifer and Vishny, "Large Shareholders and Corporate Control"; Andrei Shleifer and Lawrence H. Summers, "Breach of Trust in Hostile Takeovers," in *Corporate Takeovers: Causes and Consequences*, ed. Alan J. Auerbach (Chicago, University of Chicago Press, 1988); Larry D. Singell Jr. and James Thornton, "Nepotism, Discrimination, and the Persistence of Utility-Maximizing, Owner-Operated Firms," *Southern Economic Journal* 63, no. 4 (April 1997): 904–919). This is especially a problem in countries that provide little protection for minority shareholders (see Andrei Shleifer and Daniel Wolfenzon, "Investor Protection and Equity Markets," *Journal of Financial Economics* 66, no. 1 (October 2002): 3–27; Morck et al., 2000, *op. cit.*).

26. The Sulzbergers control the *Times* through a special class of voting shares.

27. Michelin, *Et pourquoi pas?*, 169.

28. Michelin, *Et pourquoi pas?*; Robert Ball, "The Michelin Man Rolls into Akron's Backyard," *Fortune,* December 1974, 140.

29. Diana B. Henriques, "Ideas & Trends," *New York Times*, Sunday August 18, 2002, Section 4, 6.

30. James C. Collins and Jerry I. Porras, *Built to Last: Successful Habits of Visionary Companies* (New York: HarperBusiness, 1994); Arie de Geus, *The Living Company* (Boston: Harvard Business School Press, 1997).

31. Our discussion of family roots suggests a natural tendency to pursue multiple elements of multiple Cs. As FCBs do this, balancing the Cs and their elements, they become more resilient, more "ambidextrous." The fact that our successful FCBs employed a blend of Cs prevented excess and bestowed longevity. Firms could be innovative, but in a thematic, measured way; they had clannish tight cultures, but were connected to the environment; they embraced tradition, to pave the way to the future.

32. Two places to start in the extensive strategy literature on these topics are: Teece, Pisano, and Shuen, "Dynamic Capabilities and Strategic Management"; and Michael E. Porter, "What Is Strategy?" *Harvard Business Review* (November–December 1996): 61–78.

33. Inevitably, subjective boundaries exist between strategy and the Cs, and chains of causality link them. Take as an example an excellent training program at a brand builder. One might be tempted to call the program a strategic capability—a part of strategy. But to our way of thinking, the training underlies a more immediate and inimitable source of competitive superiority: brand preservation. Training would be classified as an element of community, and brand preservation as a component of strategy. The training program, moreover, is apt to be more generic and more easily imitated, whereas brand preservation is a key building block of strategy and a function of *many* subtle practices. In short, capabilities are more complex and more directly linked to competitive advantage than the C elements that give rise to them, and they normally are a product of multiple elements.

Chapter 3

1. Levi Strauss & Co. Web site: <www.levistrauss.com>.

2. Scott Robinette and Claire Brand, *Emotion Marketing: The Hallmark Way of Winning Customers for Life* (New York: McGraw-Hill Trade, 2001).

3. Robinette and Brand, *Emotion Marketing*; Joyce C. Hall and Curtiss Anderson, *When You Care Enough* (Kansas City, MO: Hallmark Cards, Inc., 1979).

4. Samuel C. Johnson, *The Essence of a Family Enterprise: Doing Business the Johnson Way* (Indianapolis, IN: The Curtis Publishing Company Inc., 1988), 71.

5. M.R. Montgomery, *In Search of L.L.Bean* (Boston: Little, Brown and Company, 1984).

6. L.L.Bean Web site: <www.llbean.com>.

7. Emily Nelson, "The Art of the Sale—How the Beauty-Counter Staff Gets Shoppers to Buy More Than They Bargained For," *Wall Street Journal*, January 11, 2001, B1.

8. Montgomery, *In Search of L.L. Bean*, 241.

9. Karl Schoenberger, "Jeans: A Soft Heart and Frayed Earnings," *New York Times*, June 25, 2000, Section 3, 1; Louis Lee, "Can Levi's Be Cool Again? It's Trying to Woo Kids—Without Turning Off Grown-ups," *BusinessWeek*, March 13, 2000, 144–148.

10. Hall and Anderson, *When You Care Enough*; Robinette and Brand, *Emotion Marketing*, 41.

11. Hallmark Greeting Cards Co. Web site: <www.hallmark.com>.

12. Montgomery, *In Search of L.L.Bean*.

13. Ibid., 170–200.

14. Nina Munk, "Why Women Find Lauder Mesmerizing," *Fortune*, May 25, 1998, 96–106; Estée Lauder, *Estée: A Success Story* (New York: Random House, 1985); Lee Israel, *Estée Lauder: Beyond the Magic: An Unauthorized Biography* (New York: Macmillan, 1985).

15. Montgomery, *In Search of L.L.Bean*, 190.

16. Nelson, "The Art of the Sale."

17. Jenny Strasburg, "Shaking the Blues: Venerable House of Levi Seeks to Regain Grip on Youth While Keeping the Faithful," *San Francisco Chronicle*, February 3, 2002, G1; Rhymer Rigby, "Jeans Genius," *Management Today*, November 1996, 56–60.

18. Munk, "Why Women Find Lauder Mesmerizing." Richard Severo, "Estée Lauder," *New York Times*, April 26, 2004, C2.

19. Nina Munk, "The Levi Straddle," *Forbes*, January 17, 1994, 44–45.

20. L.L. Bean Web site: <www.llbean.com>.

21. Margaret Allen, *Selling Dreams: Inside the Beauty Business* (New York: Simon & Schuster, 1981), 74–75.

22. Johnson, *The Essence of a Family Enterprise*, 166.

23. Grace Mirabella, "Beauty Queen: Estée Lauder," *Time*, December 7, 1998, 183–184; Jan Pottker, *Born to Power: Heirs to America's Leading Businesses* (Hauppauge, NY: Barron's, 1992), 260–269.

24. Johnson, *The Essence of a Family Enterprise*, 86–87.

25. Nelson, "The Art of the Sale."

26. Montgomery, *In Search of L.L.Bean*, 170–200.

27. Hall and Anderson, *When You Care Enough*.

28. Thomas Goldwasser, *Family Pride: Profiles of Five of America's Best-Run Family Businesses* (New York: Dodd, Mead, 1986), 7–44.

29. Johnson, *The Essence of a Family Enterprise*, 8.

30. David Barboza, "At Johnson Wax, a Family Passes on Its Heirloom: Father Divides a Business to Keep the Children United," *New York Times*, August 22, 1999, Section 3, 1.

31. Morag Preston, "American Beauty," *The Times* (London), May 20, 2000, 14; Jacqueline Doherty, "Glamour Stock," *Barron's*, August 30, 1999, 25–28.

32. The Estée Lauder Companies Web site: <www.elcompanies.com>, and press release, January 6, 2004.

33. Georg Simmel, "Fashion," *American Journal of Sociology* 62, no. 6 (May 1957): 541–558 (reprinted from 1904).

34. Robinette and Brand, *Emotion Marketing*, 175; Hal F. Rosenbluth and Diane McFerrin Peters, *Good Company: Caring as Fiercely as You Compete. Lessons from America's Best Companies* (Cambridge, MA: Perseus Publishing, 1998), 166.

35. Sherman, "Levi's: As Ye Sew, So Shall Ye Reap"; Nicholas Bannister, "Riveting the Market Brand Values: Levi's," *The Guardian*, July 3, 1999, 26.

36. Robinette and Brand, *Emotion Marketing*, 108–109; Jeff Mauzy and Richard A. Harriman, "Three Climates for Creativity," *Research Technology Management* 46, no. 3 (May–June 2003): 27–30.

37. Rosenbluth and McFerrin Peters, *Good Company*, 166; Robinette and Brand, *Emotion Marketing*, 191.

38. *Fortune,* January 20, 2003; Mauzy and Harriman, 2003, "Three Climates for Creativity."

39. "How Hallmark Goes About Being Low-Cost Producer," *Fortune*, May 25, 1987, 31; Hallmark Web site <www.hallmark.com>.

40. Mirabella, "Beauty Queen: Estée Lauder."

41. Munk, "Why Women Find Lauder Mesmerizing."

42. Ibid.

43. Nelson, "The Art of the Sale."

44. The figurehead role is especially important at fashion-prestige brands such as Prada, Gucci, Versace, Bulgari, and Ferragamo, most of whose leaders are icons of glamour, taste, or panache.

45. Nina Munk, "How Levi's Trashed a Great American Brand," *Fortune,* April 12, 1999, 82–90; Levi Strauss & Co. Web site: <www.levistrauss.com>.

46. Hallmark Greeting Cards Co. Web site: <www.hallmark.com>; S.C. Johnson & Co. Web site: <www.scjohnson.com>; The Estée Lauder Companies, Inc. Web site: <www.elcompanies.com>.

47. Robert Lenzner and Stephen S. Johnson, "A Few Yards of Denim and Five Copper Rivets," *Forbes,* February 26, 1996, 82.

48. Doherty, "Glamour Stock."

Chapter 4

1. Dan Baum, *Citizen Coors: A Grand Family Saga of Business, Politics, and Beer* (New York: William Morrow, 2000) xxi–xxii; Russ Banham, *Coors: A Rocky Mountain Legend* (Lyme, CT: Greenwich Publishing Group, 1998).

2. Joseph C. Goulden, *Fit to Print: A. M. Rosenthal and His Times* (Secaucus, NJ: Lyle Stuart, 1988),140, 142; Harrison Evans Salisbury, *Without Fear or Favor: The New York Times and Its Times* (New York: Times Books, 1980); Gay Talese, *The Kingdom and the Power. The Story of the Men Who Influence the Institution That Influences the World: The New York Times* (New York: World Publishing Co., 1969).

3. As quoted in Robert Spector and Patrick D. McCarthy, *The Nordstrom Way: The Inside Story of America's #1 Customer Service Company* (New York: John Wiley & Sons, Inc., 1995), 27.

4. Spector and McCarthy, *The Nordstrom Way*, 44–45, 185.

5. Baum, *Citizen Coors*, 49–52.

6. Pruitt, *Timken: From Missouri to Mars*, 75. Coors did everything itself, from growing barley to making all of its own equipment. See Charles G. Burk, "While the Big Brewers Quaff, the Little Ones Thirst," *Fortune,* November 1972, 105.

7. Pruitt, *Timken: From Missouri to Mars*, 67–68, 245.

8. Michael L. Sullivan-Trainor, "A Gamble and a Long-Term View Pay Off at Timken," *ComputerWorld,* September 11, 1989, 66, 68.

9. Tom Bagsarian, "Timken: Build on Bearings," *Iron Age New Steel* 13, no. 12 (December 1997): 50–54.

10. William H. Miller, "Timken Jumps into Tomorrow," *Industry Week,* September 2, 1991, 72–73, 76–77, 80.

11. Miller, "Timken Jumps into Tomorrow."

12. Bagsarian, "Timken: Build on Bearings"; Pruitt, *Timken: From Missouri to Mars.*

13. Case, "Publisher of the Year."

14. Pruitt, *Timken: From Missouri to Mars*, 73–75, 89, 119. Auto bearings moved from 80 percent of bearings revenues in 1925 to 49 percent in 1932.

15. Pruitt, *Timken: From Missouri to Mars*, 1, 4.

16. Bagsarian, "Timken: Build on Bearings," 53–54; Pruitt, *Timken: From Missouri to Mars*, 6–8, 109.

17. Baum, *Citizen Coors*, 22–23.

18. Baum, *Citizen Coors*, 140, 304; Burk, "While the Big Brewers Quaff, the Little Ones Thirst," 105.

19. See Goulden, *Fit to Print*, 175–176. See also John Corry, *My Times: Adventures in the News Trade* (New York: Putnam, 1994), 119–121, and Salisbury, *Without Fear or Favor*, for descriptions of the general tone at the paper.

20. Spector and McCarthy, *The Nordstrom Way*, 4. Another executive said that Nordstrom's service reputation was based on word of mouth, not ads or press releases, and that it was normal that the retailer be held to a higher standard than its competitors.

21. Hints in historical accounts indicate that the Protestant ethic embodied by immigrants such those in the Coors and Timken families influenced their attitudes toward quality. Hard work, frugality, stewardship, and sacrifice were all values that translated easily into an obsession with excellence.

22. Baum, *Citizen Coors*, 41–43; Beth Mende Conny, *A Catalyst for Change: Coors and the Pioneering of the Aluminum Can* (Golden, CO: Adolph Coors Co., 1990).

23. Eric S. Hardy, "The Soul of an Old Company," *Forbes,* March 13, 1995, 70–71; Sullivan-Trainor, "A Gamble and a Long-Term View Pay Off at Timken." All of this was done with a debt to capital ratio of 15 percent versus the industry average of 100 percent. Kathy Rebello, "Steel Firm's New Mill Backs Trend," *USA Today*, May 23, 1984, C2; Tonya Vinas, "Manufacturing Deserves Investment," *Industry Week,* February 2002, 22.

24. Welles, "The Arthurian Legends."

25. Spector and McCarthy, *The Nordstrom Way*, 67. See Michael Winerip, "Canton's Biggest Employer," *New York Times*, December 2, 1996, B8, for Timken apprenticeship.

26. Baum, *Citizen Coors*, 129; Jan Pottker, *Born to Power: Heirs to America's Leading Businesses* (Hauppauge, NY: Barron's, 1992), 156.

27. Susan E. Tifft and Alex S. Jones, *The Trust: The Private and Powerful Family Behind the New York Times* (Boston: Little, Brown, 1999), 740–755. By contrast to Primis, Punch Sulzberger, the CEO and publisher, did *not* see himself as a business executive. On passport applications and immigration forms he listed his trade as "journalist."

28. Pruitt, *Timken: From Missouri to Mars*, 180, 190–191.

29. Spector and McCarthy, *The Nordstrom Way*, 235.

30. Tifft and Jones, *The Trust*, 354, 480–490; Leonard Silk and Mark Silk, *The American Establishment* (New York: Basic Books, 1980), 66–103.

31. Goulden, *Fit to Print*, 181.

32. Baum, *Citizen Coors*, 268–269.

33. Pruitt, *Timken: From Missouri to Mars*, 175, 177.

34. Pruitt, *Timken: From Missouri to Mars*; David Bottoms, "Timken," *Industry Week,* October 17, 1994, 31–32.

35. Francine Schwadel, "Courting Shoppers: Nordstrom's Push East Will Test Its Renown for the Best in Service," *Wall Street Journal*, August 1, 1989, 1.

36. Spector and McCarthy, *The Nordstrom Way*, 31–32, 68–69, 126.

37. Michael Winerip, "An American Place," *New York Times*, September 30, 1996, B6; Pruitt, *Timken: From Missouri to Mars.*

38. Spector and McCarthy, *The Nordstrom Way*, 16. See also Schwadel, "Courting Shoppers"; James C. Collins and Jerry I. Porras, *Built to Last: Successful Habits of Visionary Companies* (New York: HarperBusiness, 1994), 115–124.

39. Collins and Porras, *Built to Last*, 115–124; Spector and McCarthy, *The Nordstrom Way*, 223.

40. Goulden, *Fit to Print*; Tifft and Jones, *The Trust*.

41. This trust pays off because the family treats employees well and because they are so constant and vocal in their articulation of values. Craftsmen show a distinct slant toward quality-preserving functions such as engineering, design, and manufacturing, while underplaying

the roles of marketing and finance. At the *Times*, the news department dominated sales and marketing, while much of the time finance took a seat so far back as to be almost invisible.

42. Spector and McCarthy, *The Nordstrom Way*, 25.

43. Bryan Gruley, "In Search of Excellence: Why 'the Shopper at Nordstrom Is King'," *Detroit News*, May 9, 1993, D1; Spector and McCarthy, *The Nordstrom Way*, 16, 23, 27; Collins and Porras, *Built to Last*, 188–189.

44. John H. Sheridan, "America's Best Plants: Timken," *Industry Week,* October 19, 1992, 53–54.

45. Bottoms, "Timken." See also Robert T. Lund et al., *Designed to Work: Production Systems and People* (Englewood Cliffs, NJ: Prentice-Hall, 1993), 123.

46. Pruitt, *Timken: From Missouri to Mars*, 77–85, 141, 189; Richard J. Maturi, "Suppliers: 'We Couldn't Do It Alone Anymore,'" *Industry Week,* September 18, 1989, 22. See also Industry Week's 5th Annual Salute, *Industry Week,* October 17, 1994, 31–32.

47. The five Nordstroms on the TMT say titles mean nothing (Schwadel, "Courting Shoppers," 1); Patrick McMahon, "Nordstrom Undergoes Store Corporate Face Lift," *USA Today*, September 21, 1998, 11B; Spector and McCarthy, *The Nordstrom Way*, 76–79.

Chapter 5

1. Operator firms clearly deliver more for less to their customers. Tyson, and J.R. Simplot, for example, have reinvented the front end of the value chain, supplying processed chicken and frozen French fries, respectively, to massive clients such as McDonald's and KFC at the lowest cost, when and where they're needed; and they add more value than their rivals. Operators such as Wal-Mart and IKEA, in contrast, have excelled by supplying attractive merchandise at bargain prices, all the while garnering good margins and splendid growth.

2. John Huey, "Wal-Mart: Will It Take Over the World?," *Fortune,* January 30, 1989, 52–58; Bob Ortega, *In Sam We Trust: The Untold Story of Sam Walton and Wal-Mart, the World's Most Powerful Retailer* (New York: Times Business, 2000).

3. Daniel Gross, "Sam Walton, Wal-Mart, and the Discounting of America," in Daniel Gross, *Forbes' Greatest Business Stories of All Time* (New York: John Wiley & Sons Inc., 1996), 267–283.

4. Ortega, *In Sam We Trust*, 111; "Wal-Mart: How Big Can it Grow?" *The Economist*, April 17, 2004, 67–69.

5. Gross, "Sam Walton, Wal-Mart, and the Discounting of America," 272–274. "Wal-Mart: How Big Can it Grow?" 67–69.

6. Marcia Berss, "Protein Man," *Forbes,* October 24, 1994, 64–65; Ron Ruggless, "Don Tyson," *Nation's Restaurant News* 29 (January 1995): 213–214.

7. "The Birdman of Arkansas," *U.S. News & World Report,* July 18, 1994, 42–44; Paul Duke Jr. and Rick Christie, "Don Tyson Marshals His Flock to Fight," *Wall Street Journal*, October 13, 1988, 1.

8. Greg Muttitt, "Control Freaks," *The Ecologist* 31, no. 2 (March 2001): 52–53.

9. Ortega, *In Sam We Trust*, 131–132. See also Carol J. Loomis, "Sam Would Be Proud," *Fortune,* April 17, 2000, 130–144.

10. "How to Feed a Growing Family," *The Economist*, March 9, 1996, 63; Wayne G. Broehl Jr., *Cargill: Trading the World's Grain* (Hanover, NH: University Press of New England, 1992).

11. Gross, "Sam Walton, Wal-Mart, and the Discounting of America," 278–279.

12. Nirmalya Kumar, "The Power of Trust in Manufacturer-Retailer Relationships," *Harvard Business Review* (November–December, 1996): 92–101; Richard de Santa, "It's Just Begun," *Supermarket Business* 53, no. 1 (January 1998): 13–16.

13. Stuart Crainer, "The Swedes Are Coming," *Across the Board* 36, no. 6 (June 1999): 31–35; Stephen D. Moore, "Sweden's Ikea Forges into Eastern Europe," *Wall Street Journal*, June 28, 1993, A9; Bertil Torekull, *Leading by Design: The IKEA Story* (New York: HarperCollins Publishers, 1999).

14. Gross, "Sam Walton, Wal-Mart, and the Discounting of America," 279–280; Huey, "Wal-Mart: Will It Take Over the World?"

15. Eric Schlosser, "Meat & Potatoes," *Rolling Stone*, November 26, 1998, 68–83.

16. Schlosser, "Meat & Potatoes"; Bill Saporito, "Cashing in on Food and Drink," *Fortune*, October 12, 1987, 152.

17. Wayne G. Broehl Jr., *Cargill: Going Global* (Hanover, NH: University Press of New England, 1998): 317.

18. Alf Young, "Ikea's Customers Have Obviously Not Heard of Recession," *The Herald* (Scotland), August 13, 2002, 24; James R. Hagerty, "How to Assemble a Retail Success Story," *Wall Street Journal*, September 9, 1999, A24.

19. Broehl, *Cargill: Going Global*, 228–229.

20. Danny Miller, "Organizational Configurations: Cohesion, Change, and Prediction," *Human Relations* 43, no. 8 (August 1990): 771–789.

21. Broehl, *Cargill: Going Global*, 366. See also Randel S. Carlock, "A Classroom Discussion with James R. Cargill," *Family Business Review* 7, no. 3 (Fall 1994): 297–307.

22. Ortega, *In Sam We Trust*, 66.

23. Broehl, *Cargill: Going Global*, 317.

24. "How to Feed a Growing Family."

25. Torekull, *Leading by Design*, 87.

26. Sam Walton, with John Huey, *Sam Walton, Made in America: My Story* (New York: Doubleday, 1992).

27. Cargill, *Nourishing Potential* (Minneapolis: Cargill Publication, 2001).

28. Danny Miller and Jamal Shamsie, "Learning Across the Life Cycle: Experimentation and Performance Among the Hollywood Studio Heads," *Strategic Management Journal* 22, no. 8 (August 2001): 725–745.

29. Torekull, *Leading by Design*, 125.

30. Broehl, *Cargill: Going Global*, 279, 359.

31. Alan Liddle, "J.R. Simplot," *Nation's Restaurant News*, February 1996, 148; Charley Hannagan, "Fried Up for Frozen Foods Geddes' J.R. Simplot Plant Packages Veggies for Quick Meals," *Syracuse Herald American*, June 27, 1999, E2.

32. Kumar, "The Power of Trust in Manufacturer-Retailer Relationships"; de Santa, "It's Just Begun."; "Wal-Mart: How Big Can it Grow?"

33. Cheryl Strauss Einhorn, "Commodities Corner: Can Tyson Pullet Off?" *Barron's*, January 8, 2001, MW15.

34. Torekull, *Leading by Design*, 62.

35. Ibid., 159.

36. Ibid., 49. See also connection with clients, in Richard Heller, "Folk Fortune," *Forbes*, September 4, 2000, 66–69.

37. Ruggless, "Don Tyson." See also Kim Clark, "Tough Times for the Chicken King," *Fortune*, October 28, 1996, 88–97. These relationships tend to be especially close when two family businesses form relationships. As they typically share the same long-term values and concern for reputation, they are able to work together well to form truly productive alliances.

38. Ruggless, "Don Tyson." 214. When employees in Cargill's malt business failed to be responsive to their clients, 70 percent were let go. *See* Neil Weinberg, with Brandon Copple, "Going against the Grain," *Forbes*, November 25, 2002, 158–168.

39. Berss, "Protein Man.": 64–65.

40. Scott Kilman, "Tyson Foods' CEO Denies Rift with Father and Affirms Control," *Wall Street Journal*, June 22, 2001, B6.

41. Clark, "Tough Times for the Chicken King."

42. Broehl, *Cargill: Trading the World's Grain,* chapters 18 and 19.

43. Torekull, *Leading by Design*, 26.

Notes | 287

44. Stephen Moss, "The Gospel According to Ikea," *The Guardian*, June 26, 2000, 2.2; Torekull, *Leading by Design:* 112–119; 228–239.

45. Broehl, *Cargill: Going Global*, 366.

Chapter 6

1. Myron Magnet, "Corning Glass Shapes Up," *Fortune,* December 13, 1982, 90.

2. Robert W. Galvin, *The Ideas of Ideas* (Schaumburg, IL: Motorola University Press, 1991), 165–166.

3. W.L. Gore and Associates Web site <www.gore.com>

4. James Collins, "The Money Machine," *Time* 148, no. 16 (September 30, 1996): 46–52.

5. Ron Suskind, "The 'Other' Fidelity Is Odd Collection of Businesses—Varied Holdings Consume Time and Money of Mutual-Fund Company," *Wall Street Journal*, October 14, 1993, B4.

6. Claudia H. Deutsch, "The Horse and Cart, in Order" *New York Times*, January 7, 2001,3.

7. Edward Meadows, "How Three Companies Increased Their Productivity," *Fortune,* March 10, 1980, 93; Davis Dyer and Daniel Gross, *The Generations of Corning: The Life and Times of a Global Corporation* (New York: Oxford University Press, 2001), chapters 12 to 14.

8. Robert Ball, "The Michelin Man Rolls into Akron's Backyard," *Fortune*, December 1974, 188.

9. Hedrick Smith, *Rethinking America, A New Game Plan from the American Innovators: Schools, Business, People, Work* (New York: Random House, 1995), 324–328.

10. "Tetra Pak PET Packaging Systems S.A.: Your Partner for the Future Starting Now," *Beverage World* 115, no. 1625 (October 1996): 156.

11. Dana Milbank, "Risky Strategies Prove Profitable for Swedish Company—But Tough Rivals in Drink-Box Market May Prompt Changes at Tetra Pak," *Wall Street Journal*, July 1, 1994, B4.

12. Stephen L. Harp, *Marketing Michelin: Advertising and Cultural Identity in the Twentieth Century* (Baltimore: Johns Hopkins Press, 2001).

13. Leslie Eaton, "The Town That Glass Built Hits a Bump, and 1,000 Lose Their Jobs," *New York Times*, July 16, 2001, B1.

14. Smith, *Rethinking America*, 321.

15. Scott Kirsner, "Fidelity at Crossroads," *Boston Globe*, October 29, 2001, C1.

16. Kirsner, "Fidelity at Crossroads."

17. David Woodruff, "Michelin Hits Some Bumps as It Modernizes—Efforts Show Struggles as Old Firms Adapt to Practices of Today," *Wall Street Journal*, May 15, 2001, A21; Ball, "The Michelin Man Rolls into Akron's Backyard," 141.

18. Browning, "On a Roll: Long-Term Thinking and Paternalistic Ways Carry Michelin to Top."

19. Ball, "The Michelin Man Rolls into Akron's Backyard," 138, 186.

20. "Michelin Gets a Grip," *The Economist,* March 1, 1997, 63–64.

21. Geoffrey Smith, Joshua Kendal, and Phoebe Eliopoulis, "Can Fidelity Spend Its Way Back to Fast Growth? As Rivals Retrench, Bob Reynolds Bets Big on New Technology," *BusinessWeek*, February 19, 2001, 88–90.

22. Robert Ball, "Warm Milk Wakes Up the Packaging Industry," *Fortune,* August 9, 1982, 78–82.

23. "Michelin Gets a Grip"; Stéphane Lauer, "Michelin finit par dévoiler sa machine 'révolutionnaire': Le 'C3M', entièrement automatisé, permettrait de quadrupler les cadences," ("Michelin finally unveils its 'revolutionary' machine: The 'C3M,' entirely automated, will quadruple production"), *Le Monde*, September 22, 2001, 24.

24. Taylor III, "Why Fidelity Is the Master of Mutual Funds."

25. Ibid.

26. Collins, "The Money Machine."

27. Justin Gillis, "Corning's Latest Reinvention: Glass Firm Enters the Uncertain Gene-Chip Market," *Washington Post*, May 9, 2001, E1.

28. Ball, "Warm Milk Wakes Up the Packaging Industry," 82.

29. Milbank, "Risky Strategies Prove Profitable for Swedish Company."

30. Ball, "The Michelin Man Rolls into Akron's Backyard," 139. At Corning, the Top Management Committee was called the "Six Pack" (Dyer and Gross, *The Generations of Corning*, 373–375).

31. Ronald Henkoff, "Keeping Motorola on a Roll," *Fortune,* April 18, 1994, 67.

32. François Michelin, with Ivan Levaï and Yves Messarovitch, *Et pourquoi pas? (And why not?)* (Paris: Bernard Grasset, 1998): 60.

33. Michelin, *Et pourquoi pas?* 65–68.

34. "The Tyre Industry's Costly Obsession with Size," *The Economist,* June 8, 1991, 65.

35. Smith, *Rethinking America*, 334.

36. Alex Dominguez, "Bossless Culture Working: Goretex Maker Strikes a Chord," *Denver Post,* July 12, 1998, J5. Ann Harrington, "Who's Afraid of a New Product?" *Fortune,* November 10, 2003, 189–192.

37. Roula Khalaf, "Sleeping Partners," *Forbes,* August 1, 1994, 49. Herbert Lottman, *The Michelin Men: Driving and Empire* (London: IBTauris, 2003).

38. Dawn Anfuso, "Core Values Shape W.L.Gore's Innovative Culture," *Workforce* 78, no. 3 (March 1999): 48–53; Dominguez, "Bossless Culture Working: Goretex Maker Strikes a Chord." Michael Winereb, "Power to the People," *Sales and Marketing Management* 155, no.4 (April 2003): 30–35.

39. Jan P. Norbye, *The Michelin Magic* (Blue Ridge Summit, PA: TAB Books, 1982): 34.

40. Graham and Shuldiner, *Corning and the Craft of Innovation*, 371.

41. Michelin, *Et pourquoi pas?* 60–61.

42. Morty Lefkoe, "Unhealthy Business," *Across the Board* 29, no. 6 (June 1992): 26–31.

43. Lynnley Browning, "Fidelity's Unassuming Heir: Johnson Daughter Weighs Her Options," *Boston Globe*, August 8, 1999, A1.

44. "Management: Re-Engineering, with Love," *The Economist* 336, no. 7931 (September 9, 1995): 69.

45. Glenn Hasek, "The Right Chemistry," *Industry Week* 249, no. 5 (March 6, 2000): 36–39.

46. Graham and Shuldiner, *Corning and the Craft of Innovation*, 3.

47. Hasek, "The Right Chemistry"; Anfuso, "Core Values Shape W.L. Gore's Innovative Culture."

48. Deutsch, "The Horse and Cart in Order."

49. Michelin, *Et pourquoi pas?* 83.

50. Norbye, *The Michelin Magic*, 4.

51. Ball, "The Michelin Man Rolls into Akron's Backyard," 142–143.

52. Smith, *Rethinking America*, 324.

53. Geoffrey Smith, "Fixing Fidelity. Who Is James Curvey? He Just May Be the Man Who Saves Fidelity from Itself," *BusinessWeek*, September 14, 1998, 178.

54. Brian McGrory and Kimberly Blanton, "Fidelity Chief Carries Fortune Quietly: Johnson's Obsession Is Work, Not Wealth," *Boston Globe*, November 6, 1994, 1.

55. Taylor III, "Why Fidelity Is the Master of Mutual Funds," 56.

56. Graham and Shuldiner, *Corning and the Craft of Innovation*.

57. Browning, "On a Roll: Long-Term Thinking and Paternalistic Ways Carry Michelin to Top"; F. Michelin and F. Renard, "Ce qu'il en pense, ce qu'il en dit . . . " ("What he thinks, what he says about it . . . ") *Le Monde*, June 7, 1991, 29.

58. Norbye, *The Michelin Magic*, 6–8.

59. Michelin and Renard, "Ce qu'il en pense, ce qu'il en dit . . . "; B. Abescat, "François Michelin: le patron ermite" ("François Michelin: The Hermit Boss"), *L'Express*, April 16, 1998, 103.

60. Heather Ogilvie, "At the Core, It's the Virtual Organization," *The Journal of Business Strategy* 15, no. 5 (September/October 1994): 29.

61. "Joint Ventures and Alliances: Corning," *Financial World,* September 29, 1992, 44.

62. Abescat, "François Michelin: le patron ermite"; Lottman, *The Michelin Men.*

63. From a conversation with Professor Mike Beer in 2003.

Chapter 7

1. Seth Lubove, "A Piece of the Action," *Forbes,* May 31, 1999, 106–110.

2. Bechtel in turn would pass along to the CIA information gathered by its own people working in foreign hot spots. Laton McCartney, *Friends in High Places. The Bechtel Story: The Most Secret Corporation and How It Engineered the World* (New York: Ballantine Books, 1989), 122–125.

3. Dan Cordtz, "Bechtel Thrives on Billion-Dollar Jobs," *Fortune,* January 1975, 90–93.

4. Larry MacDonald, *The Bombardier Story: Planes, Trains, and Snowmobiles* (Etobicoke, Ontario: John Wiley & Sons Canada Ltd., 2001), 134–138.

5. Nigel Holloway, "Bombardier's Master Builder," *Forbes,* April 19, 1999, 162–166; MacDonald, *The Bombardier Story,* 140.

6. MacDonald, *The Bombardier Story,* 53–66; Miville Tremblay, *Le sang jaune de Bombardier: la gestion de Laurent Beaudoin* (Bombardier's yellow blood: The management style of Laurent Beaudoin) (Sainte-Foy, Canada: Presses de l'Université du Québec, 1994).

7. Anthony Bianco, *The Reichmanns: Family, Faith, Fortune, and the Empire of Olympia & York* (Toronto: Random House of Canada, 1997), 402–409.

8. Ron Chernow, *The House of Morgan: An American Banking Dynasty and the Rise of Modern Finance* (New York: Touchstone/Simon & Schuster, 1990), 69.

9. Shawn Tully, "The Bashful Billionaires of Olympia & York," *Fortune,* June 14, 1982, 94.

10. Bianco, *The Reichmanns,* 447.

11. Cordtz, "Bechtel Thrives on Billion-Dollar Jobs."

12. Lubove, "A Piece of the Action."

13. Steve Ginsberg, "Power Play: Bechtel Group Ditches Go-It-Alone Strategy," *The Business Journal* 17, no. 3 (July 23, 1999): 29.

14. McCartney, *Friends in High Places,* 101–103.

15. Bianco, *The Reichmanns,* 259.

16. Peter Foster, *The Master Builders: How the Reichmanns Reached for an Empire* (Toronto: Key Porter, 1986).

17. Lubove, "A Piece of the Action."

18. Mehrdad A. Baghai et al., "The Growth Philosophy of Bombardier," *The McKinsey Quarterly,* no. 2 (1997): 4–29.

19. MacDonald, *The Bombardier Story,* 69–78.

20. Bianco, *The Reichmanns,* 370.

21. Chernow, *The House of Morgan,* 65.

22. Andrew Sinclair, *Corsair: The Life of J. Pierpont Morgan* (Boston: Little, Brown & Co., 1981); Chernow, *The House of Morgan,* 58.

23. MacDonald, *The Bombardier Story,* 128.

24. Bianco, *The Reichmanns,* xviii.

25. George Wheeler, *Pierpont Morgan & Friends: The Anatomy of a Myth* (Englewood, NJ: Prentice-Hall, 1973); Chernow, *The House of Morgan,* 77.

26. Chernow, *The House of Morgan,* 122.

27. Bianco, *The Reichmanns,* 379; Foster, *The Master Builders*; Paul Goldberger, "A Dramatic Counterpoint for Trade Center," *New York Times,* May 14, 1981, 22.

28. Bianco, *The Reichmanns,* 374.

29. Stewart, *Too Big to Fail,* 105–114; Jim Powell, *Risk, Ruin and Riches: Inside the World of Big-Time Real Estate* (New York: Macmillan, 1986), 43.

30. Tully, "The Bashful Billionaires of Olympia & York," 96.

31. McCartney, *Friends in High Places,* 104–108.

32. MacDonald, *The Bombardier Story*, 129–130; G. Pierre Goad, "Salvage Strategy for Units Helps Bombardier Sell Jets," *Wall Street Journal*, April 26, 1990, B11.

33. Christopher J. Chipello, "Jet Maker Looks to the Old Economy—Bombardier of Canada Seeks a Smoother Ride with Railroad Deal," *Wall Street Journal*, September 12, 2000, A21.

34. Bianco, *The Reichmanns*, 260–261.

35. Sinclair, *Corsair*.

36. Chernow, *The House of Morgan*, 23, 26, 61.

37. Bianco, *The Reichmanns*, 269.

38. Ibid., 247.

39. Ibid., 267.

40. Laton McCartney, "Crisis at Bechtel," *Fortune*, February 29, 1988, 100–112.

41. George J. Church, "Global Builder: Stephen Bechtel," *Time*, December 7, 1998, 114–116; Cordtz, "Bechtel Thrives on Billion-Dollar Jobs."

42. The Morgans' contacts came from helping out the right parties at the right times, being true to their word, and being loyal to their partners.

43. McCartney, *Friends in High Places*, 14.

44. Ibid., 106–107.

45. Ibid., 96.

46. Bianco, *The Reichmanns*, 261.

47. Ibid., 416.

48. Ginsberg, "Power Play: Bechtel Group Ditches Go-It-Alone Strategy," 29; Cordtz, "Bechtel Thrives on Billion-Dollar Jobs."

49. Robert Thomas Crow, "The Business Economist at Work: The Bechtel Group," *Business Economics* 29, no. 1 (January 1994): 46–49; McCartney, *Friends in High Places*, 76–77.

50. Chernow, *The House of Morgan*, 32, 152.

51. Anthony DePalma, "Bombardier Rises, with Some Help from Friends in Ottawa," *New York Times*, December 25, 1998, C1; William H. Miller, "After 33 Years, a New Leader," *Industry Week*, July 5, 1999, 40–44; MacDonald, *The Bombardier Story*, 244–250.

52. Church, "Global Builder," 114–116.

53. Chernow, *The House of Morgan*, 204.

54. Ibid., 37.

55. Tully, "The Bashful Billionaires of Olympia & York," 89; Norman Peagam, "The Reichmanns Never Gamble," *Euromoney*, June 1984, 37–41.

56. Jeffrey Robinson, "From the Ground Up: How a Canadian Family Built a Real-Estate Empire," *Barron's National Business and Financial Weekly*, November 21, 1983, 52–55.

57. Baghai et al., "The Growth Philosophy of Bombardier."

58. MacDonald, *The Bombardier Story*, 128–129.

59. Holloway, "Bombardier's Master Builder."

60. Cordtz, "Bechtel Thrives on Billion-Dollar Jobs."

61. Lubove, "A Piece of the Action."

62. Anthony L. Velocci Jr., "Bombardier Disciplined in Innovation Strategy," *Aviation Week & Space Technology*, December 4, 2000, 58–61.

63. Tremblay, *Le sang jaune de Bombardier*; MacDonald, *The Bombardier Story*, 228.

64. Bianco, *The Reichmanns*, 451.

65. Tully, "The Bashful Billionaires of Olympia & York"; Chernow, *The House of Morgan*.

66. Chernow, *The House of Morgan*, 70, 322.

67. For a discussion of these kinds of organizations, see: Russell Eisenstat et al., "Beyond the Business Unit," *The McKinsey Quarterly*, no. 1 (2001): 54–63.

Chapter 8

1. Jenny Strasburg, "Shaking the Blues. Venerable House of Levi Seeks to Regain Grip on Youth While Keeping the Faithful," *San Francisco Chronicle*, February 3, 2002, G1. Michael Kahn, "Levi Explores Sales of Dockers Brand," *National Post* (Canada), May 12, 2004, FP16.

2. Nina Munk, "How Levi's Trashed a Great American Brand," *Fortune,* April 12, 1999, 82–90.

3. Karl Schoenberger, "Tough Jeans, a Soft Heart, and Frayed Earnings," *New York Times,* June 25, 2000, 3.

4. Munk, "How Levi's Trashed a Great American Brand."

5. Ibid.

6. Ibid. In 1996, Haas consolidated ownership in the hands of a tiny group of relatives with a $3.3 billion leveraged buyout (LBO).

7. Dan Baum, *Citizen Coors: A Grand Family Saga of Business, Politics, and Beer* (New York: William Morrow, 2000), 139–141, 197–198.

8. Ibid., 197–198.

9. Ibid., 317, 321, 331–332.

10. Ibid., 151.

11. Ibid., 133–135.

12. Ibid., 218–220.

13. Marcella Bernhard, "Nordstrom Loses its Luster," <Forbes.com>, January 5, 2001.

14. "Can the Nordstroms Find the Right Style? They'll Need More Than Great Service to Get Back on Top," *BusinessWeek*, July 30, 2001, 59–62.

15. Kim Clark, "Tough Times for the Chicken King," *Fortune,* October 28, 1996, 88–97; Tyson Foods, Inc, *Notice of Annual Meeting of Shareholders: February 7, 2003* (Springdale, AR: Tyson Foods Inc., 2003), 4.

16. Kim Clark, "The Bird Gets Plucked," *Fortune,* February 2, 1998, 27.

17. Joel Chernoff, "Tyson Chief Lays an Egg," *Pensions & Investments,* April 17, 2000, 2, 52; Gary Strauss, "Shareholder Wants to Oust Tyson Foods' Board: CalPers Questions Accountability, Compensation," *USA Today*, January 10, 2000, B1.

18. Clark, "Tough Times for the Chicken King."

19. Ibid.

20. Bob Ortega, *In Sam We Trust: The Untold Story of Sam Walton and Wal-Mart, The World's Most Powerful Retailer* (New York: Times Business, 2000).

21. Ibid., 240–241.

22. Ibid., 284–303.

23. Roger O. Crockett, "Motorola, Can Chris Galvin Save His Family's Legacy?" *BusinessWeek*, July 16, 2001, 72–78.

24. Mark Veverka, "False Spring," *Barron's*, April 30, 2001, 23–26.

25. Andrea Petersen, "Softer Sell: Once-Mighty Motorola Stumbled When It Began Acting That Way—Repairing Frayed Relations with Wireless Carriers Is Key for CEO Galvin—A New Button for Cingular," *Wall Street Journal*, May 18, 2001, A1.

26. Veverka, "False Spring"; see also Peterson, "Softer Sell."

27. Crockett, "Motorola, Can Chris Galvin Save His Family's Legacy?"

28. Veverka, "False Spring."

29. Petersen, "Softer Sell."

30. Floyd Norris, "Disaster at Corning: At Least the Balance Sheet Is Strong," *New York Times,* July 13, 2001, C1; Leslie Eaton, "The Town That Glass Built Hits a Bump, and 1,000 Lose Their Jobs," *New York Times*, July 16, 2001, B1.

31. Anthony Bianco, *The Reichmanns: Family, Faith, Fortune, and the Empire of Olympia & York* (Toronto: Random House of Canada, 1997), 517.

32. Ibid., 536.

33. Ibid., 665.

34. Laton McCartney, "Crisis at Bechtel," *Fortune,* February 29, 1988, 100–112.

35. Laton McCartney, *Friends in High Places. The Bechtel Story: The Most Secret Corporation and How It Engineered the World* (New York: Ballantine Books, 1989), 232.

36. McCartney, *Friends in High Places*, 232.

37. McCartney, "Crisis at Bechtel."

38. Danny Miller, *The Icarus Paradox: How Exceptional Companies Bring About Their Own Downfall* (New York: HarperBusiness, 1990); Danny Miller, "The Architecture of Simplicity," *The Academy of Management Review* 18, no. 1 (January 1993): 116–138.

39. Miller, "The Architecture of Simplicity."

40. Miller, *The Icarus Paradox.*

41. Family businesses, it is true, face an especially severe leadership challenge: They have a smaller pool of potential family succession candidates from which to draw. And they require decades-long planning and grooming to bring along numerous family and nonfamily people who might be able to serve as CEOs. They also demand a robust and empowered board and top management team that can counterbalance a CEO's weaknesses and get things back on track. (Isabelle Le Breton-Miller, Danny Miller, and Lloyd Steier, "Towards an Integrative Model of Effective FOB Succession," *Entrepreneurship, Theory & Practice* 28, no. 4 (Summer 2004): 305–328.; Ivan Lansberg, *Succeeding Generations: Realizing the Dream of Families in Business* (Boston: Harvard Business School Press, 1999); Kelin E. Gersick et al., *Generation to Generation: Life Cycles of the Family Business* (Boston: Harvard Business School Press, 1997)).

Chapter 9

1. *Special governance challenges of FCBs:* Although our winners were, for the most part, able to overcome them, the challenges of governance in family businesses are like no other. They require simultaneous attention to the needs of the family, the owners, and the business, and these can diverge. The useful three circle model of family business is a good place to begin (Ivan Lansberg, *Succeeding Generations* (Boston: Harvard Business School Press, 1999)). The three circles, one each for the family, the owners, and the business, overlap in the center to reflect multiple roles and interests—which may easily conflict. Different interests and points of view are brought to the table by the likes of, say, a family owner with management responsibility concerned with the well-being of the firm, and a family owner who merely collects dividends and therefore wants immediate return. Unless there are processes and forums for resolving these conflicts, and unless a competent family leader can address the interests of the business while also satisfying powerful owners, the family advantages we speak of will not materialize. And unless there is a process put into place for developing and selecting able leaders who can master these conflicts, family advantages will not extend beyond a single generation.

We found that virtually all our thriving companies, at least while they were thriving, had adopted effective governance structures that allowed the Cs to be realized, and minimized the damage family battles could inflict on the business. In many cases, the leader and his or her most powerful family allies had controlling ownership. Alternatively, conflict resolution mechanisms were in place to ensure the leader had a clear mandate. Frequently, there were agreements to arrange for the buyout of discontented family members, or mechanisms to ensure that the family always "voted as a block." On the positive side, there tended to be family councils or forums in which nonmanagement family owners could voice their preferences.

Beyond the family there were vehicles for motivating nonfamily managers with incentives such as bonuses or shares that would be sold back to the company upon retirement using some predetermined formula. There were also procedures in place to ensure smooth succession: to discover, train, and select the right candidate. Finally, sophisticated estate planning devices were commonly used to pass the business onto the next generation without unduly diluting control. All of these governance issues are absolutely vital to get right. Unless they are dealt with appropriately, there is little chance that the advantages we speak of will be realized over the generations. But family governance mechanisms, legal and estate issues, and conflict resolution approaches are beyond the scope of this book, and we refer readers once again to the excellent integrative works cited (see Lansberg, *Succeeding Generations*; Kelin E. Gersick et al., *Generation to Generation: Life Cycles of the Family Business* (Boston: Harvard Business School Press, 1997), and John L. Ward, *Keeping the Family Business Healthy: How to Plan for Continuing Growth, Profitability, and Family Leadership* (San Francisco: Jossey-Bass, 1987)).

2. Michael T. Jacobs, *Short-Term America: The Causes and Cures of Our Business Myopia* (Boston: Harvard Business School Press, 1991).

3. Peter S. Lynch and John Rothchild, *Beating the Street* (New York: Simon & Schuster, 1994); Benjamin Graham and David L. Dodd, *Security Analysis: Principles and Techniques* (New York: McGraw-Hill, 1940).

4. An excellent discussion of boards and their responsibilities and failings is contained in Myles L. Mace, *Directors: Myth and Reality* (Boston: Division of Research, Graduate School of Business Administration, Harvard University, 1971); Sydney Finkelstein and Donald C. Hambrick, *Strategic Leadership: Top Executives and Their Effects on Organizations* (Minneapolis/St. Paul, MN: West Publishing Co., 1996), 209–262; and Stanley C. Vance, *Corporate Leadership: Boards, Directors, and Strategy* (New York: McGraw Hill, 1983).

5. Personal communication with Don Hambrick, June 2002; see also Andrei Shleifer and Robert W. Vishny, "Large Shareholders and Corporate Control," *Journal of Political Economy* 94, no. 3 (June 1986): 461–84; Randall K. Morck, Andrei Shleifer, and Robert W. Vishny, "Management Ownership and Market Valuation: An Empirical Analysis," *Journal of Financial Economics* 20, no. 1/2 (January/March 1988): 293–315.

6. Mace, *Directors*; James P. Walsh and James K. Seward, "On the Efficiency of Internal Control Mechanisms," *Academy of Management Review* 15, no. 3 (July 1990): 421–458.

7. James G. March, "Notes on Ambiguity and Executive Compensation," *Scandinavian Journal of Management Studies* 1, no. 1 (August 1984): 53–64; Artur Raviv, "Managerial Compensation and the Managerial Labor Markets," *Journal of Accounting and Economics* 7, no. 1/3 (April 1985): 239–245; Jennifer J. Gaver, Kenneth M. Gaver, and George P. Battistel, "The Stock Market Reaction to Performance Plan Adoptions," *The Accounting Review* 676, no. 1 (January 1992): 172–182; James D. Westphal and Edward J. Zajac, "Substance and Symbolism in CEO's Long-Term Incentive Plans," *Administrative Science Quarterly* 39, no. 3 (September 1994): 367–390.

8. Robert S. Kaplan and David P. Norton, "The Balanced Scorecard: Measures That Drive Performance," *Harvard Business Review* (January–February 1992): 71–79.

9. See Danny Miller, Lloyd Steier, and Isabelle Le Breton-Miller, "Lost in Time: Patterns of Intergenerational Succession in Family Business," *Journal of Business Venturing* 18, no. 4 (July 2003): 513–531; Isabelle Le Breton-Miller, Danny Miller, and Lloyd Steier, "Towards an Integrative Model of Effective FOB Succession," *Entrepreneurship, Theory & Practice* 28, no. 4 (Summer 2004): 305–328.; see also Lansberg, *Succeeding Generations*.

10. Le Breton-Miller, Miller, and Steier, "Towards an Integrative Model of Effective FOB Succession"; see also Lansberg, *Succeeding Generations*.

11. Danny Miller, "Stale in the Saddle: CEO Tenure and the Match Between Organization and Environment," *Management Science* 37, no. 1 (January 1991): 34–52; Danny Miller, "Some Organizational Consequences of CEO Succession," *Academy of Management Journal* 36, no. 3 (June 1993): 644–659; Danny Miller and Jamal Shamsie, "Learning Across the Life Cycle: Experimentation and Performance Among the Hollywood Studio Heads," *Strategic Management Journal* 22, no. 8 (August 2001): 725–745; Danny Miller, Andrew D. Henderson, and Donald C. Hambrick, "Learning vs. Obsolescence: Two Models of CEO Tenure Effects," working paper, HEC Montreal, Montreal, 2003.

12. Jeffrey A. Sonnenfeld, *The Hero's Farewell: What Happens When the CEO Retires* (New York: Oxford University Press, 1988).

13. John G. Michel and Donald C. Hambrick, "Diversification Posture and Top Management Team Characteristics," *Academy of Management Journal* 35, no. 1 (March 1992): 9–37; Margarethe F. Wiersema and Karen A. Bantel, "Top Management Team Demography and Corporate Strategic Change," *Academy of Management Journal* 35, no. 1 (March 1992): 91–121; Ken G. Smith et al., "Top Management Team Demography and Process: The Role of Social Integration and Communication," *Administrative Science Quarterly* 39, no. 3 (September 1994): 412–38.

14. James C. Collins and Jerry I. Porras, *Built to Last: Successful Habits of Visionary Companies* (New York: HarperBusiness, 1994); James C. Collins, *Good to Great: Why Some Companies Make the Leap . . . and Others Don't* (New York: HarperBusiness, 2001).

15. See Gary Hamel and C. K. Prahalad, *Competing for the Future* (Boston: Harvard Business School Press, 1994).

16. Danny Miller, "An Asymmetry-Based View of Advantage," *Strategic Management Journal* 24, no. 10 (October 2003): 961–976.

17. David Nadler and Michael L. Tushman, *Competing by Design: The Power of Organizational Architecture* (New York: Oxford University Press, 1997).

18. Jay R. Galbraith, *Competing with Flexible Lateral Organizations* (Reading, MA: Addison-Wesley, 1994).

19. Nadler and Tushman, *Competing by Design*, 139–153.

20. Jangwoo Lee and Danny Miller, "People Matter: Commitment to Employees, Strategy, and Performance in Korean Firms," *Strategic Management Journal* 20, no. 6 (June 1999): 579–593; Danny Miller and Jangwoo Lee, "The People Make the Process: Commitment to Employees, Decision Making, and Performance," *Journal of Management* 27, no. 2 (2001): 163–189.

21. John Hagel III and Marc Singer, *Net Worth: Shaping Markets When Customers Make the Rules* (Boston: Harvard Business School Press, 1999).

22. David Halberstam, *The Reckoning* (New York: William Morrow & Co., 1986); J. Patrick Wright, *On a Clear Day You Can See General Motors: John Z. de Lorean's Look Inside the Automotive Giant* (Grosse Pointe, MI: Wright Enterprises, 1979).

Appendix A

1. James C. Collins and Jerry I. Porras, *Built to Last: Successful Habits of Visionary Companies* (New York: HarperBusiness, 1994).

2. Michael E. Porter, *Competitive Strategy: Techniques for Analyzing Industries and Competitors* (New York: Free Press, 1980); Peter H. Fuchs et al., "Strategic Integration: Competing in the Age of Capabilities," *California Management Review* 42, no. 3 (Spring 2000): 118–147; Danny Miller, "Configurations of Strategy and Structure: Towards a Synthesis," *Strategic Management Journal* 7, no. 3 (May–June 1986): 233–249; Danny Miller, *The Icarus Paradox: How Exceptional Companies Bring About Their Own Downfall* (New York: HarperBusiness, 1990); Danny Miller, "Generic Strategies Classification, Combination, and Context," in *Advances in Strategic Management, Vol. VIII*, eds. Paul Shrivastava, Jane Dutton, and Anne Huff (Greenwich, CT: JAI Press, 1992): 391–408.

3. Fuchs et al., "Strategic Integration"; Miller, *The Icarus Paradox;* Miller, "Configurations of Strategy and Structure"; Danny Miller and Isabelle Le Breton-Miller, "Challenge Versus Advantage in Family Business," *Strategic Organization* 1, no. 1 (February 2003): 127–134.

Table A-1

a. Companies 10K Report, 2002/2003.

b. Hoover's Online Company Profile, February 2003.

c. *Market Share Reporter* (Detroit: The Gale Group, 2003).

d. Neil Weinberg and Brandon Copple, "Going Against the Grain," *Forbes*, November 25 2002, 158+; Greg Muttitt, "Control Freaks," *The Ecologist*, March 2001, 52–53.

e. "Business Brief—Michelin SCA: First-Half Earnings Fell 31% on Restructuring, Higher Costs," *Wall Street Journal*, July 30, 2003, 1.

f. Richard Heller, "Folk Fortune," *Forbes*, September 4, 2000, 66–69; "Ikea to Open New Stores in China on the Back of Strong Sales," *asia.news.yahoo.com* (August 27 2003, 11:47 a.m.).

g. J.P. Morgan/Chase Web site, September 2, 2003.

h. http://www6.vjc.edu/mj/ff/Alice%20Parsons/Simplot%20Industries.htm.

i. IMD, *U.S. Company Honored as Top Business World-Wide,* IMD Press Releases, September 17, 2002 (http://www02.imd.ch/pressroom/pressreleases/article.cfm?num=81); David Barboza,

"Father Divides a Business to Keep the Children United; At Johnson Wax, a Family Passes on Its Heirloom," *New York Times,* August 22 1999, 1+.

j. "World Business Briefing Europe. Switzerland: Container Takeover Is Blocked," *New York Times,* October 31 2001, 1; Terry Slavin, "Leader of the Pack," *The Observer,* August 5, 2001.

k. Largest daily and Sunday circulation of all seven-day newspaper in the United States (Audit Bureau of Circulation reported in the NYT Annual Report 2002).

l. "How Timken Turns Survival into Growth: The Bearing Maker's CEO, Jim Griffith, Talks about the Industrial Recession," *BusinessWeek,* April 7, 2003, 26A.

m. http://www.berghaus.com/the_gear/gear_info/gore/gore_tex.asp

n. World #1 in high data rate/high frequency signal transmission cable and cable assemblies; World #1 supplier of MEAs (membrane electrode assembly) for PEM (proton exchange membrane) fuel cells, W.L. Gore Web site, 2003 <ww.gore.com>.

o. Kathleen Hickey, "We are the world," *Traffic World,* May 21, 2001, 25.

Index

Page numbers in italics refer to tables or figures.

connection (*continued*)
erosion of complements and, 188–189,
191–192, 198, 204
erosion of majors and, 195, 204
excessive focus on, 194, 204
family roots of, 45, 170–172
innovation and, 134–135, 151–152
long-standing relationships and, 174
operations and, 114, 119–122, 194
consideration, 72–73, 146
consistency, 61
construction techniques, 162
contacts, cultivation of, 172–174
continuity, 6, 32, 33–38, 233
brand building and, 64–68
craftsmanship and, 87, 88–93, 189, 190,
192–193
deal makers and, 176–178
elements of, 35–37
erosion of complements and, 199, 201,
202, 204
erosion of majors and, 192–193, 194, 204
excessive focus on, 190, 195, 204
family roots of, 37–38
superior operators and, 114–119, 195
continuous improvement. *See also* capability
development; innovation
craftsmanship and, 84–86
superior operators and, 118
contrarian deals, 168–169
Coors, Ad, 92
Coors, Adolph, 41, 92, 93
Coors, Adolph, Jr., 89, 92
Coors, Bill, 89–90, 91, 92, 97, 189, 190, 191
Coors, Jeff, 92
Coors, Joe, 191
Coors, Joe, Sr., 92
Coors, Peter, 92, 93, 190, 191
Coors Brewing Company. *See* Adolph Coors
Company
Coors family, 41, 47, 206
Cordiner, Ralph, 168
core capabilities, 35–36, 47, 49
deal makers and, 177–178
long-run approach and, 86–87, 217–218,
226–227
Corning Incorporated, 127
characteristics of, 128, 243
command and, 45–46, 47
complementary priorities at, 149, 150,
151, 152

innovation strategy at, 131, 132, 133–134,
135
long-run approach and, 218, 222, 223,
227, 228, 229
major priorities at, 139, 141–142, 145,
146, 147, 148
mismanaged priorities at, 196, 198–199,
261
cost reduction, 40, 133–134, 195, 229–230
courage, 47, 76, 216. *See also* command
deal makers and, 166
innovation and, 137–138
C priorities. *See also* assessment grid; command; community; complementary
priorities; connection; continuity; major
priorities; mismanagement of priorities;
self-assessment checklist
basis for recommendations in, 233
brand building and, 76–77
characterizations of, 33–48
configuration of, 9, 32–33, 50–51, 76–77,
207, 226
current research and, 238–247
major versus complementary priorites
and, 184, 185
mismanagement of priorities and,
183–184
overview of, 6–7, 31–33, 34
pilot study on, 236–238
strategy and, 51, 52
tensions among, 50–51
themes among, 51
types of problems with, 184
craftsmanship, 79–80, 103–104, 185–186.
See also Adolph Coors Company; The
New York Times Company; Nordstrom,
Inc.; quality; The Timken Company
assessment grid on, 252–253
command and, 102, 103, 191–192
community and, 87, 93–101, 190
complementary priorities of, 102–103,
186
configuration of four Cs and, 104
connection and, 102–103
continuity and, 87, 88–93, 189, 190
major priorities of, 87–101, 185, 190
mismanaged priorities and, 189–193
representative FCBs and, 80–81, 185
self-assessment checklist for, 264–266
strategy based on, 82–87, 185
cronyism, 194, 261, 280n

About the Authors

Danny Miller is Research Professor of Strategy at HEC Montreal and Research Chair in Strategy and Family Enterprise at the University of Alberta. He has published more than a hundred articles on business strategy and the theory of organizations, and five books, including *Organizations: A Quantum View* (with Peter Friesen), *The Neurotic Organization* (with Manfred Kets de Vries) and *The Icarus Paradox*. His current research interests are centered on building competitive capabilities and managing organizational change in family and non-family enterprises. For more than twenty years he has consulted with major U.S. and Canadian companies on shaping competitive strategy, building capabilities, improving leadership, and mastering organizational change.

Isabelle Le Breton-Miller is a Senior Research Associate at the Centre for Entrepreneurship and Family Enterprise at the University of Alberta and President of Organizational Effectiveness Research, (Montreal), a consultancy in human resources and family enterprise. Her research interests and recent publications are focused on managing succession in family business, building human and social capital, and creating competitive advantage in family enterprise.